Foreign Policy Decision-Making (Revisited)

Foreign Policy Decision-Making  (Revisited)

Richard C. Snyder
H.W. Bruck
Burton Sapin

With New Chapters by
Valerie M. Hudson
Derek H. Chollet and James M. Goldgeier

palgrave
macmillan

FOREIGN POLICY DECISION-MAKING (REVISITED)
Copyright © The Estate of Richard C. Snyder, Valerie M. Hudson,
Derek H. Chollet and James M. Goldgeier, 2002.

First published 2002 by
PALGRAVE MACMILLAN™
175 Fifth Avenue, New York, N.Y. 10010 and
Houndmills, Basingstoke, Hampshire, England RG21 6XS.
Companies and representatives throughout the world.

PALGRAVE MACMILLAN IS THE GLOBAL ACADEMIC IMPRINT OF THE
PALGRAVE MACMILLAN division of St. Martin's Press, LLC and of Palgrave
Macmillan Ltd. Macmillan® is a registered trademark in the United States,
United Kingdom and other countries. Palgrave is a registered trademark in
the European Union and other countries.

ISBN 1-4039-6075-5 hardback
ISBN 1-4039-6076-3 paperback

Library of Congress Cataloging-in-Publication Data
Snyder, Richard Carlton, 1916–
　Foreign policy decision-making (revisited) / Richard C. Snyder,
H. W. Bruck, Burton Sapin.
　　　p. cm.
　Originally published: Foreign policy decision-making. [New York] : Free
Press of Glencoe, [1962]. With new chapters by Valerie M. Hudson, Derek
H. Chollet and James M. Goldgeier.
　Includes bibliographical references.
　ISBN 1-40396-075-5 — ISBN 1-40396-076-3 (pbk.)
　1. International relations—Decision making.　2. International
relations—Methodology.　I. Bruck, H. W. (Henry W.)　II. Sapin,
Burton M.　III. Title.

JZ1253.S65　2002
327.1'01—dc21

　　　　　　　　　　　　　　　　　　　　　　　　　　2002029241

A catalogue record for this book is available from the British Library.

Design by Letra Libre, Inc.

First edition: December 2002
10　9　8　7　6　5　4　3　2　1
Printed in the United States of America.

Contents

Foreword

Burton M. Sapin

Professor Richard C. Snyder (1916–1997) was one of the leading figures in the post–World War II revolution in American political science. This revolution altered in significant ways the conceptual-theoretical underpinnings, empirical scope and foci, and methodology and research tools of the field. There can be no doubt that they changed fundamentally what and how political and governmental phenomena were studied. By no means everyone welcomed the new approaches, with criticism that scientific claims and aspirations were excessive that sound familiar today.

That Snyder was at the forefront of seeking to integrate insights from other disciplines was perhaps not surprising. He was a strong and forceful academic and intellectual leader and at the same time notably open to hearing and encouraging the views and efforts of others. Intellectually curious, one colleague recalls that he would trawl the stacks of a library seeking out the literature in other disciplines. As early as 1950 he taught an exciting graduate seminar on U. S. foreign policy–making, bringing to bear perspectives and data from the other social and behavioral sciences, including psychology, psychiatry, sociology, and anthropology. A similar pluralism informed an early course on political behavior Snyder created with his colleague H. Hubert Wilson.

Snyder, like some of his fellow "behaviorists" in the late 1940s and early 1950s, found essentially unsatisfying the leading approaches to the study of international political phenomena, including the emphasis on national power and national interests that became dominant immediately after World War II. In his view, they were not very helpful in explaining the *whys* of governmental behavior. He proposed instead that we define state action as the behavior of its official decision-makers, thus providing a clear empirical focus for studying the behavior of nation-states, as well as other political entities.

Once he broke out of the traditional political science mold of institutional description and legal analysis, and even the power approach, he saw all of the social sciences as relevant to his interests and concerns. Since political science lagged behind the other social sciences theoretically, conceptually, and methodologically, Dick Snyder had no problem in borrowing from them. He was quite willing to take the time and make the necessary efforts to understand them and to bring their theories, concepts, and data to bear on political phenomena. His approach was and remained genuinely and deeply interdisciplinary.

The origins of *Foreign Policy Decision-Making* lies in Snyder's early attempts to broaden the study of international relations and reflects concerns apparent earlier. Much of the material was initially published in 1954 as a small monograph, almost a pamphlet, entitled *Decision-Making as an Approach to the Study of International Politics* by the Organizational Behavior Section at Princeton. At a time when communication was slower, absent e-mail and the Web, but the networks closer, the monograph generated a stir befitting a challenge to the received approaches. This monograph was republished in 1962, with some additional essays, by The Free Press as *Foreign Policy Decision-Making*. It is an indication of Snyder's openness that included in this volume were chapters critical of the arguments we put forward. I should note that while Henry Bruck and I did quite a bit of the organizational work, this monograph was essentially Dick Snyder's work. Nevertheless, he put all three of our names on the publication. This is just one indication of how supportive he could be of his students and colleagues, and he treated the former as though they were the latter.

Dick Snyder essentially treated everyone as equals in the search for truth and understanding. This was not a posture or a pose. It was the way he approached the world, with a basic humility and a genuine openness to the ideas and perspectives of others, even while holding very strong views of his own. He maintained a deep-seated personal and intellectual egalitarianism, undergirded by a compassionate and respectful approach to almost all of those with whom he came in contact, believing there should be no barriers of any kind, personal or intellectual, hierarchical or generational, to the search for a deeper understanding of the socio-political world around us.

This did not mean that all views have equal validity or significance but simply that everyone should be approached with respect and others should display a willingness to pay attention to the ideas, values, and perspectives they may articulate. There are differences of viewpoint, some views might be more insightful or closer to empirical reality than others, and it is legitimate to attempt to identify the analytical shortcomings and factual errors of others. Snyder's approach was to encourage others, particularly if they stood lower in some hierarchical structure, to "do their thing," think their own thoughts, and engage in productive and creative interaction with you and with one another. Clearly, this is a stance that would add considerable clarity and balance, and improved decisions as well, to the broad realm of public policy analysis, discussion, and decision-making.

Skeptics will point out that all of this openness to the views and ideas of others may mean that decisions never get made, or may give the impression that all opinions are entitled to equal weight and respect. Anything is possible, but neither of these shortcomings is part of the Snyder heritage. Dick Snyder had strong and well-defined views on a broad range of academic, institutional, social-scientific, and political science issues, and on matters of personal behavior and ethics as well, and he pursued and attempted to implement them vigorously and persistently. All while maintaining respect for others.

As scholar, mentor, and administrator, Snyder's approach influenced a substantial number of students and other colleagues (and anyone else open to this kind of personal and intellectual support) in a number of academic fields and disciplines—in stimulating, encouraging, and liberating their talents, values, and ideas. It is comforting to realize that many of these beneficiaries of the Snyder approach have in turn brought it to bear on others, and that the republication of *Foreign Policy Decision-Making* is here complemented by two new chapters examining its impact, implications, and potential for future research. Snyder's approach, both personal and intellectual, stands as a model.[1] It is a legacy that should be encouraged and sustained.

NOTE

1. For a tribute to Richard Snyder, see Glenn D. Paige and James A. Robinson in *PS* (June 1998), available at http://www.apsanet.org/PS/june98/snyder.cfm.

Foreign Policy Decision-Making 🔲

A Touchstone for International Relations
Theory in the Twenty-first Century

Valerie M. Hudson

F*oreign Policy Decision-Making,* edited by Richard Snyder, H. W. Bruck, and Burton Sapin 40 years ago, is one of the foundational works of the subfield of Foreign Policy Analysis (FPA) in the field of International Relations (IR). As is the case with any revolutionary vision, it has taken a great deal of time—in this case, over four decades—for those who followed the initial vision to find that their work is making its way toward the heart of current debates in the larger field of which they are a part. Today, the questions are asked in a slightly different dialect than that used by Snyder, Bruck, and Sapin (hereafter "SBS"), but most of the questions are the very same ones that stirred SBS so many years ago. Familiarity with current debates makes any close reading of *Foreign Policy Decision-Making* an interesting experience, given the uncanny prescience of their concerns about issues such as:

- the agent-structure problematique
- capturing cultural effects in international affairs
- the relationship between rational choice and decision-making models
- the problem of dynamism and change in IR theory
- the "two-level game"; interrelating domestic and foreign influences on nation-state action
- the need for integration in theory-building

- broader methodological issues concerning choice of unit of analysis, preferred modes of satisfactory explanation, and appropriate data collection.

WHAT DID SBS DO?

To understand the major contribution of the SBS framework, one must understand a bit about the trajectory of IR theory since the end of World War
II. Generally speaking, realism and scientism combined after 1945 in a po-
tent mix that sought to uncover generalizable laws about state behavior. Realism emphasized the nation-state as the preferred unit of analysis, noting
the overriding primacy of state self-interest in power as a motivation for state
behavior, and stating a firm commitment to exploring international relations
as it is, not as it should be. Scientism provided a second commitment to
careful empirical investigation of phenomena, entailing data collection, creation of formal models (often statistical or mathematical in nature), and fal-
sifiability of resulting models. As the state was the unit of analysis, its
behavior was seen as best comprehended in the context of the system of
states in which it found itself. Distribution of capabilities across states was
the primary determinant of behavior within any given system.

Two metaphors began to take hold: the state as a "billiard ball" among
other billiard balls on the pool table of the international system; and the
state as a "black box," whose behavior could be estimated by the study of external forces without much inquiry into the idiosyncratic contents of the
box, such as domestic politics and leader psychology. Realism, with its emphasis on raison d'etat, combined with scientism, with its envy of the natural law explanations of physics and the seeming powerfulness of economic
models, provided a denatured perspective of international politics. It is not
difficult to see how game theoretic and rational choice analyses could therefore be constructed as the most useful approaches to the study of international relations. It is not coincidental that the development of this "states
systemic project" took place during the Cold War, which could be viewed as
the natural crucible for its development (Wendt 1999: 7). This project emphasized the importance of system-level explanations of state behavior, at the
expense of examining more micro-level explanatory levels that focus on how
and why individuals act in international relations.

Although SBS was published during the first half of the Cold War, it was
the states systemic project that continued as the mainstream of IR theory.
This is not to suggest that some glaring deficiency of the SBS framework resulted in it being overlooked—rather, it was more a result of the times. The

Cold War was unusual for the apparent robustness and stability of the bipolar structure pitting the United States and the Soviet Union against each other in an apparently predictable action-reaction cycle.

Arguably, the catalyst for the search for alternatives to the states systemic project was not a theoretical event but an actual one: the abrupt end of the Cold War. This dynamic and unforeseen process undermined the belief in system stability, its robustness, and not the least its predictability, as the collapse of the Soviet Union went largely unpredicted by IR theory. No matter how one attempted to rationalize that event in terms of states, power, and system constraints, a key element seemed missing: ideas (see the discussion in Brooks and Wohlforth, 2002; English 2002; Brooks and Wohlforth, 2000–2001). A new wave of theorizing, generally called constructivism, attempted to show that ideational factors could alter perceptions of power and system structure. As one influential article phrased it, "Anarchy is What States Make of It" (Wendt, 1992). Yet, oddly, much of this challenge came from scholars who still clung to the primacy of states as actors—scholars that were arguably still within the states systemic project. The theoretical mix simply changed to: states, power, system structure, *and* ideas.

Thus, at the beginning of the twenty-first century, even the constructivist turn in IR theory seems lacking the answers to certain key questions: Where did these ideas come from? How were they disseminated? How did they become persuasive? How did they become the new basis for state action? The standard mix of variables cannot give us a satisfying account, and thus the search for alternative visions in IR continues (Hudson, 2001). And so it is that the republication of SBS comes at an opportune moment—for much of what SBS stood for in 1962 is precisely what is needed now in IR theory. The difference is that in 1962, this could not be recognized, generally speaking. But in 2002, I think there is a good chance that it will. The republication of SBS might have a significantly greater effect on the larger field of IR today than the framework was able to produce 40 years ago.

THE THEORETICAL INTERSECTION
OF MATERIALISM AND IDEALISM IN IR

The single most important contribution of the SBS framework to IR theory is to identify the point of theoretical intersection between the most important determinants of state behavior: material and ideational factors. The point of intersection is *not* the state, and that is where classic and even contemporary IR theory is lacking and needs augmentation, according to SBS.

The point of intersection is the *human decision-maker*. As the SBS essay puts it, "The description and explanation of national behavior has also suffered from the common fallacy of *misplaced concreteness or reification,* exemplified chiefly by the subtle transformation of the word "state" from a proper analytical abstraction into a symbol allegedly standing for a concrete entity— that is, an object or person having an existence of its own apart from real persons and their behaviors."

If our IR theories contain no human beings, they will erroneously paint for us a world of no change, no creativity, no persuasion, no accountability. And yet virtually none of our mainstream IR theories over the decades of the Cold War placed human beings in the theoretical mix. By asserting that analysis on the level of individual human beings was the key to fully understanding state and system phenomena in international relations, Snyder, Bruck, and Sapin were proposing nothing less than a theoretical handstand for IR theory:

> It is one of our basic methodological choices to define the state as its official decision-makers—those whose authoritative acts are, to all intents and purposes, the acts of the state. *State action is the action taken by those acting in the name of the state.* Hence, the state is its decision-makers. State X as *actor* is translated into its decision-makers as actors. It is also one of our basic choices to take as our prime analytical objective the re-creation of the "world" of the decision-makers as *they* view it. The manner in which *they* define situations becomes another way of saying how the state oriented to action and why. . . . Of all the phenomena which *might* have been relevant, the actors (the decision-makers) finally endow only some with *significance*.

Adding human decision-makers as the key theoretical intersection confers some advantages generally lacking in IR theory. Let us explore each in turn:

The Possibility of Theoretical Integration in IR

In IR, there are quite a number of well-developed theoretical threads, studying phenomena such as institutions, systems, group dynamics, domestic politics, and so forth. Often we refer to the "levels of analysis problem" in IR, which is that many theoretical efforts posit that phenomena can be (best) explained by a focus on a certain level of analysis, such as domestic politics or the international system. Attempts at integration are typically absent or even resisted. The formidable task of weaving these threads together has been stymied by the insistence on retaining the state as a "metaphysical" actor. If one replaces metaphysics with a more realistic conceptualization of "actor," the weaving becomes feasible, albeit certainly complex. SBS points out that one must insist that the individual decision-maker be the locus of theoretical integration across levels of analysis:

> The central concept of decision-making may provide a basis for linking a group of theories which hitherto have been applicable only to segment of international politics or have not been susceptible of application at all. . . . By emphasizing decision-making as a central focus, we have provided a way of organizing the determinants of action around those officials who act for the political society, Decision-makers are viewed as operating in dual-aspect setting so that apparently unrelated internal and external factors become related in the actions of the decision-makers.

This "dual-aspect setting" is familiar by a different name, that of the "two-level" game that state decision-makers must play: the simultaneous play of the game of domestic politics and the game of international politics (Putnam, 1988).

In addition, other types of theory that have not been well developed in IR, such as theory of how cultural factors and social constructions within a culture affect state behavior, can now be attempted with a greater probability of success. It is interesting to note that SBS are emphatic that IR theory must at some point address the issue of culture, but that it was not until the 1990's that serious work on this subject by IR scholars became more accepted as informing the major theoretical questions of the discipline (e.g., Katzenstein, 1996; Lapid and Kratochwil, 1996; Hudson, 1997). But SBS had presaged this: "Any conceptual scheme for analyzing state behavior must attempt to account for the impact of cultural patterns on decisions. If the decision-maker is viewed as a culture-bearer it would seem possible to lay the foundations for tracing the possible effects of common value orientations held by most members of a whole society upon the deliberation of members of decisional units." Only a move toward placing human decision-makers at the center of the theoretical matrix would allow the theorist to link to the social constructions present in a culture. To SBS, the long-standing neglect of cultural factors by IR theorists stemmed from their reticence to make this move.

The task of the IR theorist, as SBS see it, is as follows: "State X orients to action according to the manner in which the particular situation is viewed by certain officials and according to what they want. The actions of other actors, the actor's goals and means, and the other components of the situation are related meaningfully by the actor. His action flows from this definition of the situation." The engine of theoretical integration, then, is the definition of the situation created by the human decision-makers.

The Possibility of Manifesting Agency in Explanations of International Affairs

Scholars in IR have struggled with the "agent-structure" problematique for some time now. Although no final resolution will ever be accepted, as this is a perennial philosophical conundrum, what is accepted is that IR theory currently provides much more insight into structure than agency. This is a severe theoretical handicap, for to lack a robust concept of the "agent" in IR means to be at a disadvantage when trying to explain or project significant change and noteworthy creativity in international relations.

SBS fully recognized this problematique, and gave a response at odds with the dominant emphasis on structure. For them,

> Adoption of the action-situational analysis makes it possible to emphasize that state behavior is determined but to avoid deterministic explanations. Some of the awkward problems of the objective-subjective dilemma are avoided by the attempt to see the world through the decision-maker's eyes. We adhere to the nation-state as the fundamental unit of analysis, yet we have discarded the state as a metaphysical abstraction.

Furthermore, it is very difficult to grapple with the issue of accountability in international affairs if the theoretical language cannot, in a realistic fashion, link acts of human agency in that realm to the consequences thereof. That a standing international court to try individuals for crimes against humanity is now in the offing suggests that the broader world community hungers after ideational frameworks that manifest the agency embedded in international affairs. A shift toward the SBS "handstand" would empower IR scholars to make an appreciated contribution in that regard.

The Possibility of a Fuller Sense of Explanation in IR, as well as Complementarity with Rational Choice Formalizations

The third major advantage is to move beyond description or postulation of natural law-like generalizations of state behavior to a fuller and more satisfying explanation for state behavior that requires an account of the contributions of human beings. Social science is unlike the physical sciences in that what is analyzed—humans as social beings—possess agency. Description of an act of agency, or assertion that natural law was operative in a particular case of the use of agency, cannot fully satisfy, for we know that agency means the agent could have acted otherwise. What is required is almost an anthropology of IR that delves into such agency-oriented concepts as motivation, emotion, and problem representation. Indeed, much of the early empirical work based on SBS (see, for example, Snyder and Paige, 1962) does resemble a more anthropological or "verstehen" approach.

But SBS felt there was a larger issue at stake here—there were two complementary but distinct approaches to IR: "(1) the description and measurement of interactions; and (2) decision-making—the formulation and execution of policy. Interaction patterns can be studied by themselves without reference to decision-making except that the 'why' of the patterns cannot be answered." Furthermore, exploration of only the first of these approaches would prohibit IR from reaching its potential as a *social* science:

> We believe that the phenomena normally studied in the field of international politics can be interpreted and meaningfully related by means of [the decision-making approach] as we shall present it. It should be clearly understood that this is *not* to say that *all* useful work in the field must or can be done within the decision-making framework. . . . However, and the qualification is crucial, if one wishes to probe the "why" questions underlying the events, conditions, and interaction patterns which rest upon state action, then decision-making analysis is certainly necessary. We would go so far as to say *that the "why" questions cannot be answered without analysis of decision-making.*

The supposed incommensurability of rational choice and "verstehen" methods is familiar and unfortunate. Presaging current research on psychological and cultural factors and the corresponding calls for "thin" rationality to be complemented by "thick" analysis of worldviews and values, SBS explicitly rejected the idea that this latter approach was somehow in theoretical conflict with more formal theories of choice:

> It has been the practice of some scholars, particularly in economics and logic, dealing with the theory of choice or decision-making to propose what are essentially rational models of rational actions, models in which the actor is not only predicated as acting rationally but also as having complete information. These are not, however, completely adequate for application to situations characterized by risk, uncertainty and incomplete information. It should be made very clear that it is not our intention to disparage in any way efforts at formalization which much of necessity make numerous simplifying assumptions.

These formal models have resulted in discussion and clarification for which any students of organizational decision-making must be grateful.

In what, then, does the complementarity lie? According to SBS, it is in the derivation of the rule of choice and specification of the preferences and preference orderings of the individuals involved in the decision. Rather than preferences and decision rules arising, as did Athena, fully formed from the head of Zeus, they derive from a myriad of factors, including culture, personality, evolution of shared organizational understandings, the exigencies of domestic politics, and so forth. To use the predictive power of rational choice theory, one must first feed it accurate and detailed information about specific decision-makers, and the context in which they are operating. As SBS put it, "[W]e might summarize our comments on the nature of choice as follows: information is selectively perceived and evaluated in terms of the decision-maker's frame of reference. Choices are made on the basis of preferences which are in part situationally and in part biographically determined."

SBS saw that the two traditions need each other: rational choice without study of human decision-makers can only aspire to be vague and pray not to be inaccurate; yet, without rational choice, a conceptualization of the strategic elements of choice may not be realizable. Furthermore, it is becoming recognized that the style of analysis outlines by SBS is not only crucial to understanding foreign policy, but to understanding *all* choice. Again, Snyder and his colleagues foresaw this: "[W]e believe that, analytically, all decision-making in formal organizations can be handled the same way."

After decades of mutual suspicion, IR theory is slowly but perceptibly drawing nearer to a state of truce between the two decision-making traditions—a truce based upon the very foundations Snyder and his colleagues described over 40 years ago.

"SBS" SCHOLARSHIP TODAY:
WHERE TO FIND IT, HOW TO DO IT

If the foregoing explication of the advantages to be realized from a re-evaluation of the SBS framework has been at all persuasive, the reader may rightfully ask at this point: Where do I find recent scholarship in the SBS tradition? And if I were interested in making this theoretical move myself, how would this be accomplished? What are the methodological implications of such a move?

First, let it be said that SBS never aspired to theoretical hegemony in the IR field. They felt that all avenues of theorizing should be explored— the only caveat being that each should be open to the insights of the other. As the SBS essay puts it, "The task [of IR theorizing] will be noticeably lighter if the moods and procedures of the active scholars permit and encourage us to stand on one another's shoulders instead of holding each other at arm's length." If Richard Snyder were alive today, perhaps what he would most lament has been an unaccountable insularity among the "invisible colleges" of IR (Hermann, 1998). I do not think he would urge today's scholars to abandon whatever they were doing and follow in the SBS tradition instead, but I do think he would ask if they had read any good SBS-type scholarship lately.

The SBS style of scholarship, including as it does the human decision-maker at the center of its theoretical enterprise, of necessity includes the collection of information about the individual(s) in the decision-making roles, the organizational context in which the decisions are made, the communications network (structure, process, and content) pertinent to the decisions being studied, the cultural and ideational setting of the decision, the sequence over time of decisions made and modified according to feedback received, and the dynamic co-construction occurring between each of these factors. SBS-style scholarship is, therefore, fundamentally interdisciplinary in nature.

It also requires a heroic data collection effort; heroic either in terms of the sheer amount of effort required to amass the necessary primary source material, much of which may be classified, or heroic in the sense of the creative construction of means to infer information that either does not exist or cannot be accessed. It was representative of SBS's openness that in the original 1962 edited volume they included an essay by Herbert McClosky, who opined,

> The inordinate complexity of the [SBS] scheme as it has so far been outlined is unquestionably its greatest shortcoming, one which in the end may prove its undoing. . . . A research design that requires an investigator to collect detailed information about such diverse matters as the social system, the economy, the foreign situation, the actors, the perceptions, the motivations, the values, the goals, the communication problems, the personality—in short, that asks him to account for a decision-making event virtually *in its totality*— places a back-breaking burden upon him, one that he could never adequately accomplish even if he were willing to invest an exorbitant effort. If the mere magnitude of the task does not frighten him off, he is likely to be discouraged by the unrewarding prospect of having to collect data about a great number

of variables whose relative importance he can only guess at and whose influence he cannot easily measure in any event. (McClosky, 1962: 201)

This is really the crux of the matter. If such research cannot be performed, then the state of current IR theory makes sense: abstractions are of necessity at the heart of our theories, agency vanishes, and to the extent that we speak of the power of ideational forces, we can only speak of them in a vague way, as if they were elusive mists that float through the theoretical landscape. But a rebuttal could be as follows: even if only a few IR scholars are willing to undertake such work, it salvages the entire enterprise of IR theorizing from irrelevance and vacuity. One can justify using shorthand if there is a full language underlying that use. We can justify theoretical shorthand in IR (e.g., using the metaphysical state as an actor) if we understand what spelling our sentences out in the underlying language (i.e., taking the human decision-maker as the theoretical focus) would look like and what the meaning of those sentences would be in that fuller language. If *someone* is willing to write in the full language, we can still translate the shorthand. It is only if the shorthand completely replaces the fuller language that we are truly impoverished in a theoretical sense in IR. It is when we stop wincing slightly when the abstraction of the state is used as a theoretical actor, when we feel fully comfortable with the omission of the real human actors behind the abstraction, that we have lost the theoretical battle and doomed IR as a field of study.

Furthermore, SBS would not concede that the totality of an event must be known to pursue this style of research:

A careful refinement of analytical purposes and delineation of research targets may help considerably to reduce the burdens of numbers and complexity of phenomena. The desire to "see" everything at once is a natural one, but it represents another siren song for it is based on the assumption that the social world can or must be reconstituted to the last detail which is neither possible, necessary, nor desirable. . . . A tradition of raw empiricism in political science (of great value in itself) has contributed both to despair and to unsound methodological assumptions. In particular, case studies, which should become the basis for generalization, have somehow supported the notion that about any policy or event there is *too much* to be known, much of it unknowable. . . . It is one thing to assume that all factors have a similar relevancy under *all* conditions. It is another to specify *potential* relevancies under *particular* conditions. . . . Accordingly, the perfection of concepts and categories should provide a basis for handling international phenomena *without* having to "see" and to "grasp" everything at once.

The best of the most recent works in the SBS tradition follow this advice: they do not seek to understand the totality of a decision-making event. Rather, they seek either to uncover the main micro-level determinants of decision-making in a generalizable sense, or they seek to weave together hitherto disparate strands of IR theory that can only be linked through the theoretical intersection that is the human decision-maker. What follows is not a comprehensive survey, by any means, but merely a starting place for those who would like to acquaint themselves with the current incarnation of SBS-style research.[1]

Construction of Meaning and Framing of Situations by Human Agents in IR, including Horizon/Template Analysis

Arguably at the heart of necessary micro-foundational theoretical work in IR, some very innovative studies of situational interpretation and problem representation by human agents in foreign policy exist. Indeed, Sylvan and Voss's edited volume, *Problem Representation in Foreign Policy Decision Making* (Sylvan and Voss, 1998), is a must-read in this regard, for it contains an excellent survey of the diverse methodological approaches to this important issue. Turning to efforts by individual scholars, G. R. Boynton's longstanding research agenda on interpretation of new foreign policy situations by human agents is noteworthy in this regard. For example, in a 1991 piece, Boynton uses the official record of hearings of congressional committees to investigate how committee members make sense of current events and policies. By viewing the questions and responses in the hearing as an unfolding narrative, Boynton is able to chart how "meaning" crystallizes for each committee member, and how they attempt to share that meaning with other members and with those who are testifying. Boynton posits the concept of "interpretive triple" as a way to understand how connections between facts are made through plausible interpretations. An interpretive triple is the means whereby human decision-makers create links between hitherto unrelated concepts by means of a third concept that he already understands to be linked to each. Boynton is then able to illuminate how plausibility is granted to an interpretation—in effect, ascertaining which interpretations are plausible within the social context created by the hearings.

Helen Purkitt has pioneered the use of the "think aloud protocol" in international relations to discern what happens in the "pre-decision" phase of foreign policy (Purkitt, 1998). Verbalizations by human agents as they ponder a hypothetical problem in foreign policy are used by Purkitt to inquire as to the parameters of the reasoning used. She discovers that background of the reasoners do influence their reasoning, but perhaps her more important finding is that problem representations are being made typically after consideration of only two to four factors. Furthermore, these representations are made and then "harden" fairly quickly.

Hudson (1999) attempted to address the construction of meaning and the representation of foreign policy problems in a different way: by exploring the horizon of imagination present within a culture. Creating several hypothetical foreign policy scenarios, she outlined numerous possible responses of a nation to each, and then inquired of average citizens in three countries what they thought their own country would do, and what they thought the other countries would do. For most scenarios, distinctive patterns of horizon visualization could be discerned within each culture. In two cases, respondents were able to imagine responses that Hudson could not! It appears that an understanding of "who we are" plays into the understanding of "what it is we do," and new foreign policy situations will be rendered intelligible in part by imagining what it is that would be done in that situation. This research has much in common with a dramaturgical approach to intelligibility in IR (see, for example, Etheredge, 1992).

Persuasion and Diffusion Undertaken by Framing/Meaning Entrepreneurs within IR; Analysis of Interaction between Competing Entrepreneurs

Once representations have begun to be formed by human agents in foreign policy, collective action can only follow when agreement has been reached with others that a particular representation or set of representations are the appropriate basis for state action. To that end, diffusion of representations must occur, followed by persuasion and competition for persuasive power within a social context. "Entrepreneurs" of framing and meaning will be the agents studied in such research. There are some excellent examples of innovative work in this area.

For example, Lotz (1997) asks how it was that Americans ever acquiesced to the North American Free Trade Agreement (NAFTA). After all, Mexico, to most Americans, is constructed as "foreign" in a way Canada is not. Traditionally, it would not be seen as either possible or desirable to link the economic fate of the United States to such an alien culture. Indeed, American public opinion was very divided on this issue, with a large bloc of undecideds. Knowing that the Gore-Perot debate of 1993 was crucial in swaying the significant undecided bloc, Lotz analyzes the rhetoric of the debate to show how Gore and Perot used different versions of American national identity (what Lotz calls "myth"). Gore successfully outmaneuvered Perot by recasting the American Dream portion of the myth to make NAFTA seem a natural extension of it. This discursive maneuver had real empirical effects, including arguably the passage of NAFTA.

Andrea Grove and Neal Carter (1999) make an important contribution to this area of research through their study of the interaction between the persuasion attempts of Gerry Adams and the persuasion attempts of John Hume to sway their countrymen in Northern Ireland to respond to the initiatives of third parties to the conflict there. Comparing the rival discourse of the two men, Grove and Carter are able to analyze the horizons of possibility for each man and the groups which follow them. They are then able to map out the maneuvering room Adams and Hume have left themselves by adhering to their particular stories of the conflict. Even more boldly, Grove and Carter go on to suggest how the pressure and influence of third parties, such as the United States, who possess their own story of the Northern Ireland conflict, could either succeed or fail depending on the state of the internal debate between Hume and Adams.

Sylvan, Majeski, and Milliken (1991) examine the mountains of written material generated by the U.S. national security establishment with reference to the conduct of the Vietnam War. They question the war policy recommendations in this material: When did a statement become a "bona fide" recommendation, to which other agents had to pay attention? How did such statements fit into the flow of recommendations and counter-recommendations? How did persuasion occur? Sylvan et al. schematically map the river of recommendations in order to answer such questions.

Change and Learning by Human Agents in IR

Levy (1994) provides a useful overview of efforts to capture social learning in IR theory. Here I will highlight but two efforts that address this concern.

Using Bonham's technique of cognitive mapping, Bonham, Sergeev, and Parshin (1997) are able to detect the emergence of new knowledge structures within the minds of Kennedy and Khruschev during the negotiations of the Partial Test Ban Treaty of 1963. These new knowledge structures improved mutual understanding, and allowed for greater reflexivity in the interactions between the two men. The authors suggests that such a "shared reality-building process" may be a prerequisite for successful negotiations between two antagonists.

Glenn Chafetz and his colleagues (Chafetz et al., 1997) use national role conception (NRC) analysis to trace identity change over time. This is an interesting use of NRC, for usually NRCs are utilized to explain the persistence, not the change, of state behavior over time. Their case study is that of Ukraine, in its first years of existence. During that time of flux, Ukraine was asked to relinquish its nuclear weapons. First refusing and then acquiescing over the period of several years, Chafetz et al. argue for a process of subtle change in NRC over this time period from role conceptions that required nuclear weapons as a tangible manifestation to conceptions that did not require such weapons. Tracking statements by highly placed officials in Ukraine, Chafetz et al. are able to demonstrate who was making what statements that were then built upon by others.

The Study of Human Agents as They Interact in Groups in IR

The study of how individual human agency is transformed by interaction with other human agents in small groups has a long and distinguished history in FPA. The work of Janis (1982), of course, is paradigmatic in this regard. The newest work is even more nuanced and insightful, if that is possible, than the old. A fine recent volume, *Beyond Groupthink* (Hart et al., 1997) is invaluable as another excellent survey of the cutting edge approaches in this field of study. Turning to individual efforts, Beasley (1998) tackles the aggregation problem inherent in group research directly, by offering new methods for "consider[ing] the group as a complex forum for the interaction of decision makers and to begin to apply our insights regarding individuals to the collective level" (109). He explores six aggregation principles, and empirically investigates the degree to which each could be said to have been used in his case study of the British Cabinet meetings of 1938. These principles include simplicity, single representation embellishment, factionalism, common decomposition, common alternatives, and expertise. He discovers that the group aggregation principle that emerges may alter other aspects of the group context, such as propensity toward groupthink itself.

Sylvan and Haddad (1998) investigate how group environments mediate individual cognition. Using an experimental model, they study small groups of subjects who are discussing a given foreign policy problem and attempting to come up with a decision as to what to do about it. They discover that such small groups attempt to create a co-authored "story" of what is taking place. The co-authorship then allows for the action decision to be made collectively. The group interaction surrounding the creation of this story is punctuated by moments of rival story lines colliding. The social working-through of these collisions can be traced to moments where participants ponder what Sylvan and Haddad call the "it depends" challenge. When one participant says, "It depends . . . (on what we mean, on what we want to do, etc.)," the group as a whole must work its way back to a consistent story line through persuasion and analysis.

Construction of National Role Conception
Identity by Human Agents Within the Nation

National role conception research, originated by Holsti (1970), is still a very useful approach to questions of national identity formation (Walker, 1987). Holsti specifically tied NRC to human agency by making individuals' articulations of national identity the measure of NRC. More recently, using eclectic methods such as discourse analysis, process-tracing, and computational modeling, Sanjoy Banerjee has traced the origins and evolution of identities in conflict. For example, Banerjee traces Indian and Pakistani national identities as individual human agents, such as Jinnah and Nehru, constructed them for their followers (Banerjee, 1991, 1997).

In addition to the work of Glenn Chafetz, mentioned above, Marijke Breuning has empirically demonstrated how differences in NRC lead to the creation of different institutions and the enactment of different policies by nations that, materially speaking, are very similar (Breuning, 1997, 1998). Once, again, as with Holsti, Banerjee, and Chafetz, the operationalization of NRC in Breuning's studies (individual discourse) lead one directly back to human agency.

Emotion and Affect of Human Agents
and its Influence in World Affairs

There is very little work on the role of emotion and strong affect in international relations. Yet if a robust theory of agency is to be developed in IR, and given that emotions are very strong forces affecting the representations and reactions of human beings, such study must at some point be undertaken. I am familiar with only two studies in this area, one by Crawford (2000), and one by Cottam and McCoy (1998). Both of these works argue that emotion "colors" rational choice in profound ways that the analyst ignores at his peril. As Cottam and McCoy argue, "Emotions, once aroused, can control cognitions" (1998: 122). Although both studies are more metatheoretic than theory-building, it will be worthwhile to track future progress in this research area.

Integrative Efforts that Attempt to Retain Agency in IR

Attempts to integrate theory in the sense of channeling both material and ideational factors through the human decision-maker intersection are extremely rare. Part of the problem may be, echoing Rose, that such integrative work demands country- or area-expertise (Rose, 1998). However, at least one integrative FPA project attempted to "shoot the moon": to integrate across all levels of theory as well as to draw upon country/area expertise. This was the effort of the now-defunct CREON 2 project. Interestingly, though having met its fate several years ago, the empirical pinnacle of its research is only now making its way into print: the summer 2001 special issue of *International Studies Review* lays out its theoretical framework and empirical results.

CREON 2 envisioned a model in which the constraining and enabling elements of the international system and the national society, coupled with an analysis of the situation at hand, would be routed through a theoretical component called the ultimate decision unit. Within this ultimate decision unit, one would find theoretical clusters corresponding to those originally postulated by the SBS framework: personality of individual decision-makers, organizational setting, communications networks, and so forth. This overall model would require inputs from country experts before it could be applied to any discrete situation. Since the principal investigators were not themselves country experts, they entered into scholarly collaboration with IR researchers who were. The result is a fascinating effort at radical integration of IR theory, while retaining an account of human agency at the center of the theoretical enterprise. One wonders if we will ever see its like again in IR theory. Perhaps with the republication of SBS, a new generation of scholars will arise to take up that challenge once more.

SUMMARY

The advantages SBS continues to offer IR theory cannot be minimized, especially at this moment in history. In the wake of the collapse of the Soviet bloc, in the wake of terrorism on U.S. soil perpetrated by a small group of foreign terrorists and applauded by many in the world, it is theoretically foolish to retain a primary focus on system-level variables, or even on enduring structural constraints. Humans appear to have almost an infinite capacity for wriggling out of macro-level structures and constraints. This is not to say that we should not have theories about system and structure and how these condition human behavior but, rather, that we cannot stop there and consider our theoretical task to have been responsibly completed. If ideas do matter in international affairs, one must move below the state level to find the unit of analysis that can think of those ideas, and be persuaded by the ideas of others, and that can be motivated to act and even change action on the basis of ideas. As SBS exhorted so many decades ago, we must bring human beings back into the IR theoretical enterprise, and put them at the intersection of all other forces about which we theorize.

Forty years has not only brought IR closer to the questions SBS addressed but has brought methodological breakthroughs, as well. Many of the works cited in the section on current scholarship employ statistical and computational tools unknown in 1962. Simultaneous, then, with the renewed interest in an SBS-type approach, is a dampening of criticism such as that offered by McClosky and others that the research was too demanding and complex. Now new methodological technologies exist to facilitate this type of research. The existence of works such as those surveyed in the previous section shows that this work can be done at a high level of theoretical and methodological sophistication. And if it can be done, then it *should* be done, for otherwise IR theory will lose its ground. If that ground were to be lost completely, then what we will be able to say through IR theory will be very little indeed.

The debt of the field of international relations to the research program initiated by SBS should not be underestimated. Some are conscious of this debt, other not. Perhaps the republication of the SBS framework is a step toward greater recognition of what is owed to those pioneers of 40 years ago. A close reading, or rereading, of Snyder, Bruck, and Sapin's work makes clear how much we should have already known in IR. A reevaluation of this "path not taken" 40 years ago might point the way to a healthier conceptualization of the main theoretical tasks that face us in International Relations today.

NOTES

1. There are numerous empirical pieces that catch the vision of reincorporating agency into IR. Some of these empirical pieces have made their way into top journals and highly visible edited volumes, for they grow out of research traditions that have sociologically based standing in the states systemic project. The work of Jeffrey Checkel (1993, 1999), Elizabeth Kier (1996), and Vaughn Shannon (2000) are prominent and praiseworthy examples of falsifiable narrative attempts to restore agency—agency embedded in social context—to IR. However, since most IR scholars would be familiar with this work, it would not be as helpful to tour that literature. We will concentrate on the SBS-type scholarship emanating from the field of FPA.

REFERENCES

Banerjee, Sanjoy (1991) "Reproduction of Subjects in Historical Structures: Attribution, Identity, and Emotion in the Early Cold War," *International Studies Quarterly*, Volume 35, No. 1, 19–38.

Banerjee, Sanjoy (1997) "The Cultural Logic of National Identity Formation: Contending Discourses in Late Colonial India," in Valerie M. Hudson (Ed.), *Culture and Foreign Policy.* Boulder, CO: Lynne Rienner, 27–44.

Beasley, Ryan (1998) "Collective Interpretations: How Problem Representations Aggregate in Foreign Policy Groups," in Donald A. Sylvan and James F. Voss (Eds.), *Problem Representation in Foreign Policy Decision Making.* Cambridge: Cambridge University Press, 80–115.

Bonham, G. Matthew, Victor M. Sergeev, and Pavel B. Parshin (1997) "The Limited Test-Ban Agreement: Emergence of New Knowledge Structures in International Negotiation," *International Studies Quarterly,* Volume 41, No. 2, June, 215–240.

Boynton, G. R. (1991) "The Expertise of the Senate Foreign Relations Committee," in Valerie M. Hudson (Ed.), *Artificial Intelligence and International Politics.* Boulder, CO: Westview Press, 291–309.

Breuning, Marijke (1997) "Culture, History, Role: Belgian and Dutch Axioms and Foreign Assistance Policy," in Valerie M. Hudson (Ed.), *Culture and Foreign Policy.* Boulder, CO: Lynne Rienner, 99–124.

Breuning, Marijke (1998) "Configuring Issue Areas: Belgian and Dutch Representations of the Role of Foreign Assistance in Foreign Policy," in Donald A. Sylvan and James F. Voss (Eds.), *Problem Representation in Foreign Policy Decision Making.* Cambridge: Cambridge University Press, 303–32.

Brooks, Stephen G. and William Wohlforth (2000–2001) "Power, Globalization, and the End of the Cold War: Reviewing a Landmark Case for Ideas," *International Security* 25:3, 5–53.

Brooks, Stephen G. and William Wohlforth (2002) "From Old theory to New Theory in Qualitative Research," *International Security* 26:4, 93–111.

Chafetz, Glenn, Hillel Abramson, and Suzette Grillot (1997) "Cultural and National Role Conceptions: Belarussian and Ukrainian Compliance with the Nuclear Nonproliferation Regime," in Valerie M. Hudson (Ed.), *Culture and Foreign Policy.* Boulder, CO: Westview Press, 169–200.

Checkel, Jeffrey T. (1993) "Ideas, Institutions, and the Gorbachev Foreign Policy Revolution," *World Politics.* Volume 45, No. 2, 271–300.

Checkel, Jeffrey T. (1999) "Norms, Institutions and National Identity in Contemporary Europe," *International Studies Quarterly.* Volume 43, No. 1, March, 83–114.

Cottam, Martha, and Dorcas E. McCoy (1998) "Image Change and Problem Representation after the Cold War," in Donald A. Sylvan and James F. Voss (Eds.), *Problem Representation in Foreign Policy Decision Making.* Cambridge: Cambridge University Press, 116–146.

Crawford, Neta C. (2000) "The Passion of World Politics: Propositions on Emotion and Emotional Relationships," *International Security.* Volume 24, No. 4, Spring, 116–156.

English, Robert D. (2002) "Power, Ideas and New Evidence on the Cold War's End: A Reply to Brooks and Wohlforth," *International Security* 26:4, 70–92.

Etheredge, Lloyd (1992) "On Being More Rational Than the Rationality Assumption: Dramatic Requirements, Nuclear Deterrence, and the Agenda for Learning," in Eric G. Singer and Valerie M. Hudson (Eds.), *Political Psychology and Foreign Policy.* Boulder, Co: Westview Press, 59–78.

Grove, Andrea K., and Neal A. Carter. (1999) "Not All Blarney is Cast in Stone: International Cultural Conflict in Northern Ireland," *Political Psychology.* Volume 20, No. 4, 725–766.

Hart, Paul, Eric K. Stern, and Bengt Sundelius (Eds.), (1997) *Beyond Groupthink: Political Group Dynamics and Foreign Policy-making.* Ann Arbor: University of Michigan Press.

Hermann, Margaret G. (1998) "One Field, Many Perspectives: Building the Foundations for Dialogue," *International Studies Quarterly.* Volume 42, No. 4, December, 605–24.

Holsti, Kal J. (1970) "National Role Conceptions in the Study of Foreign Policy," *International Studies Quarterly.* Volume 14, 233–309.

Hudson, Valerie M. (Ed.), (1997) *Culture and Foreign Policy.* Boulder, CO: Lynne Rienner.

Hudson, Valerie M. (1999) "Cultural Expectations of One's Own and Other Nations' Foreign Policy Action Templates," *Political Psychology.* Volume 20, No. 4, December, 767–802.

Hudson, Valerie M. (2001) "Manifest Agency, Foreign Policy Analysis, and IR Theory: The Other Agent-Structure Debate and Its (Higher) Stakes," paper presented at the 42nd annual conference of the International Studies Association, Chicago, February 20–24.

Janis, Irving (1982) *Groupthink.* Boston: Houghton-Mifflin.

Katzenstein, Peter J. (Ed.), (1996) *The Culture of National Security: Norms and Identity in World Politics.* New York: Columbia University Press.

Kier, Elizabeth (1996) "Culture and French Military Doctrine Before World War II," in Peter J. Katzenstein (Ed.), *The Culture of National Security: Norms and Identity in World Politics.* New York: Columbia University Press, 186–215.

Lapid, Yosef and Friedrich Kratochwil (eds.), (1996) *The Return of Culture and Identity in IR Theory (Critical Perspectives on World Politics.* Boulder, CO: Lynne Rienner.

Levy, Jack (1994) "Learning and Foreign Policy: Sweeping a Conceptual Minefield," *International Organization.* Volume 48, No. 2, Spring, 279–312.

Lotz, Hellmut (1997) "Myth and NAFTA: The Use of Core Values in U.S. Politics," in Valerie M. Hudson (Ed.), *Culture and Foreign Policy.* Boulder, CO: Lynne Rienner, 73–98.

McClosky, Herbert (1962) "Concerning Strategies for a Science of International Politics," in Richard C. Snyder, H.W. Bruck, and Burton Sapin (Eds.), *Foreign Policy Decision-Making.* Glencoe, IL: The Free Press, 186–205.

Purkitt, Helen E. (1998) "Problem Representations and Political Expertise: Evidence from 'Think Aloud' Protocols of South African Elite," in Donald A. Sylvan and

James F. Voss (eds.), *Problem Representation in Foreign Policy Decision Making*. Cambridge: Cambridge University Press, 147–86.

Putnam, Robert D. (1988) "Diplomacy and Domestic Politics: The Logic of Two-Level Games," *International Organization* 42 (summer): 427–60.

Rose, Gideon (1998) "Neoclassical Realism and Theories of Foreign Policy," *World Politics*. Volume 51, No. 1, October, 144–72.

Shannon, Vaughn P. (2000) "Norms are What States Make of Them: The Political Psychology of Norm Violation," *International Studies Quarterly*. Volume 44, No. 2, June, 293–316.

Snyder, Richard C., H. W. Bruck, and Burton Sapin (1954) *Decision-Making as an Approach to the Study of International Politics*. Foreign Policy Analysis Project Series No. 3, Princeton, NJ: Princeton University Press.

Snyder, Richard C., H. W. Bruck, and Burton Sapin (Eds.), (1962) *Foreign Policy Decision-Making*. Glencoe, IL: The Free Press.

Snyder, Richard C., and Glenn D. Paige (1962) "The United States Decision to Resist Aggression in Korea: The Application of an Analytical Scheme," in Richard C. Snyder, H.W. Bruck, and Burton Sapin (eds.), *Foreign Policy Decision-Making*. Glencoe, IL: The Free Press, 206–49.

Sylvan, David, Stephen Majeski, and Jennifer Milliken (1991) "Theoretical Categories and Data Construction in Computational Models of Foreign Policy," in Valerie M. Hudson (Ed.), *Artificial Intelligence and International Politics*. Boulder, CO: Westview Press, 327–46.

Sylvan, Donald A. and Deborah M. Haddad (1998) "Reasoning and Problem Representation in Foreign Policy: Groups, Individuals, and Stories," in Donald A. Sylvan and James F. Voss (Eds.), *Problem Representation in Foreign Policy Decision Making*. Cambridge: Cambridge University Press, 187–212.

Sylvan, Donald A., and James F. Voss (Eds.), (1998) *Problem Representation in Foreign Policy Decision Making*. Cambridge: Cambridge University Press.

Walker, Stephen G. (Ed.), (1987) *Role Theory and Foreign Policy Analysis*. Durham, NC: Duke University Press.

Wendt, Alexander (1992) "Anarchy is what States Make of It: The Social Construction of Power Politics," *International Organization*. Volume 46, No. 2, Spring, 391–425.

Wendt, Alexander (1999) *Social Theory of International Politics*. Cambridge: Cambridge University Press.

Decision-Making as an Approach to the Study of International Politics

Richard C. Snyder
H. W. Bruck
Burton Sapin

PREFACE

The authors want to express here their firm conviction that a field such as international politics is not just a hodge-podge of ideas that in the past for one reason or another have been shoved under the same tent. It is rather a set of empirical problems, meaningfully related and having very specific, researchable referents. These problems, regardless of their origin, must be analyzed with tools appropriate to the enterprise. To that end we have found it necessary to manufacture our own scheme of analysis by drawing heavily on the works and methods of scholars not normally consulted by political scientists. We have documented these sources in the hope that others may find them useful. We have had to employ words and concepts that may appear strange to the reader.

We must comment frankly on two possible kinds of misunderstanding to which our paper may give rise. First, we shall be grateful and more than satisfied if our effort stimulates others in a modest fashion and if it provides a point from which more accurate bearings may be taken. We would be guilty of the most unforgivable naïveté and unbearable self-confidence were we to overestimate the impact of this work on so large and complex a field as international politics. Second, we would like to dispel the notion that we are offering a kind of Rube Goldberg contraption, cleverly designed to do in a hundred-odd pages that for which others need many volumes. If the reader follows the argument closely, he will, we trust, find a challenge. We cannot, however, overemphasize that we are not presenting a field of learning. Rather, these are some ways of thinking about, or a posture with respect to, a field of learning. On both these counts we are aware of the risks.

Our intellectual debts are many. Some of the pre-eminent scholars whose writings we have drawn upon are acknowledged in the various citations. Others are more immediate and no less extensive. Without the original and continued interest and good offices of Professor Harold Sprout of the Department of Politics, the project could not have been undertaken. Thanks to Professor Wilbert E. Moore we have had the opportunity of participating in the Organizational Behavior Section at Princeton University. We have thus had the privilege of benefiting from the analytical prowess of a group of scholars representing virtually all the social science disciplines. These men helped us lay the foundations for our approach. In addition to Professor Moore, the director, we owe an especial debt to Professor Harold Garfinkel (now of the Department of Sociology, University of California, Los Angeles). Other members of the Section to whom we owe much are Dr. Elliot Mishler (Office of Population Research, Princeton University), Professor Gresham Sykes (Department of Sociology), and Professor Gordon B. Turner (Department of History). Professor Edgar S. Furniss, Jr., of the Politics Department, consultant to the Foreign Policy Analysis Project, took a substantial part in the early formulations which later turned out to be an integral part of our analysis. Professor Percy Corbett of the Center of International Studies at Princeton has given valued criticism and welcome intellectual support. Professor Marion J. Levy, Jr. (Department of Sociology), Professor Richard W. VanWagenen (Director, Center for Research on World Political Institutions), Dr. Harold Stein (Woodrow Wilson School of Public and International Affairs, Princeton), and Dr. David E. Apter (Visiting Fellow, Center of International Studies) also read the manuscript and made helpful suggestions. A special debt is owed by one of the authors, Mr. Bruck, to the Social Science Research Council for a fellowship which gave him an opportunity to develop some of the ideas incorporated in this essay.

Needless to say, none of the persons whose help we have acknowledged bears any responsibility of the views presented here. This study was made possible by funds granted by the Carnegie Corporation of New York. That

INTRODUCTION

The primary purpose of this essay[1] is to present a tentative formulation of an analytical scheme which we hope may serve as the core of a frame of reference[2] for the study of international politics. Eventually the outline followed here will be expanded into a full-length monograph in which points neglected for lack of space will be given fuller treatment and in which other points will be pursued where logical implications lead. The contents of this monograph will be approximately as follows:

Part I

Part II

Part III

Part IV

14. Problems of Research
15. Summary and Conclusion

We only intend at this time, therefore, to suggest in a general way the nature of the analysis we are trying to develop. Even in this abbreviated form, however, we feel our scheme may be of sufficient substance and clarity to permit our colleagues to comment constructively on its possible contribution to teaching and research while the process of development is still going on. Actually, our frame of reference and its central decision-making focus will have to remain tentative; we are convinced that we stand on the threshold of a period of measurable intellectual growth in which flexibility and tentativeness are not only imposed by circumstances but required by the rules of sound scholarship.

1. SCOPE AND METHOD

Some Preliminary Considerations

Before we discuss our basic assumptions, certain points must be brought out into the open immediately. The individual reader will forgive us if we try in part to anticipate the reactions of groups of readers to our presentation. We do this not to demonstrate our capacity to "second guess" our audience, but because we believe enough in the potential value of this kind of intellectual enterprise that we do not want to alienate some readers *unnecessarily.*

First, many will recognize that the general kind of analysis we are urging in this essay has actually been familiar to historians and political scientists for many years and has been attempted by them, sometimes with marked success. Good historiographers have long taken for granted the necessity of probing the minds of decision-makers in terms of their official behavior. Certain problems we emphasize here have been understood and discussed by such political scientists as George Catlin, Arthur Bentley, Charles Merriam, Harold Lasswell, Herbert Simon, and others. Among younger writers we share much with David Easton. While we can claim no inherent superiority over these predecessors, we have tried to build on their work and to synthesize a number of basic factors which hitherto have been treated somewhat in isolation. We recognize, too, that many readers have engaged in essentially the same type of analysis without having the time to systematically work out its implications.

Second, in the words of one of our colleagues at Princeton, it may appear that we have manufactured a sledge hammer to crack a small nut. Closely related to this is the possibility that the tools presented are perhaps over-refined in view of the "crude, imperfect, and spotty materials" with which students of international politics must work. We shall have more to say about this as we go along. At the moment, we will admit freely that there are many significant questions which can be asked—and even answered with varying degrees of satisfaction—without using a global scheme like the one we are outlining below. As we shall have occasion to reiterate later, we are confronted with the imposing task of studying a whole field of political science. But more important, we would insist that asking the right questions is fundamental to all scholarly inquiry. Furthermore, questions rarely suggest themselves. A conceptual scheme may be of substantial help in asking *all* the possibly significant questions, in asking them in fruitful form, *and* in uncovering some of the subtle analytical problems raised by apparently pertinent and self-evident questions.

Third, the reader may wonder, before he has covered many pages, whether we are discussing international politics or all of political science. The query is a proper one. Actually, we have concluded, tentatively, that if our approach meets various tests suggested later, it will have value for the analysis of other than international political phenomena.[1] There are obviously some qualifications necessary, due to special features of interstate relations. However, our feeling is that basically the decision-making core of our scheme, as well as the comments on the nature of a frame of reference, are equally applicable to the study of domestic politics or comparative politics.

Fourth, the scheme advanced here must eventually be applied and tested in various ways. The approach has been employed in both graduate and undergraduate teaching at Princeton with enough positive success to be encouraging. Foreign Policy Analysis Series No. 4, a research note on the role of the military in American foreign policy, represents another kind of trial run. Professor Edgar S. Furniss, Jr., of Princeton University will shortly prepare a case study of foreign policy-making in France within the framework of the present analysis. Henry Bruck—one of the authors—will also analyze, comparatively, commercial treaty-making in Ottawa and Washington. These should be viewed as nothing more than a recognition on our part that our system must prove itself.

Finally, in the pages which immediately follow, we have attempted to state some crucial methodological propositions. Some of our readers may find these painfully obvious. Others may become somewhat impatient. To still others, the word *methodology* is a scare word. We have not intended to bore or torture the reader. If any justification is needed, we would ask that two primary factors be kept in mind. Our obligation under the Carnegie Corporation's grant is to evaluate critically the study of international politics, not to make a substantive contribution to knowledge in the field. Thus, we are engaged in *a study of the study* of international politics; we cannot escape problems of method. In addition, we believe that political science currently suffers, on balance, from a lack of *sound* theory and conceptualization, not from too much theory. If the reader shares this last sentiment, he will perhaps be persuaded that a few pages of elementary methodology are not irrelevant to our purposes.

Underlying Assumptions and Principles

It seems only fair at the outset that we attempt to state briefly some of our basic assumptions and principles. The clearer we are about these, the less likelihood of serious or petty misunderstandings. Naturally, others may hold different assumptions and principles, in which case the differences between us will be clear. Naturally, too, we can be judged as to whether we have been true to our own premises.

Assumption One: That a fundamental need in the field of international politics at this time is more effective and more explicit conceptualization

What follows is, in effect, an exercise in *explicit* conceptualization. We stress explicitness in part because we feel that if our analytical apparatus is brought out into the open, our work can be more easily shared and tested. Much of the work of scholars in this field cannot be replicated, and, therefore, an important test of soundness and usefulness is missing. We would be presumptuous to claim novelty, but we do claim a greater degree of explicitness and systematization than is now typical of writing in this field.

The practical uses of conceptualization need no elaborate demonstration. Teachers are always under the necessity of planning courses. Time is limited. What is to be stressed? How can a course which is just a set of isolated topics be avoided? How a great mass of material to be organized? How can the subject be packaged coherently for the student? Similarly, the research is confronted by questions which can only be answered on basis of preconceptions. Aside from available time and data, library facilities, and so on, how will he choose what he will do? His choice must be made and must be made in terms of some criteria. These are surely familiar considerations, but we do always associate them with the nature of existing conceptualization in the field.

At this particular stage in the development of systematic analysis of international politics, the construction of concepts, categories, and a specialized vocabulary is both essential and appropriate. We realize, of course, that this sort of activity may command more than its due share of scholarly attention, can become an end in itself, can be sterile of results, and can be logically valid yet unrelated or unrelatable to empirical facts. Nonetheless, the perfection of analytical tools—if guided by strict application of certain rules of logic and scientific investigation—does not need to be wasteful or misleading.

All attempts to describe and explain human behavior require that what has already transpired be recaptured—not in all its original detail, but selectively according to a scheme employed by the reporter or observer. As a matter of fact, this goes on in daily life with all sorts of common-sense concepts being used. For example, we say Congressman Jones made a speech praising free trade because he is trying to get re-elected, or Congressman Jones attacked Congressman Smith for personal reasons. Such are common-sense explanations of motivation. They are not statements of fact but inferences based on an assumption or a pre-existing interpretative scheme. Normally we do not analyze these underlying factors or question them. In systematic investigations they cannot be taken for granted. A complicating factor is that many premises are hidden, many preconceptions implicit. However, the issue in social analysis is not conceptualization vs. no conceptualization, but what kind. Even the statement: "let the facts speak for themselves" is based on certain assumptions concerning the nature of facts, particularly that the selection and relationships of facts are suggested by the facts themselves without any operations by the observer.

It should also be recognized that any conceptual scheme—if poorly constructed and unwisely used—can be a "blinder" which only permits the observer to see what he wants to see and find what he expects to find. These are mechanical difficulties which can be remedied by rigor and vigilance. Nor do they refute the need for some way (or ways) to determine *what kinds of facts are relevant, how they are to be characterized, and how relations among them are to be explored.* The notion that the scholar who engages in conceptualization necessarily lives in a dreamworld far removed from so-called reality is untrue. Pending systematic investigation, concepts must always be checked against known facts, and fruitful concepts really result from a combination of rules of scientific procedure, imagination, and empirical knowledge.

Our first assumption is, then, that the attempt to establish a frame of reference which will embrace the political phenomena included in the study of international politics and the attempt to define certain central concepts for the analysis of state behavior represent a proper expenditure of intellectual resources by some scholars at this stage in the development of political science.[2]

Assumption Two: That any interpretative scheme must meet certain tests

When a science is young—and we mean the study of politics, not the practice of it—diverse ideas and investigative enterprises are to be welcomed. Yet it does not follow that every man's "approach" to the study of international politics is equally useful and valid. When the range of empirical phenomena is as broad as it is in this field, certainly there are many legitimate kinds of interests which students may have, and there are many kinds of researches which ought to be carried on. The variety of interests and problems open to any observer of a large area of social behavior, as well as the variety of methods of analysis, can be taken for granted. On the other hand, we ought to know—as a group of practicing scholars—why we disagree on these matters. Many discussions of scope and method fail to reveal the real bases of disagreement. One political scientist likes a historical approach, another likes an institutional approach, still another likes a power approach. Often the choice seems based on what suits the temperament of the individual teacher, not on rational intellectual calculation. In other words, because a wide choice is possible does not mean that every choice is equally legitimate in terms of criteria which should predominate in social science work.

We should like to emphasize that the attempt to order a total area of observation, that is, to discuss a field such as international politics *in general,* is clearly not the same thing as conducting a specific research operation on a limited topic or phase of the total subject. We are attempting to gain a broad and useful perspective on the sum total of ideas, data, courses, and activities which constitute a branch of learning. A research project is usually limited and may be designed to answer only one question. Not only is a field made up of many such questions and problems, but it would be manifestly ridiculous to take a cumbersome system of analysis into a limited research project. We would hope, of course, that a general scheme might aid in the smaller project—chiefly, perhaps, in suggesting researchable questions.

Furthermore, there would appear to be only a limited number of ways to define a field of learning (as distinct from specific interests, problems, and issues), and these can be evaluated according to accepted criteria. But we certainly would not argue that there is only *one way* to organize the data which comprise objects of study. All systems of analysis rest on two kinds of value judgments: first, those which affect the selection of data or problems to be emphasized and principles to be taught; second, those which affect the construction of the systems of analysis. In the first case, it may be decided to teach students the way toward peace by concentrating on the causes of war. In the second case, it may be decided to probe the prerequisites of peace by means of a concept of security-community.[3] In any event these value judgments ought to be made explicit, and all such systems ought to be constructed on the basis of rules of logic and concept-formation. Hence, we assume our scheme must stand or fall according to agreed tests. One of these tests is the extent to which it makes possible a more meaningful interpretation of existing data, suggests new and fruitful research efforts, and raises meaningful empirical questions about the phenomena of international politics which otherwise would not be asked. In short, interpretive schemes must meet three kinds of tests: operational, predictive, and efficiency.

Assumption Three: That the basis for a general theory of international politics does not exist at this time

Again we must emphasize the present stage in the intellectual development of our field. We have assumed that an attempt at an inclusive framework for existing and later theories makes more sense *now* because empirical data and preliminary conceptualization are as yet inadequate to support a general theory. A general theory must, of course, be sufficiently integrated to accommodate all phenomena and all logical relationships. We do not know enough about international politics to construct such a theory. We hope one possible by-product of our studies may be the exposure of gaps in our knowledge. However, this is not to say that the analysis of foreign policy and international politics ought not to be pushed to a higher level of generalization. Nor do we argue that the renewed interest in general theories of human behavior in the social sciences will not contribute to progress in the study of international politics.[4] On the contrary, our feeling is that these are of major importance. But so far as the present inquiry is concerned, there is more immediate profit—and less methodological difficulty—in an attempt to create a frame of reference within which flexibility can be preserved and "middle range theories"[5] can be stimulated and related to each other.[6]

We recognize nonetheless that the line between a general theory and a frame of reference is not as sharp as we have implied. Our analysis contains definite "intimations" of a general theory. We are moving toward such a theory, though at the moment our analysis has too many loose ends to be more than a frame of reference. The next step will be to put our categories together in terms of logical relationships. We hope meanwhile that the foundations for a general theory have been laid.

The Nature of a Frame of Reference[7]

Since we have said that we are attempting to create a frame of reference for the study of international politics, it might be helpful to say something about what it means as applied to a field of study.

1. First of all, it is an ordering enterprise. It consists of specifying a way or ways of segregating phenomena for description and explanation, normally, by means of definition, classification, categorization, and assignment of properties to what is to be observed—all in varying degrees of complexity and detail. The operations are basic to descriptive analysis and make it possible to isolate the factors which are presumed to account for the observed elements. *This involves a good deal more than labeling things.* For example, suppose we call the number of males aged nineteen to twenty-six in any nation a "power factor" or one kind of a power factor, namely, a "demographic factor." All we have done really is to suggest a listing of isolated factors. Unless we know more about the two categories of "power factor" and "demographic factor" and, above all, about the relationships among the factors, we have little more than a label or a synonym.

If carefully done, the segregation of phenomena for study should make it possible to locate the particular field of interest in a larger intellectual context. To put the matter in a simple-minded way, in the case of international politics we are concerned with human social behavior, not with all social behavior but with political behavior under certain specified conditions. Aside from being self-evident, what is gained by such a statement? For one thing others are also studying human behavior, and if we can relate our work to theirs, perhaps help from them will be possible. There is another problem too. Suppose we take Gardner Murphy's study of India, *In the Minds of Men* (1953),[8] and other products of UNESCO's "Tensions Project" such as Hadley Cantril (ed.), *Tensions That Cause Wars* (1950).[9] Does Murphy's study throw any light on all nations or just India? How can the Murphy study and the report on international frictions be related to each other and to the general study of international politics? These are recurring questions and cannot be answered unless the field is given more than perfunctory definition.

It would appear that this process of identification or drawing of boundaries is also one prerequisite for relating the study of international politics to other areas of political science, to other social sciences, and to other academic disciplines in a profitable, meaningful way. Thus far, we have not effectively linked Area Studies, Comparative Government, Public Administration, Political Theory, and Political Parties, to say nothing of History, Philosophy, and the Social Sciences, to International Politics.

2. Secondly, a coherent frame of reference should make explicit the value clusters which govern the social and intellectual purposes of observers and teachers who employ it. Thus, if there is a Marxist or World Government value cluster which serves as an organizing principle and if the frame of reference is coherent and explicit, that fact should be abundantly clear. Purposes can be classified roughly as follows: criticism; reform; reliable description; explanation; prediction; teaching; pure research; and applied research. These are not mutually exclusive, and several may be served simultaneously by a single investigative enterprise. The distinction among various purposes is so important that some examples are in order. Here are several simple propositions with designation as to purpose indicated in parentheses:

a. The President needs more staff help (criticism)
b. There should be a joint Executive-Congress committee on foreign policy (reform)
c. The President (or someone acting for him) opens all treaty negotiations (description)
d. The President is more powerful in foreign policy matters because he has more opportunity to act (explanation)
e. The less information Congress has on a major foreign policy issue, the more likely it is to oppose the President (prediction)

Pure research would be represented by a question of this type: under what conditions will the President's interpretation of his role be more significant in predicting his behavior than the written rules which bind him? Applied research would be represented by this question: how can the President handle his relations with Senate leaders so that his Constitutional prerogatives will not be impaired and so that the Senate will feel it has been fully consulted?

An adequate frame of reference ought to alert the user to possible incompatibility of purposes. For example, to the extent that predictive power is developed with respect to decision-making, an observer should be able to make certain statements about the probable consequences of an alteration of the conditions under which decisions are made, that is, "reform." In this instance, scientific knowledge may contribute to the solution of an essentially engineering problem. But the critic who tries to bring about a change by arguing from a priori assumptions which are not to be tested is performing a quite different kind of intellectual operation from the observer who holds such assumptions as problematical—as subject to empirical verification of some sort. Similarly, conveying "understanding" to students may be quite different from designing a research project. Some frames of reference will accommodate both, others will not. Doubtless a graphic and interesting class hour can be built around outstanding personalities and their interpretations of the so-called "gap" between President and Congress, but such an approach might not serve to suggest *researchable questions.* This brings up the point that training students as enlightened citizens and training them as future researchers may be quite different things and involve quite different problems. Again, judging a policy-maker's actions is not necessarily the same as trying to portray the world of the policy-maker as it exists for him.

3. Perhaps the heart of any frame of reference, as we are using the term here, is the explicit revelation of the observer's general posture toward his subject—how he relates himself to the phenomena under study and how he chooses to handle these phenomena. This third characteristic of a frame of reference actually embraces several components concerning which the observer should be demandingly self-conscious. Every student of social behavior makes certain assumptions about the social world in which he lives and in which he carries on his investigations—some of these are moral, some philosophical, and some methodological. Thus, some scholars do not believe that precise knowledge about human behavior is possible—or, to take the extreme of this position—that social science is possible. Now these scholars are certainly entitled to this belief. The point here is that the consequences of so believing are great for the kind of frame of reference employed and the frame of reference ought to make it explicit.

To take another example, some observers or scholars apparently postulate an *objective reality* which is knowable and describable by an investigator and which, when described, constitutes the *real* social world. Others, on the contrary, assume *multiple subjective realities* which, when described, also constitute the social system in terms of which human behavior is to be explained.[10] To suggest the difference this choice makes, let us suppose that there is a dispute between the State Department and the Defense Department. If one assumes objective reality, it follows logically that the dispute and its context can be described—that there is a single, coherent whole which an outside observer can put together and in terms of which he can then interpret action. Thus he may say that the two agencies are disputing because they both have "ignored" certain facts or because they "see" the problem or situation differently. In either case it is assumed that there is *a* situation composed of relevant factors which is affecting the behavior of the two agencies whether they realize it or not. To assume multiple realities, on the other hand, is to assume that *there is no one objective situation* common in all respects to all the participants. Rather, the views the individual participants have of their situation will overlap (that is, agree) and also will show discrepancies. *Both* the overlap and discrepancies are regarded by the observer as defining the situation. Anything the participants ignore is not a part of the situation, though any subjective errors the participants may make are. In the first case, an objective situation is recreated by the observer on the basis of what the participants tell him *plus* what he knows which they do not. In the other case, the situation is recreated on the basis of how the participants each define it.

Methodologically, many models[11] are available to the observer—models based on statistical inference, organizational charts, process analysis, system analysis, actors and action,[12] and so on. Within these, further choices are possible. "Model" is an ambiguous term in social science. But it is so closely related to frame of reference that a brief comment is required. Actually, of course, a model is an analytical tool—fashioned by the observer for his own purposes or chosen from existing stocks. It is an artificial device for *comparing, measuring, experimenting,* and *guiding observation*—all with respect to empirical phenomena. One of the most important functions of models is to generate hypotheses which otherwise might not occur to the observer and which can be tested by reference to factual data.

A familiar device (or model) is that of a rational bureaucracy. No one ever saw a completely rational organization, but the observer specifies the characteristics of such an organization (what it would be like if it did exist) and then measures or describes the extent to which a real organization conforms to the specifications. To take another example, one can also assume rational policy-makers whose behavior will manifest certain properties. When these properties do not appear in the behavior, one already has a basis for saying something about the differences between what the model predicts and what actually happens, and about the reasons for the differences.

4. A frame of reference will also consist of a definition or characterization of the range of empirical phenomena to be described and explained, along with the concepts which establish the criteria of relevance for specifying the factors or determinants to be employed. To illustrate, let us deliberately choose a set of factors which all students would agree is important but which is not always geared effectively into the analysis of state behavior, namely, *class structure*. Unless a scheme includes an explicit category entitled *social stratification* which directs attention to certain domestic social phenomena, an observer might or might not eventually reach these data. In the absence of this category, two possibilities would appear to be open: the first, the observer may work backward from a particular problem, thus reaching the class factor among others; second, the observer—*if* he had some special interest

in class or some other reason—might ask the general question: how do social classes affect foreign policy? The first possibility has an unfortunate random quality—important factors may be easily missed. The second is
cumbersome and time-consuming. Other questions must follow; what are
classes? which definition of class should be used? how are the connecting
links to foreign policy to be established? Furthermore, unless a more basic
category such as social stratification is employed, scholars tend to argue
about the meaning of class, and the vital distinction between class and stra-
tum may be ignored.[13]

One possible reason for the early neglect of power factors in the study of
international politics was the lack of categories which would have alerted
students to such factors. Later shortcomings in the power approach can be
traced in part to inadequate categories. To describe and explain state behavior, therefore, it is necessary to begin with definitions and categories which
specify the way in which such behavior is to be described and the way in
which the determinants of such behavior are to be identified. The set or sets
of concepts which comprise the frame of reference should normally point to
possible relationships among the factors so isolated.

5. When properly developed, concepts can be used as the basis for gen-
erating hypotheses which can then be tested against existing empirical
knowledge or future observation. If the categories and concepts are inclusive
and suggestive, it should be possible to decide tentatively what kinds of theories are appropriate for the phenomena included in the over-all analytical
scheme and to suggest ways of applying these theories. To these ends, some
of the implications of the definitions and concepts employed should be indicated explicitly. Thus, a frame of reference functions as a *basis* for developing and applying theories—theories of varying degrees of complexity and
on various levels of generalization. One reason for the neglect or ignorance
of the applicability of existing and developing theories of human social behavior to the study of international politics has been the lack of a conceptual scheme which would suggest possible applications. For example, under
the heading of "communications theory" there is a cluster of analytical tools
including insights and hypotheses concerning mass media, organizational
behavior, small groups, and intra- as well as cross-cultural phenomena. The
problem is *how* to use these, for they are vitally important to our field. But
it is also part of the problem to do so in a way which will make the analysis
of state behavior more coherent, not more confused. Communications theories point in several directions to the flow of information and interpretative
cues among policy-makers, between policy-making groups, between various
publics, between policy-makers and the general public, between govern-

ments, and between national groups on the nongovernmental level. How can these be both explored and linked in terms of an over-all system?

In another sense, a frame of reference may be likened to an umbrella. It may make it possible to link or relate apparently unrelated data and propositions by providing new and perhaps broader categories. Thus, both cultural differences and armaments are significant categories. Can they be related to each other and, in turn, to a more general category? We think the answer is yes, with success depending on the adequacy of the frame of reference.

6. A frame of reference may or may not have a *major informing notion* or a focus around which its constituent elements may be organized. The frame of reference we are attempting to construct does have a central concept or, better, a set of concepts—namely, *decision-making*. By saying that our scheme rests on this central analytical device, we are really stating our tentative conclusion that the decision-making approach is *one* fruitful method of alerting the observer to the major determinants of state behavior and of analyzing such factors. We believe that the phenomena normally studied in the field of international politics can be interpreted and related meaningfully by means of this concept as we shall present it. It should be clearly understood that this is *not* to say that *all* useful work in the field must or can be done within the decision-making framework. One may describe particular events, conditions, and interactions between states without necessarily probing the nature and outcome of the processes through which state action evolves. However, and the qualification is crucial, if one wishes to probe the "why" questions underlying the events, conditions, and interaction patterns which rest upon state action, then decision-making analysis is certainly necessary. We would go so far as to say *that the "why" questions cannot be answered without analysis of decision-making.*

Purposes of This Project

We are assuming, then, that at this stage the attempt at a comprehensive frame of reference makes more sense than an attempt at a general theory. And we are assuming that this attempt requires us to be explicit about our intellectual purposes and operations. If the scheme is successful on technical grounds, there remain further tests, for we have also assumed that a preliminary effort at conceptualization would substantially aid certain other basic purposes we have in mind:[14] (1) to take stock of the intellectual underpinnings of the field of international politics; (2) to classify and to evaluate critically existing "approaches," "theories," and systems of analysis; (3) to prepare a selected, annotated bibliography of the literature of international politics; (4) to formulate some major problems of research in this area of human behavior. All of these purposes are related to one fundamental long-range ambition—the establishment of adequate intellectual foundations for a genuine analytical science. It ought to be said at once that we expect only to make limited, yet measurable, progress toward these goals. If these goals are accepted by other scholars as appropriate and feasible, it will take the work of many laboring over time to make a substantial progress. The task will be noticeably lighter if the moods and procedures of the active scholars permit and encourage us to stand on one another's shoulders instead of holding each other at arm's length. Discrete, isolated intellectual effort often results in unnecessary duplication. Perhaps, eventually, an agreement on what we know and do not know about international politics and on what *kinds* of knowledge[15] (for example, scientific, intuitive, a priori, and so on) are socially valuable and technically possible will pave the way for piling up relatable empirical studies from which generalizations can be drawn and continuously codified.

Even if the foregoing assumptions turn out to be adequate and accepted, we do not feel that we are in any way excused from confronting the difficult problems of research in this field of learning. A conceptual scheme is not a research design or a substitute for one. Nor can we remain intellectually honest without at some point stating some hypotheses and laying down some of the conditions under which low-level predictions[16] are possible. We shall try also, as we proceed, to support our analysis with real hypothetical examples. To keep categorization from becoming a sterile exercise, we shall suggest the "difference it makes" to use certain concepts.

2. SOME GENERAL CHARACTERISTICS OF THE PRESENT STUDY OF INTERNATIONAL POLITICS

The assumptions and purposes outlined above have grown in part out of our conviction concerning the state of learning in international politics.

Ferment and Discontent

There has been almost constant ferment in the field since the publication of the pioneering works of Schuman[1] and Spykman.[2] These works were themselves the symbols of an intellectual revolt. In the meantime, dissatisfaction with existing explanations and teaching methods has continued unabated.[3] There might be several reasons for this. First, the factors relevant to adequate explanations of state behavior have multiplied because the social complexity and significance of the impact of relations between states have increased far more rapidly in the past twenty years[4] than at any previous time. A greater range of factors affect, and in turn are affected by, the actions of national states. Second, simultaneously the progress of social science techniques and the gradual accumulation of reliable knowledge (particularly through the social research of World War II)[5] have alerted observers to the existence and significance of factors hitherto ignored or taken for granted. Thus, in a sense, the phenomena of international politics have become more numerous and complicated because students have become more sophisticated. Simple notions of causality are no longer acceptable. As tradition and precedent have been weakened as forms of international social control, attention has been turned to "human" factors, much as in the case of industrial relations and public administration. Third, recent events and developments such as totalitarianism and ideological warfare have prompted scholars to inquire into the so-called irrational or nonrational elements of politics and into communications among societies. The need for many varieties of valid social knowledge as a basis for sound policies has also stimulated a more thorough and systematic analysis of political behavior at the international level. It is not a long jump from an awareness of the relevance of anthropological data for the efficient administration of occupied islands in the Pacific during and after World War II to the application of the concept of culture to an understanding of international conflict.

The combination of social and intellectual developments has therefore opened up at once new problems as well as new opportunities. As we have become more realistic in our grasp of the complexities of international politics, the list of relevant phenomena has grown longer, and the determinants of state action appear to be increasing proportionately. This is apparent especially if one probes a single case in great detail. Accordingly, there has been an almost random search for variables and some discouragement over the possibility of exhaustive categories which will facilitate the establishment of relationships among variables. Another result has been explanatory theories built around single-factor analysis. Still another is a series of separate topics, studies, and fields of interest which are unrelatable, primarily because they are on different levels of abstraction. In sum, there is no commonly accepted, comprehensive frame of reference for the study of international politics which systematically defines the field and establishes categories for its analysis.

The Confusion of Purposes

Often the purposes of writers on international politics are unidentified and thoroughly intermixed. There is nothing wrong per se with an author having multiple purposes, provided these are kept separate and made explicit. Nor does it need to be argued that the gathering of reliable data concerning state behavior has a direct relevance to the sound evaluation of foreign policies or that the capacity to predict the consequences of patterns of action involved in decision-making might help the policy-makers to solve some of their organizational problems. However, to repeat a point made earlier, an analysis of what values *should* govern foreign policy decisions may throw little light on what values *do* in fact govern and *how.* The literature on the idealism-realism theme illustrates clearly the way in which *what is* and *what-ought-to-be* may become confused for analytical purposes. Actually, this is primarily a controversy over the desirability or undesirability of certain policies or strategies. Yet participating writers often make explanatory comments which presume to portray the factors which *do*—as well as *should*—influence the policy-makers, without adequate or appropriate analytical supports for the conclusions. For example, the criticism that American foreign policy is too moralistic and/or legalistic implicitly suggests that certain implied values are dominant, though it does not explain why or how.

The Implicitness of Intellectual Operations

Much more serious is the intellectual confusion which flows from the fact that many of the key assumptions, concepts, and definitions which figure in present writing are *implicit* and often, apparently, not even clearly understood. The words "security," "policy," "state," "objective," "power," "national interest," "peace," and so on appear over and over again in the literature. Yet it is relatively rarely that the implied assumptions and definitions connected with them are recognized or spelled out. Several important kinds of consequences may follow.

First, it is exceedingly difficult to evaluate or test empirically the systems of analysis based on such implicit operations. Such operations may in fact slip by unnoticed. In systematic analysis, assumptions, concepts, and definitions constitute the rules which the observer is to employ, and he is limited as well as helped by them. One result of implicitness is that limitations may be ignored. Simplifying assumptions are necessary and useful, but once made they cannot be ignored—that is, the observer cannot proceed to make statements which violate the assumptions he has made. One does not eliminate the impact of, say, motivational factors on certain behaviors by making assumptions about them; one only holds them constant or temporarily beyond need of investigation. Many of the assumptions made in the analysis of international politics concern the motives of state. When made explicitly—which means they are subject to the tests of validity and usefulness—confusion can be avoided. But often a particular writer will assume a single motive—that is, a drive for power—and then proceed to describe and explain phenomena which cannot be accounted for except by abandoning the assumption originally made. Discrepancies of this kind are usually treated as exceptions. This permits retention of the assumption without regard for its inherent limitations.

Second, there is no magic in assumptions—they may be false or implausible. Assumptions ought to be examined carefully. Third, implicitness tends to separate the basis of a statement from the statement itself. Fourth, and also very serious, unless the bases for propositions about data are made explicit, comparison is difficult. Earlier it was suggested that one possible defect in contemporary analysis is that one scholar cannot always employ the approach of another and arrive at identical results. Replication depends on underlying operations being made clear.

Lack of Researchable Issues and Operational Definitions

Many of the propositions commonly accepted and used by students of international politics are not expressed in researchable form—it would be difficult if not impossible to verify them by empirical investigation.[6] Basic concepts—such as "national interest"—when they are defined are not operationally defined in the sense that empirical referents can be identified easily. It is one thing to insist that the observer has a right to define his terms any way he sees fit provided only that he is clear and consistent. It is another to insist that all definitions are of one kind (that is, nominal, operational, postulational, extensional, and so on) and are of equal clarity and utility. There appears to be substantial semantic confusion traceable to this source. Many distinctions and dichotomies—among them "realism" versus "idealism"—are false or misleading.[7]

Needless to say, constructive research has not been enhanced by the mistaken employment of *metaphors,* especially when they are based on concepts borrowed from the natural sciences. A case in point is the mechanical model drawn from Physics which has become the basis for postulating equilibrium in the so-called power relations of states.[8] The description and explanation of national behavior has also suffered from the common fallacy of *misplaced concreteness or reification,* exemplified chiefly by the subtle transformation of the word "state" from a proper analytical abstraction into a symbol allegedly standing for a concrete entity—that is, an object or system having an existence of its own apart from real persons and their behaviors.[9] This is closely related to the failure often to distinguish between *analytical and concrete structures* of policy-making institutions. Since this is an immensely significant distinction it ought to be explained briefly. Suppose we think of a Wednesday morning meeting of the National Security Council. All the members are seated around the conference table discussing problems. In toto, this would exemplify a concrete structure. Now suppose we think of one aspect of this decision-making unit, namely, *the authority relationships* existing among the members—the President is the superior officer, the Secretary of State is first among equals, the Director of the C.I.A. ranks below the Secretary of Defense, and so on. This exemplifies an *analytic structure,* that is, an abstraction of certain relationships. We shall have occasion to return to this point later.[10]

Nor has it been helpful in the study of international politics to employ common-sense notions of motivation and to employ motivational concepts properly applicable only to an isolated individual human being without regard to his social role or his role as a policy-maker. We have already made this point in another connection. Two further examples will suffice: "statesmen rationalize because they do not want their true motives known" and "the Secretary of State behaves the way he does because he is emotionally insecure." The first is a hypothesis drawn from lore or from everyday experience, the second is essentially a hypothesis which applies to individuals viewed as psychic organisms. Basically, the issue is one of appropriateness. As a matter of fact, common-sense constructs are not dangerous or misleading per se—they can be very helpful in the early stages of any systematic analysis. If allowed, however, to dominate conceptualization and empirical research, the results can be stultifying indeed. Common-sense constructs are designed to facilitate social action, not to explain it.

"Personality" and "Informal Factors"

Two fairly recent foci of political interest and theorizing—the concept of *personality* and the concept of *informal factors*—constitute at once a source of strength and weakness for further intellectual ordering of the field of international politics. The more sophisticated contemporary theories of personality undergirded by case studies and experiments are more serviceable than the one-dimensional models of some classical political theorists.[11] They dovetail nicely with the well-established preoccupation of some diplomatic historians with the individual statesman. However, emphasis of this kind also serves to intensify a tendency which has already produced unfortunate by-products in the analysis of state behavior, one of which is to view the decision-maker in isolation rather than as a part of a social system (that is, governmental institutions). Concentration on the personality of diplomats or policy-makers—without making explicit the relevant assumptions about their roles in a governmental context—unleashes the ugly specter of the problem of not being able to decide which aspects of the individual's personality are really crucial to an explanation of his behavior qua decision-maker.

Belated discovery of the nature and importance of so-called informal[12] factors in administrative behavior and in the larger context of the non-governmental social factors which condition the actions of officials obviously has enriched and liberated political science. On the other hand, the resulting tendency to talk ambiguously about *the political process*[13] and about the *real* locus of decision-making as being outside the boundaries of the formal structure of government has diverted attention from the significance of formal organizational factors. In the process of liberating us from the confines of the legal-institutional approach, little provision has been made for analytical concepts to link the policy-makers and domestic social factors beyond the concept of *access*[14] which, though necessary and fruitful, leaves a gap—a gap between the interaction of officials and nonofficials and *the decision-making behavior of the officials.* For example, the concept of access does not offer any visible means to explain why, after a conversation with a paid lobbyist, a senator will go to the floor of the Senate and vote the way the lobbyist wanted him to. That is, if the conversation is the *only* variable (and it is a big if) and if no bribe is involved, how is the Senator's behavior to be explained? To say he was "influenced" by the lobbyist begs all the crucial questions.

The Wide Range of Phenomena in International Politics

One of the characteristics of international political[15] relationships generally is the wide range of phenomena to be identified, described, and accounted for. Thus the student appears to be confronted with an almost insurmountable task. The list of possible relevant factors and determinants required to *explain* the behavior of states seems infinite. Admittedly, the phenomena are complex. However, problems of relevance and cruciality, and the relationship between phenomena and explanatory principles arise from sources other than the inherent nature of the phenomena. There is, of course, no necessary one-to-one relationship between the complexity and number of empirical phenomena on the one hand and the complexity of explanatory systems on the other. To take an absurd case, perhaps 179 pressure groups may be suspected of being involved in a particular foreign policy issue. Provided one has an adequate model (or scheme) for handling the possible impact of a *single* pressure group, 179 groups make more work but do not complicate the model. This is the familiar pitfall of insufficient generalization. An apparent multiplicity of factors may be due to incomplete or faulty categorization. Apparent complexity may result from an attempt to relate propositions which are unrelatable as stated and from an attempt to be exhaustive in listing or accounting for *all* occurrences which are connected with a given event or set of events. A careful refinement of analytical purposes and delineation of research targets may help considerably to reduce the burdens of numbers and complexity of phenomena. The desire to "see" everything at once is a natural one, but it represents another siren song for it is based on the assumption that the social world can be or must be reconstituted to the last detail which is neither possible, necessary, nor desirable.

It would take a large umbrella indeed to cover the hurly-burly of empirical events, the actions being taken, the conditions which affect the actions, and the "problems" which we think of when we think of foreign policies and the numerous, ongoing contacts between nations. All of these occurrences and states of affairs are going on or did go on *simultaneously*. How can all this be "fitted together"—the atomic bomb, the race issue in South Africa, the cold war, the revolution in Egypt, the European coal-steel community, the death of Stalin, the negotiation of a trade agreement between Canada and Mexico, a speech by the President of the United States, and so on indefinitely? As a matter of fact, one of the first kinds of questions about a scheme such as we are presenting here is: how do you "fit in" something like the Bricker Amendment or the fact that the Secretary of Defense and the Secretary of State "dislike" each other? It is not always clear what "fit in" means. Whatever it means it is perfectly clear that these two requirements must be met to avoid swamping the observer: first, he must ask himself what precisely he wishes to describe and explain; second, he must ask himself how he can best *typify* and *generalize* so description and explanation can proceed *economically.* It is one thing to assume that all factors have a similar relevancy under *all* conditions. It is another to specify *potential* relevancies under *particular* conditions. Obviously, if one has constructed a workable model of an atom, one can understand certain things about atoms. Accordingly, the perfection of concepts and categories should provide a basis for handling international phenomena *without* having to "see" and to "grasp" everything at once.

The foregoing suggests an important point. At the present time political science lacks—or appears to lack—useful *typologies*. Essentially, a typology is a grouping of phenomena or data or analytic structures according to assumed or verified *common properties*. Thus, "factors" that otherwise have unique properties or different properties can be considered as potentially relatable under limited conditions. This facilitates the search for comparability as well as relationships. Above all, any prediction would require the ability to generalize from one situation to another on the basis of enduring relevancies based on common properties. The present lack of typologies apparently stems in part from the stress on *differences* among phenomena rather than on *uniformities*. It should be noted that a useful typology will usually involve more than simple classification.

The impression of overwhelmingness of data in the study of international politics is due partly to the fact that traditionally it has been primarily a descriptive discipline. Much historical reconstruction seems to rest on the accumulation of a great mass of detail which has a tendency to emphasize the *uniqueness* of events, conditions, cases, and developments. Unfolding a story causes general properties and common elements which might link different occurrences to be lost. How can one comprehend the past in all of its detail, all of its ramifications, all of its discontinuities? The task is hopeless if one thinks only in terms of discrete phenomena. A tradition of raw empiricism in political science (of great value in itself) has contributed both to despair and to unsound methodological assumptions. In particular, case studies, which should become the basis for generalization, have somehow supported the notion that about any policy or event there is *too much* to be known, much of it unknowable.

We stress this point on the unwieldiness of the field because we feel that it has contributed to unfortunate extremes of approach to an analysis of state behavior. Some writers have sought refuge in a single, over-simple concept such as "power." Others have despaired of finding organizing principles and have confined themselves to highly factual presentation of discrete topics—the state, diplomacy, economic instrumentalities, and so on. Many widely used textbooks appear to be grab-bags, leaving the reader with an impression of incoherence. The more ground these books cover, the less integrated they are.

3. CONTEMPORARY APPROACHES TO THE STUDY OF INTERNATIONAL POLITICS

In the previous section we undertook a brief review of what we think are some of the major characteristics of our field because such reminders may enable readers to "locate" our position and purposes more easily. By spelling out these obvious points—which generally are passed over—we make our ideas clearer. To carry this one step further we shall comment in summary fashion on contemporary approaches to the study of international politics.

When students, teachers, and researchers discuss approaches to the study of international politics, usually everything from intuitive hunches to full-blown theoretical systems is included. It is perhaps natural, though unfortunate, that theory is such a loose word even among social scientists. Often theory is employed as a synonym for concept, frame of reference, simple hypotheses, and principle or law. While these ambiguities do not seem to interfere with communication on a common-sense basis, they may be a severe handicap not only to rigorous analysis and inquiry, but to a fruitful assessment of any field of learning. Theory is also employed to include the operating rules of the policy-maker and the social proverbs which circulate in any cultural context. Difficulties arise not so much from multiple meanings as from the suppression of the differences and their analytical consequences. We have already noted that nature of a frame of reference and how it differs from theory in the technical sense. At another time we shall discuss more adequately the nature of concepts and theories particularly as they relate to the work in international politics. Suffice it to say here, the term "approach" means many things not excluding the purposes and philosophical disposition of various writers. It may be more important to characterize a given author as a *realist* (again, in a technical philosophical sense) than to identify him with the power school of thought. It may be as important to know that an author is trying to demonstrate errors in a nation's foreign policy as to know that he employs an assumption of inevitable conflict among states. Finally, "approach" may merely call attention to a focus of interest evident in recent writings, such as the role of ideals versus self-interest in the formation of foreign policy.

We wish to make it very clear that what we intend here is no destructive criticism. We do not imply that any scholar's work as a whole or in part, is good or bad or should or should not have been undertaken. It would be ungracious, improper, and fallacious to make sweeping condemnations of the labors of our colleagues in this field. When we say that we are attempting to "evaluate critically" the existing ways of defining and organizing the study of international politics, we mean that we are interested in trying to identify and characterize the various intellectual properties involved. To say that a writer's system is based on single causation does not necessarily mean such a practice is *wrong* per se or *lacks utility*, but only that certain analytical consequences follow and that the criteria for judging any frame of reference or testing hypotheses should be applied if one wishes to be rigorous. Once again it is necessary to emphasize the range of choice open to the observer-teacher, both with respect to general schemes which encompass the field and to specific research problems. However, choice is always related to purpose, and it can be established by objective rules that certain choices of analytical system are not appropriate for certain purposes the observer may entertain.

Theories, Categories, Frames of Reference, Concepts, Foci of Interest

If one peruses the most influential texts and the existing periodical literature one can list the chief kinds of preoccupations and interests contemporary scholars in the field of international politics appear to have:

NATIONAL INTEREST—(a) as an explanation of state behavior involving the notion that policy-makers and diplomats discover, define, and preserve the "national interest"; (b) a formula or formulas employed by statesmen to guide their choices and to legitimate choices already made; (c) reference to value conflicts and to competing clusters of values which might guide policy choices

POWER THEORIES—three basic varieties: (a) balance of power (and its own variations); (b) the national power equation—a quantitative reckoning of certain ingredients such as natural resources, population, productive capacity, and so on; (c) capabilities analysis—power factors plus an estimate of a state's capacity to mobilize its power effectively, to make sound decisions, and to execute them properly, plus analysis of the capacity of other states to resist and to carry out objectives of their own

EQUILIBRIUM AND STABILITY ANALYSIS—a distant cousin of one variety of the balance of power idea which implies a delicate relationship among power factors, fundamental national needs and tolerance for conflict short of war which can or cannot be upset by a rapid change in one of the components; a stable equilibrium would be one in which a substantial shift in one of the components or in the relationship among them would be required to destroy the equilibrium

THE GEOPOLITICAL APPROACH—(a) the Haushofer School; (b) emphasis on geography as a crucial factor in the determination of state behavior; (c) non-deterministic and nonpolicy-oriented consideration of geographical factors

IMPERIALISM—historical and contemporary studies in the development and consequences of dominance-submission relationships; simple and elaborate economic and psychological hypotheses to account for the phenomena

NATIONALISM—regarded as a basic force behind the evolution of the nation-state and as underlying both aggressive behavior and the legitimate striving for independence and self-determination; also viewed as a basic cause and catalyst of international conflict

WAR AND PEACE—a long and deep interest in the causes, nature, and consequences of war and the conditions of peace; the cooperation-conflict continuum has been closely related

COMMUNITY—again, an enduring interest in the possibility, desirability, and actual degree of community at the supranational level; also closely related to the war-peace focus

THE MARKET APPROACH—most international trade and monetary theory and the description of trade relations can be categorized as viewing the exchange of goods and services among nations in essentially market terms

LAW AND INSTITUTIONS—perhaps until 1930 the dominant emphasis in the field: description and interpretation of legal norms and the institutional arrangements through which national conduct and formal interstate collaboration were regulated; the legal-institutional approach laid primary emphasis on the significance of formal rules in the conduct of states

VALUE THEORY—recently some scholars have attempted to apply value theory to the behavior of nations in an effort to avoid some of the difficulties found in power theories and the national interest focus; an attempt has been made to push analysis beyond the familiar catalogue of national objectives to discover possible sources

MEANS-ENDS ANALYSIS—the attempt to identify and classify the objectives, techniques, and strategies observable in the actions of states; generally speaking objectives are postulated, and there has been relatively more accent on techniques

Commentary on These Approaches

This list is only meant to call to mind the major areas of interest displayed by scholars and is not intended as a truncated critical evaluation. Enough has been said, however, to permit comment which in turn should make it easier to identify the differences in our analysis.

1. To repeat an earlier assertion: Despite all the writing done which can be categorized under the foregoing headings, key words and concepts have remained ambiguous and for the most part undefined. Multiple purposes have remained undifferentiated, and the various schemes (or even combinations) are *not* agreed upon as *the* unifying devices for the field. Serious criticisms have been leveled at all of them, and there seems to be widespread dissatisfaction with their usefulness as pedagogical techniques.

2. It should be noted that the intellectual history of any field of learning will be shaped by two sets of factors: the interests and capacities of professional scholars *and* social events and conditions such as wars, revolutions, and so on. Thus, there are noticeable fads and trends. This is not the proper place to trace the developments in this field since 1930, but several points are deserving of comment. First, though there is now growing interest in the systematizing of the study of international politics, there is only a handful of articles and chapters of books dealing with the nature of the field.[1] Second, much of the attention now focused on national interest and the realist-idealist conflict by American scholars stems in large part from the influences of what can only be called a period of "re-examinism" with respect to American foreign policy from 1947 to 1954. The attempt to discover "error" in official policy and to establish enduring criteria for "sound" strategies has had its impact on the study of international politics. Realistic critics[2] have alleged that adherence to moral principles and failure to recognize the "power essence" of interstate relations have led to unwise and ineffective policies. It has been fashionable to "whip Wilsonianism" and to herald the Founding Fathers as hard-headed, politically sophisticated analysts. United States policy-makers have been condemned for being idealistic and for trying to espouse the welfare of all mankind. Third, the reaction against power-realism, both as policy criticism and as an approach to understanding the international political process, has already set in. Not only is the power approach criticized on logical and methodological grounds but on ethical grounds as well. Not only is power analysis attacked for not accounting for all available empirical evidence but its supporters are condemned for their policy views. It is being asserted that ideals do and must play a significant role in the policies and actions of states and that the assertion and implementation of ideals are in themselves ways of influencing the conduct of others. Those who insist upon a realistic stability based on an equilibrium of power free of moral connotations are condemned as neutral with regard to the very core of the great international conflicts of the day.

3. Despite the increased attention paid to "error" in national policy, no objective definition of error has been forthcoming. It is to be noted that none of the well-known approaches listed above, except for the probing of values presumed to effect the decisions of statesmen, make any provision for reconstructing the world as it might seem to the statesmen. Therefore, the question of the appropriateness of the criteria (even when these are explicit, which often they are not) for judging policies arises. Capabilities analysis has certainly thrown new light on a range of possible reasons for policy failures and ineffectiveness. In most cases, "error" tends to be defined by the observer's rules—which may be quite inappropriate because these ignore the policy-maker's situation and make no attempt to take his views into account.

4. All of the empirical phenomena described and interpreted in the text-books and periodical literature of international politics can be grouped under four major headings: (a) interaction between states: patterns, systems, processes; (b) historical trends: chronological descriptions and explanation; (c) policy formation and execution; and (d) discrete events, including cases and problems. A casual survey indicates clearly that by far the greater proportion of research and writing has been expended on categories (a) and (b). Within (a), relatively more attention has been paid to describing the inter-actions than to discovering the "why" of such interactions. Also within (a), relatively more attention has been paid to governmental rather than non-governmental interaction, to institutional rather than noninstitutional pat-terns. Finally, attention has been concentrated on the allocation of goods and services (economic patterns), the opposite ends of the conflict-coopera-tion continuum, and the dominance-submission relationships.

These relative emphases, along with neglect of policy-making, perhaps partially explain the failure until recently to take into account sociological variables in state behavior. Emphasis on historical description has served to accent the need for perspective and to show how we arrived where we are, but it has not helped to answer the question why certain sequences of events have occurred with the consequences which followed. Historical explanation has often been based on concepts and categories which are difficult to apply to contemporary developments and has been couched in terms of imper-sonal forces to which are imputed a causal power.

Underlying Assumptions of Contemporary Approaches: The Objective-Subjective Dilemma

No systematic attempt has been made so far to examine the methodological presuppositions of the various schemes noted above and their analytical con-sequences. These approaches—or aspects of them—can be categorized ac-cording to certain characteristics. Most of the writing—*insofar as it is interpretive*—can be fitted into what may be called an "objective reality" group and an "ethical principles" group.

Objective Reality

This is primarily an inductive school of thought[3] which basically insists that objective conditions exist and are knowable on the basis of rules which would yield identical results to all investigators or observers. Objective real-ity in effect determines or prescribes the behavior of states.[4] This obviously leads essentially to a deterministic type of explanation. Writing which falls in this category assumes: a particular kind of rational man—who is capable of choosing wise, effective courses of action on the basis of an awareness of reality; a particular kind of relationship between the observer and the empirical phenomenon—namely, that objective reality can be reconstructed without distortion by the observer's operations; and that knowledge of all the relevant empirical phenomena exists or can be obtained. Implicit in much of the work of the national interest school is, therefore, the assumption that national interest is objectively real—it exists and hence is knowable to students and statesmen alike. Once known it will automatically produce correct policies or at least it should. Marxist thought is also typical of this group in that state interaction and motivation—both objectively real—are determined by relationships of production and distribution, and "right" conduct or the nature of world politics is clear to the man who knows the key (the dialectic).

One assumption in the geopolitics school is that geographical location—itself an objective factor—determines the conditions under which state action will take place. Statesmen are, essentially, prisoners of circumstances and can only be free to the extent of discovering what circumstances will permit.

Ethical Principles

This is a deductive kind of analysis. There is a basic assumption of universally applicable values. Empirical investigation or argument is limited to spelling out such values, comparing existing conditions to what *should* be, and outlining reforms. It is also assumed that it is only necessary to provide the conditions, by means of education, a return to religion, or a new moral approach, for the conscious recognition of the correctness of these values in order to assure their realization. Once again, a rational policy-maker is assumed—this time one who will know what to do and will do it successfully once he understands the nature and implications of the postulated universal values. Much of the literature characterized by prescriptive and ethical-deductive propositions (including some elements of both national interest and Marxist schools) explains international conduct in terms of its deviation from a set of absolute standards and norms which if adhered to would automatically produce certain consequences. Thus war, exploitation, rivalry, destructive competition, and waste in the relations of states arise from "false" views of reality and from ignorance (willful or otherwise) of principles of right conduct. Examples of ethical deductive thinking are "Manifest

Destiny" and "The American Century," which imply that American values are everywhere applicable and, therefore, there is an imperative to expand. "One World" and other related philosophies based on the assumption of community and the brotherhood of man are also illustrative.

The realism-idealism dichotomy is now seen to involve more than a conflict of values which should or do influence the choices of policy-makers. It reveals also basically different methodological assumptions concerning the observation and interpretation of international politics. Both kinds of schemes run rather apparent risks that their assumptions may be incorrect or too simple to account for observed phenomena. This is, of course, a common risk of investigation, but in both these cases, the system of postulates is so rigid that modification beyond a certain point destroys the scheme. The assumption of objective reality and the imputation of motivation to abstractions called states would seem to beg many of the most significant questions concerning state behavior which at present remain unanswered. Each group would appear to be trapped in the objective-subjective dichotomy for different reasons. In the case of the first group, how does one tell when the observer's operations yield a *faithful* portrait of reality? How does one know that an observer's mind and a statesman's mind are in tune? In the case of the second group, how does one know whether the diagnosis is accurate if the prescriptions are never tested? How does one predict the condition under which ethical principles would be effective from the principles themselves?

Indeed, apart from the fact that the key terms in the two kinds of thinking are rarely operationally defined, it is often not clear whether national interest, balance of power, or geographical conditions are an *explanation* of what motivates statesmen, a *guide to action* which *should* be taken by statesmen, or an *analytic category*, that is, a variable to be studied. The search for eternal causes, for deterministic theories, and for sweeping judgments leaves the observer of international politics feeling vaguely uneasy. Too much is left unaccounted for.

Simple Description and Scientific Analysis

Not all writing in the field fits neatly into the two categories just discussed. Certainly most of the interpretive schemes which go beyond mere labeling do. On the other hand, much of our material is in a raw state—simple descriptive propositions. Empirical materials are obviously the basis of any system of analysis. But when these are classified for purposes of interpretation and establishment of relationships, a third avenue of approach is open: a commitment to scientific analysis. The interest is then in what goes on in interstate relations *and why.* The purpose is explain and to explain according to rules which are quite different from those which govern the other two schools of thought. When this choice is made by the observer, he pledges himself to face openly the subjective-objective dilemma—which is really the issue of the observer's relation to his data—and to concentrate on the accumulation of reliable knowledge on the assumption that prescription is based on, but is not a substitute for, analysis.

One of the reasons for dissatisfaction with the dominant kinds of writing is that the classifications involved are determined less by the nature of the evidence than by the dictates of the particular a priori assumptions employed. The exceptions and qualifications made by various writers suggest that their categories leave considerable data "unboxed." Another is that the built-in notion of rationality characteristic of the objective reality school and the ethical-deductive school appears to *condemn* all policy-makers to one of three unfortunate classes—the misguided, the helpless, and the evil.[5] Once again, the observer is assumed to have omniscience, and the statesmen is assumed to be confronted only by black-and-white situations and alternatives.

We have not meant to argue that all of any one scholar's writing or all of any particular piece of writing can be put in one of the three categories just discussed. Actually this is a way of *typifying* the intellectual operations currently in use. One reason for the mixture of all three in the same book or even on the same page is the confusion of purposes which we have stressed previously. Nor have we meant to argue that the first two kinds of writing are "bad" or useless. Rather, we have argued for making the differences explicit in the conviction that claims which cannot be supported by a given analytical scheme constitute a violation of the norms of the scholarly enterprise.

Recent Trends

A bird's eye view of thirty years of intellectual development in the field of international politics reveals obvious trends aside from the one toward more systematic analysis. First, there has been a noticeable tendency to balance the earlier institutional approach with the more recent behavioral approach. Second, interest has broadened from simply the interaction of states to include the analysis of the "why" of patterns of interaction. This requires inquiry into policy-formation. Third, an effort is being made to break the confining effects of the realist-idealist polarity which in turn has grown out of a reaction to idealistic reformism in the 1930's and to the power emphasis of the 1940's.

4. TOWARD A NEW FRAME OF REFERENCE
FOR THE STUDY OF INTERNATIONAL POLITICS

Special Difficulties in the Field of International Politics[1]

The characteristics and tendencies sketched briefly in the previous section have reinforced our conviction that the time is ripe for students of international politics to intensify the re-examination of the field. We have indicated that the study of international politics has been marked by fallacies and by particular methodological difficulties which may overtake any area of social research.[2] It is now necessary to add that there are characteristics of the phenomena of international politics which serve to differentiate in degree (if not in kind) this category of political action from all others. Such characteristics may help to reveal some of the reasons why progress toward more orderly analysis has been delayed.

Several of these are well known. First, data are notoriously hard to come by because governments are prone to suppress many things which the scholar must know and wants to know. Diplomatic records and memoirs are published years after the events occurred. Negotiations are held in secret or semi-secret. Security regulations—necessary and otherwise—hide many vital facts. Busy administrators have been known to have little sympathy for the scholarly curiosity of the academic man. Withal, only the most naïve could close his eyes to this basic handicap. We shall return to this handicap in another place. Here we need only note two things: the lack of plentiful, verified factual information—admitted and bemoaned by all—has not prevented the growth of a thriving field of learning in American colleges and universities, and perhaps the consequences of the disability have been misinterpreted if not exaggerated.

Second, as already noted, a large number of factors appear to affect the behavior of states. "Appear" is the proper word here because, as already noted, the imperfection of selective devices (classification and categorization) has endowed the search for relevant factors with an unnecessarily random quality. Instead of developing efficient analytical procedures for interpretation of the data, observers in the field have tried to compensate for a feeling of inadequacy in the face of many and complex phenomena by making simplifying assumptions about these phenomena. A distinction between assuming only one dominant motive on the part of statesmen on the one hand, and constructing a model to handle multiple motives on an orderly basis on the other, might have suggested different ways of grouping phenomena and thinking about possible relationships. Similarly, the lack of attention to typologies has apparently caused numbers of factors (or data) to be confused with generalized *properties*. Obviously a common property running through many phenomena makes it possible to say something about all by a statement concerning one with respect to that property.

Third, and most obvious of all, the field embraces a very wide range of phenomena—many events and actions. Because of the number of political entities involved and because of the vast quantity of interactions among them, the sheer succession of events and occurrences which *in general* are the focus of study in the field or which *may* be relevant to particular patterns of interaction or problems is enormous. In any given edition of an adequate newspaper, the reader is presented with abundant evidence of "so much happening." Thus, the possibilities of relevant, significant events are multiplied considerably over what would be true of domestic politics in one nation. In brief, this means the problem of selectivity—always difficult—is intensified.

Another difficulty is broadly cultural in nature. Heterogeneity of phenomena is, of course, a challenge to systematic description and generalization. The nations of the world represent widely diverse cultures and social systems. Diversity is a complicating factor in domestic politics, but again, the degree of difference is noteworthy. It is often said—and often correctly—that intranational differences are greater than international. However, as a general rule, it must be said that the unifying factors in the former case are more of a countercheck to diversity than in the latter. It is not only that the social and cultural differences among nations account in part for certain interaction patterns—notably conflict—but that such differences complicate the attempts to explain why states take the actions they do. We *know*—in various meanings of the word—a great deal about how individual political systems are structured and how various governmental functions are performed in various societies. We know somewhat less about the processes of policy formation and about the particular influences of cultural factors. In the absence of a general scheme for genuinely comparative analysis of political systems, it is difficult if not impossible to isolate and generalize about the connections between culture patterns (in the broadest sense) and the actions of states. For example, one might cite the confusion and disagreement over the impact of cultural factors on the behavior of Soviet policy-makers. Given a divided world, the multiplication of politically significant national units, and the breakdown of the common codes which stabilized internal relations during the nineteenth century, it would seem necessary for any attempt to order the study of international politics to face this problem

squarely and to suggest at least its major implications. So far, the most coherent efforts have been embraced by "national character" analysis, the nature and limitations of which will be discussed at another time.

Two further problems remain: the problem of *simultaneity* and the
problem of *chance*. We shall take the latter first. An amazingly small
amount of attention has been paid to the possible significance of accident
when a relatively large number of actions and interactions occurs. The
tempting quest for causality—especially of the ultimate or eternal variety—has led in part to a search for a *logical* explanation for events which
are essentially the results of chance, that is, the intersection of actions in
the political realm which produce new events or conditions unintended
by those who took the separate actions in the first place. Chance is therefore that which happens that is not for the sake of some end.[3] Chance is
caused by nothing. Many events and conditions of international politics
fall in this category of absolute singularity even though the sequences of
action which they in turn set off do not. The peculiar conjunction of separate actions can be viewed in part as the *unanticipated consequences* of action, but this probably does not cover all instances since it is the
criss-crossing of independent and unrelated actions which constitutes
chance and not simply the consequences of any particular action. Conflict is usually thought of in terms of a clash of wills and the pursuit of
objectives each of which cannot be achieved except at the expense of another. However, one might at least question whether some conflict is not
accidental and whether the incidents which breed conflict are not the result of a chance patterning of action.

The problem of *simultaneity* grows out of the fact that no state engages
in separate, isolated actions, with one following the other in chronological
sequence. *Within* governments a number of actions are being decided upon
and implemented at the same moment in time. Between states a number of
interactions coexist. This has a number of implications usually neglected in
international political analysis. Examples or cases are sometimes discussed as
though these were all that was happening. The actions of other states have
an obvious impact on the action of any one state, but equally important—
in perhaps a different sense—are the effects of given states' actions on each
other. For one thing, the burden of simultaneous responses to external demands may be a crucial determinant in the timing of actions and the nature
or amount of policy-making resources which are devoted to specific actions.
Thus, one aspect of the "failure" of our China Policy might be the excessive
demands of the European scene. The knowledge of simultaneous actions

would seem to be one of the more important kinds of information of interest to the state's policy-makers. This point also suggests a modification of the term *the* national interest.

Definition of International Politics

Definition of phenomena to be observed and explained is not, of course, identical with definition of methods of observation and explanation. Both will be spelled out as this essay proceeds. Suffice it to say here, we believe that those who study international politics are mainly concerned with the actions, reactions, and interactions among political entities called national states. Emphasis on action suggests *process* analysis, that is, the passage of time plus continuous changes in relationships—including the conditions underlying change and its consequences. Since there is a multiplicity of actions, reactions, and interactions, analysis must be concerned with a *number of processes.*

Action arises from the necessity to establish, to maintain, and to regulate satisfying, optional contacts between states and to exert some control over unwanted yet inescapable contacts. Action is planful[4] in the sense that it represents an attempt to achieve certain aims, and to prevent or minimize the achievement of the incompatible or menacing aims of other states.

The action-reaction-interaction formulation suggests that sequences of action and interaction are always closed or symmetrical. This may be diagrammed State A ←→ State B which implies a reciprocal relationship. Such is clearly not always the case. Many sequences are asymmetrical, that is, State A ——→ State B ——→ in which case State A acts, State B reacts, but there is no immediate further action by A in response to B's action. With more than two states involved, of course, there are other possibilities— as suggested by:

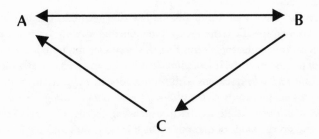

Given the fact that relationships may be symmetrical or asymmetrical and given the fact that action sequences though initiated at different times are nonetheless carried on simultaneously, there will be both the appearance and the possibility of *discontinuity* (that is, discontinuous processes) within the total set of processes which link any one state with all others. The process of state interaction is not, to repeat, always a sequence of action and *counteraction,* of attempt and frustration, of will opposing will. Nor should it be assumed that the process *necessarily* has an automatic chess-game quality or that reactions to action are necessarily immediate or self-evident. Not all national purposes are mutually incompatible, that is, it is not necessary that one nation's purposes be accomplished at the expense of another set of national purposes. One state may respond to the action of another without opposing that action per se; it may or may not be able to block that action effectively; it may or may not want to do so. The response may be in the form of inaction (calculated inaction we shall regard analytically as a form of action), or it may be in the form of action quite unrelated to the purposes of the state which acted first. Much diplomacy consists in probing the limits of tolerance for a proposed course of action and in discovering common purposes. As action unfolds, purposes may change due to resistances or altered circumstances and hence, often, head-on conflicts are avoided or reduced in impact. For these reasons the processes of state interaction are much less orderly than—hopefully—the analysis of these processes.

State action and therefore interaction obviously takes many forms—a declaration, a formal agreement, regulation of relationships, discussion, a gift or loan, armed conflict, and so on. Reactions take the same forms only they are viewed as responses. Since we are dealing with planful actions (rather than random behavior),[5] interaction is characterized by *patterns,* that is, recognizable *repetitions* of action and reaction. Aims *persist.* Kinds of action become *typical.* Reactions become *uniform.* Relationships become *regularized.* Further comment on the identification and characterization of patterns will be made below.

Thus far, there would probably be few disagreements except relatively minor ones on specific terminology. Now the question is: how is the political process (remembering always that this connotes multiple processes and *kinds* of processes) at the international level to be analyzed? Clearly there are *what, how,* and *why* questions with respect to state interaction. In order to be true to our previously stated philosophy, we should recognize that there is more than one possible approach, depending on the purposes of the observer and on the kinds of questions which interest him most.

"The State as Actor in a Situation"

This diagram will serve as a partial indication of the fundamental approach adopted in this essay. A complete analysis of the diagram and its major implications must be reserved for the longer monograph.

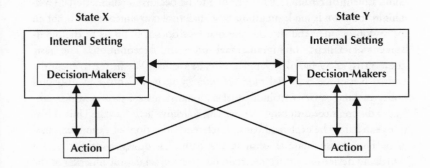

Commentary

1. The first aspect of this diagrammatic presentation of an analytical scheme is the *assumption* that the most effective way to gain perspective on international politics and to find ways of grasping the complex determinants of state behavior is to pitch the analysis on the level of *any state*. An understanding of *all* states is to be founded on an understanding of *any one* state through the use of a scheme which will permit the analytical construction of properties of action which will be shared in common by all specific states. That is, the model is a fictional state whose characteristics are such as to enable us to say certain things about all real states regardless of how different they may appear to be in some ways. Therefore, if the scheme is moderately successful, we should be able to lay the foundation for analyzing the impact of cultural values on British foreign policy and on Soviet foreign policy even though the values are different in each case and produce quite different consequences. "State X," then, stands for all states or for any one state. We have rejected the assumption that two different analytical schemes are required simply because two states behave differently.

It should be added immediately that theoretical progress in the study of international politics will require eventually a *typology*[6] of states based on basic political organization, range of decision-making systems, strengths and weaknesses of decision-making systems, and types of foreign policy strategies employed. This will facilitate comparison, of course, but it will also make it possible to take into account certain significant differences among states while at the same time analyzing the behavior of all states in essentially the same way.

2. We are also assuming that the nation-state is going to be the significant unit of political action for many years to come. Strategies of action and commitment of resources will continue to be decided at the national level. This assumption is made on grounds of analytical convenience and is not an expression of preference by the authors. Nor does it blind us to the development or existence of supranational forces and organizations. The basic question is solely how the latter are to be treated. We prefer to view the United Nations as a special mode of interaction in which the identity and policy-making capacity of individual national states are preserved but subject to different conditioning factors. The collective action of the United Nations can hardly be explained without reference to actions in various capitals.

3. The phrase "state as actor in a situation" is designed primarily as a shorthand device to alert us to certain perspectives while still adhering to the notion of the state as a collectivity.[7] Explicit mention must be made of our employment of action analysis and (both here and in the detailed treatment of decision-making) *of some of the vocabulary* of the now well-known Parsons-Shils scheme.[8] We emphasize vocabulary for two reasons. First, as new schemes of social analysis are developed (mostly outside of political science), there is a great temptation to apply such schemes quickly, one result being the use of new words without comprehension of the theoretical system of which they are a part. Second, we have rejected a general application of the Parsons-Shils approach as an organizing concept—for reasons which will emerge later. At this point we may simply note that our intellectual borrowings regarding fundamental questions of method owe much more to the works of Alfred Schuetz.[9]

Basically, action exists (analytically) when the following components can be ascertained: actor (or actors), goals, means, and situation. The situation is defined by the actor (or actors) in terms of the way the actor (or actors) relates himself to other actors, to possible goals, and to possible means, and in terms of the way means and ends are formed into strategies of action subject to relevant factors in the situation. These ways of relating himself to the situation (and thus of defining it) will depend on the nature of the actor—or his orientations. Thus, "state X" mentioned above may be regarded as a participant in an action system comprising other actors; state X is the focus of the observer's attention. State X orients to action according to the manner in which the particular situation is viewed by certain officials and according to what they want. The actions of other actors, the actor's goals and means, and the other components of the situation are related meaningfully by the actor. His action flows from his definition of the situation.

4. We need to carry the actor-situation scheme one step further in an effort to rid ourselves of the troublesome abstraction "state." It is one of our basic methodological choices to define the state as its official decision-makers—those whose authoritative acts are, to all intents and purposes, the acts of the state. *State action is the action taken by those acting in the name of the state.* Hence, the state is its decision-makers. State X as *actor* is translated into its decision-makers as actors. It is also one of our basic choices to take as our prime analytical objective the re-creation of the "world" of the decision-makers as *they* view it. The manner in which *they* define situations becomes another way of saying how the state oriented to action and why. This is a quite different approach from trying to recreate the situation and interpretation of it *objectively,* that is, by the observer's judgment rather than that of the actors themselves.

To focus on the individual actors who are the state's decision-makers and to reconstruct the situation as defined by the decision-makers requires, of course, that a central place be given to the analysis of the behavior of these officials. One major significance of the diagram is that it calls attention to the sources of state action and to the essentially subjective (that is, from the standpoint of the decision-makers) nature of our perspective.

5. Now let us try to clarify a little further. We have said that the key to the explanation of why the state behaves the way it does lies in the way its decision-makers as actors define their situation. *The definition of the situation*[10] is built around the projected action as well as the reasons for the action. Therefore, it is necessary to analyze the actors (the official decision-makers) in the following terms: (a) their *discrimination* and *relating* of objects, conditions, and other actors—various things are perceived or expected in a relational context; (b) the existence, establishment, or definition of *goals*—various things are wanted from the situation; (c) attachment of *significance* to various courses of action suggested by the situation according to some criteria of estimation; and (d) application of *"standards of acceptability"* which (1) narrow the range of perceptions, (2) narrow the range of objects wanted, and (3) narrow the number of alternatives.

Three features of all orientations emerge: *perception, choice,* and *expectation.*

Perhaps a translation of the vocabulary of action theory will be useful. We are saying that the actors' orientations to action are reconstructed when the following kinds of questions are answered: what did the decision-makers think was relevant in a particular situation? how did they determine this?

how were the relevant factors related to each other—what connections did the decision-makers see between diverse elements in the situation? how did they establish the connections? what wants and needs were deemed involved in or affected by the situation? what were the sources of these wants and needs? how were they related to the situation? what specific or general goals were considered and selected? what courses of action were deemed fitting and effective? how were fitness and effectiveness decided?

6. We have defined international politics as processes of state interaction at the governmental level. However, there are nongovernmental factors and relationships which must be taken into account by any system of analysis, and there are obviously nongovernmental effects of state action. Domestic politics, the nonhuman environment, cross-cultural and social relationships are important in this connection. We have chosen to group such factors under the concept of *setting*. This is an analytic term which reminds us that the decision-makers act upon and respond to conditions and factors which exist outside themselves and the governmental organization of which they are a part. Setting has two aspects: *external* and *internal*. We have deliberately chosen setting instead of environment because the latter term is either too inclusive or has a technical meaning in other sciences. Setting is really a set of categories of *potentially relevant factors and conditions* which may affect the action of any state.

External setting refers, in general, to such factors and conditions beyond the territorial boundaries of the state—the actions and reactions of other states (their decision-makers), the societies for which they act, and the physical world. Relevance of particular factors and conditions *in general* and *in particular situations* will depend on the attitudes, perceptions, judgments, and purposes of state X's decision-makers, that is, on how they react to various stimuli. It should be noted that our conception of setting does *not* exclude certain so-called environmental limitations such as the state of technology, morbidity ratio, and so on, which *may* limit the achievement of objectives or which *may* otherwise become part of the conditions of action *irrespective* of *whether* and *how* the decision-makers perceive them.[11] However—and this is important—this does not in our scheme imply the substitution of an omniscient observer's judgment for that of the decision-maker. Setting is an analytical device to suggest certain enduring kinds of relevances and to limit the number of nongovernmental factors with which the student of international politics must be concerned. The external setting is constantly changing and will be composed of *what the decision-makers decide is important*. This "deciding" can mean simply that certain lacks—such as minerals or guns—not imposed on them, that is, must be *accepted*. A serious native revolt in South Africa in 1900 was not a feature of the external setting of United States decision-makers; it would be in 1963. Compare, too, the relatively minor impact of Soviet foreign activities on the United States decision-makers in the period of 1927 to 1933 with the present impact.

Usually the factors and conditions referred to by the term *internal setting* are loosely labeled "domestic politics," "public opinion," or "geographical position." A somewhat more adequate formulation might be: some clues to the way any state behaves toward the world must be sought in the way its society is organized and functions, in the character and behavior of its people and in its physical habitat. The list of categories under B (see p. 64) may be somewhat unfamiliar. There are two reasons for insisting that the analysis of the society for which X acts be pushed to this fundamental level. First, the list invites attention to a much wider range of potentially relevant factors than the more familiar terms like morale, attitudes, national power, party politics, and so on. For example, the problem of vulnerability to subversive attack is rarely discussed by political scientists in terms of the basic social structure of a particular nation, that is, in terms of B3. Nor is recruitment of manpower often connected with the way the roles of the sexes are differentiated in a society. Second, if one is interested in the fundamental "why" of state behavior, the search for reliable answers go beyond the *derived* conditions and factors (morale, pressure groups, production, attitudes, and so on) which are normally the focus of attention.

7. The diagram suggests another important point. Line BC is a two-way arrow connoting rightly an interaction between social organization and behavior on the one hand and decision-making on the other. Among other things this arrow represents the impact of domestic social forces on the formulation and execution of foreign policy. BC implies that the influence of conditions factors in the society is felt through the decision-making process. But line DB is also important because it indicates that a nation experiences its own external actions. State action is designed primarily to alter factors and behavior or to otherwise affect conditions in the external setting, yet it may have equally serious consequences for the society itself. We need only suggest range of possibilities here. Extensive foreign relations may enhance the power of the central government relative to other regulatory institutions. Particular programs may contribute to the redistribution of resources, income, and social power. For example, the outpouring of billions in foreign aid by the United States since 1945 has contributed to the increased power and influence of scientists, military leaders, engineers, and the managerial group. The people of a state experience foreign policy in other ways—they

may feel satisfaction, alarm, guilt, exhilaration, or doubt about it. There will be nongovernmental *interpretations*—perhaps several major ones—shared by various members or groups of the society. Such interpretations may or may not be identical with the prevailing official interpretation. There will also be nongovernmental expectations concerning state action which, again, may or may not correspond to official expectations. Discrepancies between nongovernmental and governmental interpretations and expectations may have important ramifications. For one thing, public support and confidence may be undermined if state action produces consequences which fundamentally violate public expectations.

The point to be made here is that the diagrammatic expression of our scheme shows that the impact of domestic social factors (line BCD) must be viewed also as a part of a larger feedback process as indicated by line BCDBC.

8. Another significant set of relationships emerges from the diagram in line ABE. The external and internal settings are related to each other. Among others, two implications may be stressed here. First, because we have defined international politics as interaction process at the governmental level, it may appear that we are making the focus unduly narrow, thus ignoring a whole host of private, nongovernmental interactions. Nothing could be further from the truth. Societies interact with each other in a wide range of ways through an intricate network of communications—trade, family ties, professional associations, shared values, cultural exchanges, travel, mass media, and migration. While all of these patterns may be subject to governmental regulation (in some form), they *may* have very little to do with the origins and forms of state action. At any rate, the question of the political significance of intersocietal, intercultural, nongovernmental interactions requires an analytical scheme which will make possible some understanding of how such interactions condition official action. This in turn requires a much more systematic description of interactions than we now have, plus a way of accounting for their connection with state action.

One can, however, study the interactions connoted by line ABE for their own sake with only a slight interest in their political aspects. In this case, it seems proper to say that the focus is international relations rather than international politics.

Nongovernmental international relations do not enter the analysis of state behavior *unless* it can be shown that the behavior of the decision-makers is in some manner determined by or directed toward such relations. For example, assume a bitter, hostile campaign against a foreign government by powerful

United States newspapers and assume the campaign is well publicized in the other nation. By itself this would constitute an asymmetrical interaction between two societies. It would not become a matter of state interaction unless or until the following happened: (a) an official protest to the U.S. State Department by the foreign government; (b) retaliation against United States citizens in the foreign country; (c) disturbance of negotiations between the two governments on quite another issue; (d) arousal of public opinion in the foreign country to the point where the effectiveness of United States policies toward that country was seriously affected; (e) the pressure generated by the campaign in the United States caused the decision-makers to modify their actions and reactions vis-à-vis the other state; (f) the United States government officially repudiated the criticism and apologized to the other government. This same *kind* of argument would hold for all types of nongovernmental relations except that there would be varying degrees of directness (that is, change in intersocietal relations ⟶ change in state action) and indirectness (that is, change in intersocietal relations ⟶ change in social organization and behavior ⟶ derived condition or factor ⟶ change in state action) and therefore different time-sequences.

Second, while the most obvious consequences of state action are to be looked for in the reactions of other states along the lines CDE4C in the diagram, changes in the external setting can influence state action along the lines CDE3A3BC, that is, indirectly through changes in nongovernmental relations which ultimately are recognized and taken into account by the decision-makers.

9. To get back to the center of the diagram, it should be noted that CD is a two-way arrow. The rest of this essay is concerned with the nature of decision-making, but it can be said here that in addition to the feedback relationships CDBC and CDE3A3, DC connotes a direct feedback from an awareness by the decision-makers of their own action and from assessments of the progress of action. This is to say that state action has an impact on decision-making apart from subsequent reactions of other states and apart from effects mediated through the state's social organization and behavior.

10. So far as this diagram is concerned, most attention in the field of international politics is paid to interactions CDE4CD. CD represents action(s); DE (particularly DE4) represents consequences for, or impact upon, the external setting; EC represents new conditions or stimuli—reactions or new actions (E4C). Therefore, CDECD represents the action-reaction-interaction sequence.

Obviously these lines stand for a wide range of relationships and kinds of action. What should be emphasized here is that interactions can be really understood fully only in terms of the decision-making responses of states to situations, problems, and the actions of other states. The combination of interaction and decision-making can be diagrammed as:

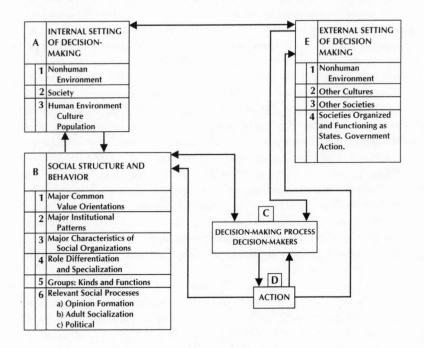

STATE "X" AS ACTOR IN A SITUATION
(Situation is comprised of a combination of selectively relevant factors
in the external and internal setting as interpreted by the decision-makers.)

Naturally if one thinks of all the separate actions and reactions and all the combinations involved in the governmental relationships between one state and all others, it seems unrealistic and somewhat absurd to let a few lines on a diagram represent much. Indeed, all would be lost unless one could speak of *patterns* and *systems*. Patterns refer to *uniformities* and *persistence* actions and sets of relationships. "Nationalism," "imperialism," "internationalism," "aggression," "isolationism," "peace," "war "conflict," and "cooperation" are familiar ways of characterizing kinds of actions and reactions as well as patterned relationships among states. These terms are, of course, both descriptive and judgmental—they are shorthand expressions covering complicated phenomena and also may imply approval or disapproval, goodness or badness.

System in this context refers to the modes, rules, and nature of reciprocal influence which structure the interaction between states. Five kinds of systems—there are others—may be mentioned: *coalitions* (temporary and permanent); *supranational organization; bilateral; multilateral* (unorganized); and *ordination-subordination* (imperial relationships and satellites). Once again, the way these interactions and relationships arise and the particular form or substance they take would seem to be explainable in terms of the way the decision-makers in the participating political organisms "define their situation." As we have said elsewhere,[12] there seem to be only two ways of scientifically studying international politics: (1) the description and measurement of interaction; and (2) decision-making—the formulation and execution of policy. Interaction patterns can be studied by themselves without reference to decision-making except that the "why" of the patterns cannot be answered.

Summary

To conclude this brief commentary, it may be said that the diagram presented on page 64 is designed in the first instance to portray graphically the basic perspectives of our frame of reference: *any* state as a way of saying something about *all* states; the central position of the decision-making focus; and the integration of a wide range of factors which may explain state action, reaction, and interaction.

The lines of the diagram carry *two* suggestive functions. First, they alert the observer to possible (known and hypothetical) relationships among empirical factors. Thus, the diagram simultaneously invites attention to three interrelated, intersecting empirical processes—state interaction (CDEC) at the governmental level, intersocietal interaction (ABE) at the nongovernmental level, and intrasocietal interaction (BCDB) at both the governmental and nongovernmental level. These processes arise, to put the matter another way, from decision-makers interacting with factors which constitute the dual setting, from state interaction as normally conceived, and from the factors which constitute internal and external settings acting upon each other.

Second, the diagram is intended to suggest possible analytic and theoretical relationships as well. The boxes indicate ways of specifying the relevant factors in state behavior through the employment of certain concepts—decision-making, action, setting, situation, society, culture, and so on—which provide, if they are successfully developed, criteria of relevance and ways of handling the empirical phenomena and their interrelationships. There are in existence a large number of tested and untested hypotheses, general and "middle range" theories, applicable within each of the categories comprising the diagram. The central concept of decision-making may provide a basis for linking a group of theories which hitherto have been applicable only to a segment of international politics or have not been susceptible of application at all. We may cite two examples. The concept of culture is clearly suggested by A2, B2, and E2 which specify empirical phenomena branded analytically as cultural in the technical sense. Based on this important social science concept is the derived concept of National Character—typical behavior patterns uniquely (or allegedly so) characteristic of one nation. Suggestive as national character analysis has been, it has been thus far impossible to bridge the analytic gap between behavior patterns at the cultural level and state action on the governmental level. Communication theory (really a cluster of related theories) has been applied almost exclusively to mass media (B6) and to techniques of state action (D). Only recently has an attempt been made to apply recent developments in communication theory to intersocietal interaction[13] and to decision-making.[14]

Before proceeding to a discussion of decision-making, there are other analytical problems which must be faced.

Supplementary Definitions and Concepts

The Path of Action Concept

No scheme which professes to account for the dynamic quality of international politics can carry decision-making to the point of action (D) and then skip to the reaction of another state or to the impact on the external setting. The troublesome factor of time must be considered and if relationships and processes are to be described and explained, a further operation is necessary to make CDEC *flow.* Furthermore, the kinds of feedback noted above must be drawn together. For *any* action, the simple diagram would be:

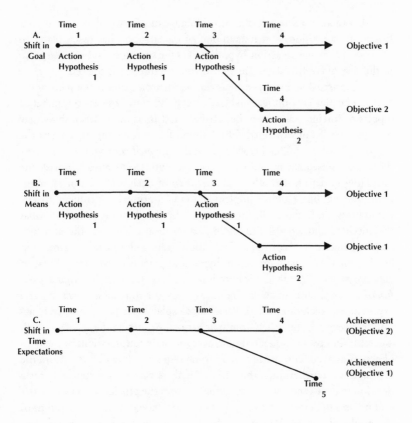

At time (1)—the point in time when action is initiated—the "action-hypothesis" (1) expresses the particular combination of ends and means involved in a particular action and the expectations embodied in the decision. At time (2) the action-hypothesis (1) may have remained the same, or may have been replaced by action-hypothesis (2). If the latter, a change in the *direction* of action (that is, the goal or goals) or a change in the strategy of action (that is, means) is implied. Changes in time perspectives, that is, *when* and *by when* calculations, may have been revised. Between time (1) and time (2) several things may be expected to occur. Presumably "progress reports" have been made, discrepancies between what was expected and what happened may have been discovered, new conditions may have arisen, and certain elements of the original action-hypothesis may have been reconsidered.

Whether there is a directional or other change or not, whether there is con-firmation or revision, a *new* definition of the situation has taken place. In the case of a change in action-hypothesis (1) the situation has been *redefined;* in the case of confirmation, the new definition duplicates the old.

If the original action-hypothesis can be identified and if the path of ac-tion can be plotted with reasonable accuracy and completeness, a number of aspects of foreign policy may be clarified, and their interrelationships may be suggested if not explained. The notion of action-hypothesis reflects the fact that decision-making involves in a real sense *prediction* and *testing*—pre-diction of consequences and testing of assumptions. As already noted, the unfolding of action—in effect the *execution* of decisions—is not an auto-matic process but requires implementation, continual adjustment to cir-cumstances, and, above all, interpretation by the decision-makers of what they decided and what the unfolding action means. The way the decision-makers perceive the "path of action" would seem to be a crucial element in any explanation of why the action-hypothesis persists or is altered. Presum-ably one way that precedent is born is by the persistence of the original *com-bination* of appraisal of the situation, strategy (or strategies) of action, and expectations (including time). Persistence explains the patterns of state ac-tion. However, the feedback from state action operates on the society as well, and authoritative or influential nongovernmental interpretations of the path of action may be (and usually are in some respects) quite different from the official ones. Furthermore, the decision-makers who were responsible for a decision may be (and usually are) different from the officials who execute de-cisions, and therefore the two groups may not share the same perceptions of the results of action. Also, it may be that still other officials may differ in their interpretation of consequences.

At any rate, the action-hypothesis may persist doggedly—here something close to willfulness may be discernible—despite changes in relevant factors or conditions, or it may be altered rather drastically. In between there may be changes in tactics, in time calculations, or a scaling down of intentions, that is, a willingness to "settle for less" than was hoped for originally.

The Concept of Successive, Overlapping Definitions of the Situation

Having sketched in the path of action concept, we must return to the prob-lem of simultaneity.

Clearly no state pursues just one path of action, but many—differing in nature and magnitude, and separable. Each action requires a *separate* defi-nition of the situation, and thus many *situations* are being defined simultaneously. The diagram indicates that the definition is built around an action, an action-hypothesis. In other words, the situation is defined *in terms of* something—a problem or a condition or the necessity for action. The definition of the situation for any state is, then, a series of definitions, each having a specific focus.

As time elapses, successive definitions—again built around a particular action—occur and, in fact, constitute the path of action. Starting at time (1) with an action-hypothesis, (Action A), which has emerged from the decision-making process, the objectives embodied therein are successively defined and refined as action unfolds. The shaded area between the successive definitions simply indicates that each new definition (which is not necessarily a radically different one) is not an isolated operation. There will always be a substantial carry-over from one to another. This can be in the "givens" which affect the first stage of action. By "givens" is meant that the particular group of decision-makers who define the situation at the time (1) will probably take into account preceding actions, other contemplated actions, and the standing rules of procedure. The rules binding on the decision-makers will heavily condition the interpretation of the prevailing conditions and what is perceived to be relevant to the problem presented.

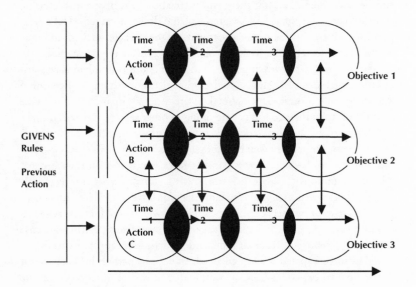

The circle surrounding Action A and policy hypothesis (1) is an analytical device for postulating a boundary between what the decision-makers considered relevant to their decision and what they considered irrelevant. In other words, the actor-situation approach to social analysis alerts the observer to the *discrimination of relevances*—to the *selection* and *valuation* of objects, events, symbols, conditions, and other actors. These relevancies are, so to speak, carved from a total number of phenomena present in the overall setting (internal and external) of action. Of the phenomena which *might* have been relevant, the actors (the decision-makers) finally endow only some with *significance*. As already mentioned, some relevancies will be "given," and among the "givens" will be certain cues to the determination of other relevancies. The situation—as defined—arises from selective perception. This does not mean, of course, that the decision-makers are necessarily unaware of phenomena beyond the boundary line but only that the label "relevant" has not been attached to such phenomena.

The circle is not only a boundary between relevance and nonrelevance, but there is a pattern of relationships among the selected components of the situation. Evaluation by the decision-makers includes much more than assignment of importance or significance. Two types of relationships within the defined situation may be mentioned. First, there will be relationships among factors in the setting—both within the external and internal settings and between them. Second, there will be relationships between the setting and the plans, purposes, and programs of the decision-makers. These relationships are established by the judgments of the decision-makers and may or may not correspond to what an "objective" observer might establish.

The two-way arrow linking A, B, and C (and also n-number of actions) again is suggestive of analytical and empirical relationships. It is common knowledge that groups of policy-makers are often aware of, and often take account of, what their colleagues are doing in other sectors of decision-making. It is also obvious that action taken by one group may have serious consequences for the action taken by another. Thus, the simultaneous pursuit of multiple paths of action creates consequences which may in turn become relevant conditions for any one action system. *Inconsistencies* of foreign policy are often viewed as though the same decision-makers inadvertently chose two objectives or two sets of objectives both of which could not be achieved at same time. Actually, it would appear that inconsistencies (in the sense used here) often result from an independent definition of the situation followed by unanticipated consequences which become part of the feedback for another course of action. Lack of coordination is sometimes regarded as the basic difficulty here, but once again, it may be that it is not necessarily the lack of awareness or information on the part of one group of decision-makers which causes the "clash" of objectives. Rather, it may be that the situation confronting one group is defined in such a way as to rule out the possibility of clash, and this assumption or prediction is upset by events.

Independent definitions are linked not only by mutual impact (either through actual consequences or calculations of such consequences by the decision-makers), but also by the fact that at any one time there will be a reservoir of policy directives applicable to most situations. Each problem or action will have its own past, but all will to a certain extent share the same past. Whether and to what extent decision-makers are equally bound by some rules depends on the circulation of common definitional elements among them.[15] However, a possible cause for lack of coordination among policies and actions may lie in the diverse interpretation of common general rules. We are mindful of the fact that the "givens" referred to above probably have a hard core of identical meaning for all decision-makers aware of them. Beyond this hard core are possibilities of disagreement.

Situational Analysis and Types of Situations

The foregoing suggests in brief the nature of the analytical consequences which follow from a choice to approach state action from an actor-situation point of view. "Situation" is an analytical concept pointing to a pattern of relationships among events, objects, conditions, and other actors organized around a focus which is the center of interest for the decision-makers (and hence for the observer). In turn the situation is related to a larger setting from which it has been abstracted by the actors, including other situations and the broader relationships surrounding them too.[16]

While no extended treatment can be given to the problem at this time, we ought to recognize that a systematic frame of reference for the study of international politics will require several typologies, one of which will be concerned with *situations* as defined by decision-makers. We shall suggest only a crude formulation at this stage:

1. *Structured vs. unstructured situations*—pointing to the relative degree of ambiguity and stability; a situation for which the decision-makers find it difficult to establish meaning may be characterized by change as well as intrinsic obscurity.
2. Situations having different degrees of *requiredness*—that is, the amount of pressure to act and its source (from within the decisional system or from the setting).

3. The *cruciality* of situations—their relatedness to, and importance for, the basic purposes of the decision-makers.
4. Kinds of *affect* with which the situation is endowed by the decision-makers—threatening, hostile, avoidance-inducing, favorable, unfavorable, and so on.
5. How the problem is *interpreted* and how its *major functional characteristic* is assigned—political, moral, economic, military, or a combination of these.
6. The *time* dimension—the degree of permanence attributed to various situations.
7. The degree *to which objective factors impose* themselves on the decision-makers—the number of uncontrollable factors and imponderables.

Perhaps the chief advantage of such a breakdown is to remind us of the fact that certain objective properties of a situation will be partly responsible for the reactions and orientations of the decision-makers and that the assignment of properties to a situation by the decision-makers is indicative of clues to the rule which may have governed their particular responses.

The Concept of Objective.[17] The existing literature is long on the discussion of kinds of objectives and short on what the term implies analytically. In fact, it is difficult to find a definition of objective. This becomes somewhat important if one is interested in the identification of empirical and/or nonempirical referents. However, current writing has gone so far as to distinguish between long-term and short-term objectives, and between positive and negative objectives. It is also recognized that objectives may be related to each other—either in terms of their comprising a program or a strategy, or in terms of the impact of the pursuit of one objective on the pursuit of others. Some writers have pointed out that techniques or means can—by a subtle transformation—become ends in themselves. Beyond this, the most that is really done by way of analysis of objectives of state action is to classify them as power or security, economic, moral, prestige, and ideological. National security, usually regarded as a basic objective, is rarely subject to an attempt at definition.[18] The connection between national objectives and national interests remains somewhat unclear.

We shall define objective as essentially an "*image*" of a future "state of affairs"—a "set of conditions" to be fulfilled or a "set of specifications" which when met are to be regarded as the achievement of what was desired by the decision-makers. There are *four aspects* of the future state of affairs, related of course, but separable for analytical purposes. First, we may employ a military term, *target*, to identify the specific achievement element of the objective. An example would be the raising of the standard of living in France under the Mutual Security Program. Second, we may specify a *generalized directional element* which refers to the ultimate state of affairs envisaged and to the relationship to other objectives or to a total strategy. An example would be the strengthening of Western Europe—via higher living standards in France as well as other measures. Third, there are *expectations* concerning certain consequences, that is, conditions, relationships, and events which are expected to be different from what might have been in the absence of the action embodying the objective. An example would be the heightening of resistance to the internal appeals of communism in France. Fourth, every objective will have a *time dimension* whether it is definite or indefinite. An example would be the five-year duration planned originally for the European Recovery Program.

Objectives are thus the directional aspect of state behavior—such behavior is *toward* something. Even avoidance behavior eventually is behavior toward something else. Individual components of objectives may change without necessarily bringing about a marked change in direction. Since objectives reflect motives, the analysis of objectives requires the analysis of motivation. Indeed, motives are inferred from objectives which are, in turn, inferred from sequences of behavior. An objective is the *projection* of action, and to formulate an objective means to rehearse the future in the imagination. Now if we link up this attempt to operationalize the term "objective"— albeit crudely—with our earlier comments on the path of action, it is clear that the actual substance of the target and the actual state of affairs which becomes acceptable to the decision-makers must depend on the unfolding of action. There may, therefore, be considerable discrepancy between the original expectational element and the objective which materializes.

Accordingly, two factors already alluded to may give foreign policy objectives an indeterminate quality: one is directional shifts along the path of action discussed above and the other is the probable existence of *different*—though not necessarily competing—interpretations of the components of various objectives. This confronts the observer with choices of the time period on which his analysis will focus. He can take a "depth sounding" by attempting to establish the empirical referents for a particular objective (or set of objectives) at *one moment* in time, or he can attempt to trace the evolution as indicated by the unfolding action. An evolutionary analysis might serve to isolate the static and dynamic properties of objectives. Differing interpretations of objectives pose the problem of identification of the authoritative interpretation and assessing the consequences of different interpretations.

The task of operationalizing the term *objective* and of discovering the content or properties of concrete national objectives is not made easier by the fact that the decision-makers often do *not* operationalize their statements of objectives, that is, specify in detail what the envisaged state of affairs would look like. One reason for this is that much state action is purely verbal, consisting of declarations and conversational exchanges. Hence, symbols may be substituted for actual conditions.[19] In this case, objectives may only *indirectly* correspond to a concrete state of affairs. What are the possible referents of the term "national security"? When the Secretary of State says that such and such an action is designed to preserve national security, what does he mean? Military safety? Relief from psychological pressure?

The Concept of Policy. Once again we note the rather strange fact that despite all the writing on foreign policy little effort has been made to clarify this ambiguous term. What does it mean to have a policy about something? We suggest that for purposes of the analytical scheme being outlined here, policy be considered to have *two* components. The sources of policy and the processes by which it is formulated and executed must be left out of account for the moment. One component is *action* as defined—action which has occurred, is occurring, and which is projected. The other component is *rules,* that is, guides to action. Rules have a threefold aspect: (1) the substance of a response to some future situation—for example, to oppose the next Communist invasion anywhere by American arms; (2) the occasion for a response or the conditions under which a particular response will be made—for example, no action will be taken by the United States on its own with respect to the Suez Canal, but, when asked by Great Britain for a view, the United States will oppose complete Egyptian control; (3) the interpretation of future events and circumstances—any move by the Soviet Union to reduce atomic stockpiles will be regarded as an empty gesture. Thus, policy embraces *action* and *rules* of action, reaction or interpretation. Accordingly, policy can be anticipatory, cumulative, specific, and general. "To have a policy" means action and/or rules with respect to a problem, contingency or event which has occurred, is occurring, or is expected to occur. Action and rules may be among the givens preceding a definition of a situation by the decision-makers.

Possible Advantages of the Present Scheme

As presented thus far, our approach can be sharply differentiated from the ones outlined in a previous section. This frame of reference is designed to be more inclusive. It attempts to provide a limited number of categories for the phenomena of international politics and to provide cues for the identification of key variables or factors which may explain state behavior. It also attempts to specify the location and possible nature of the interrelationships among factors which are relevant to state behavior.

Adoption of the action-situational analysis makes it possible to emphasize that state behavior is determined but to avoid deterministic explanations. Some of the awkward problems of the objective-subjective dilemma are avoided by the attempt to see the world through the decision-maker's eyes. We adhere to the nation-state as the fundamental level of analysis, yet we have discarded the state as a metaphysical abstraction. By emphasizing decision-making as a central focus, we have provided a way of organizing the determinants of action around those officials who act for the political society. Decision-makers are viewed as operating in dual-aspect setting so that apparently unrelated internal and external factors become related in the actions of the decision-makers. Hitherto, precise ways of relating domestic factors not been adequately developed.

We have suggested that the problems of *time* and *simultaneity* can at least be clarified by the concepts of path of action, by the definition of the situation, and by the specifications of the properties of objectives. The concept of situation requires investigation of how relations among past action, existing rules, strategies of action, and particular aspects of the setting are established by the decision-makers.

The whole problem of national interest is bypassed by the adoption of the definition of the situation device. As is well known, considerable ambiguity and intermixture of purposes characterize the national interest concept. The term itself is rarely defined, and it appears to be assumed that everyone understands what is implied. If one analyzes the usage, it is by no means clear whether national interest refers to the more fundamental values which must be protected or which guide the choice of strategies, to the specific objectives which are formulated with respect to particular problems, to the meaning attached to events and conditions, to the results of policies, to policies themselves, or to some or all of these. We propose to translate the term into our frame of reference by saying that the "national interest" is given form and substance through the definition of the situation by the decision-makers and through the evolution of action from one situation to another. *The* national interest is, in reality, a cluster of definitions which share certain attributes, notably the rules which affect or bind all groups of decision-makers.

5. THE DECISION-MAKING APPROACH

We come now to a more detailed discussion of the central part of the diagram presented earlier. Having said that we wish to think in terms of decision-makers and how they orient to action, it is necessary to consider them as participants in a *system of action*. The concept of *system*[1] is above all an ordering device employed by the observer which implies certain defined types of relationships and patterns of activities having some persistence over time. The characteristics of the system determine to a considerable extent the manner in which the decision-makers relate themselves to the setting. The type of social system with which we shall be primarily concerned is an *organization*. Therefore, *the definitions of the situation which we consider to be central to the explanation of state behavior result from decision-making processes in an organizational context.*

The Organizational Context

Existing treatises on International Politics seem to ignore or assume the fact that decision-makers operate in a highly particular and specific context. To ignore this context omits a range of factors which significantly influence the behavior of decision-makers (and therefore state behavior), including not only the critical problem of *how* choices are made but also the *conditions under which* choices are made.

To assume the organizational factors is perfectly permissible if one is interested only in *what* was decided and in interaction patterns among states. But for purposes of analyzing state behavior in general such assumptions beg most of the crucial questions. We are convinced that many of the abortive attempts to apply personality theory, culture theory, and small group theory to the analysis of foreign policy have been due to a failure to consider the peculiar social system in which decision-makers function. Often, as remarked earlier, the individual policy-makers are treated as though they performed their duties in a vacuum.

There is in existence at present a very large literature on organization to which substantial contributions have been made by virtually all the social sciences. We shall not take the time here to review this literature. It is necessary to point out, however, that there is no single, comprehensive, unified theory of organization.[2] Numerous choices are available to the student, depending upon his purposes and the problems he seeks to treat. Upon these will depend in turn his definitions and his selection of concepts. We shall try to make our choices as explicit as possible.

Elsewhere we have stated that we are concerned primarily with process analysis. This means we are treating *the organizational system in action.* Consequently, we have chosen to treat certain major features of organizational structure as specifications to be taken for granted. The consequences of this choice will be elaborated below. In the meantime, however, it may be helpful to list some of the features of the organizational structure we shall assume:[3]

1. The *personnel* of formal organizations gain their livelihood from membership, have a limited working life, and differ in skills
2. Specific, limited, hierarchized *objectives*—either given or decided by the organization
3. *Internal specialization or division of labor,* which implies:
   a. recruitment and training (including in-service)
   b. universalistic standards of placement
   c. functionally specific role relationships among members based on organizationally defined patterns of behavior
   d. two kinds of specialization—vertical (delegation to levels of authority) and horizontal (boundaries of coordinate units and roles)
4. *Authority and control,* which imply:
   a. normatively sanctioned power distributed unequally throughout the organization
   b. superior-subordinate relationships to insure coordination of specialized activities
   c. motivation for exercise and acceptance of authority
   d. pyramidal structure of power
5. *Motivation*—members are moved to participate in cooperative pursuit of organizational objectives or activities related to such objectives
6. *Communication*—circulation of orders, directions, information
7. *Relationships are formalized and routinized,* serving to:
   a. insure predictability of behavior
   b. allocate roles according to competence
   c. depersonalize relationships and insure continuity with personnel turnover
8. *Positions and careers "professionalized"* in terms of operating codes and procedures, lines of career development, criteria of advancement

This check-list of structural specifications to be taken for granted does not mean that we are consciously begging any vital questions having to do with organizational behavior as we will define it below. Indeed, the list is a reminder that the actors who participate in decision-making are members of a certain type of social structure (not society in the more general sense), and that when we come to discuss spheres of competence, internal specialization is relevant, or when we come to discuss motivation, recruitment and training are relevant.

Organizational Decision-Making

Social structures characterized by the features listed above constitute the organizational context within which the types of decisions with which we are concerned are made. The specific characteristics of decisional units will be discussed below.

Despite the obvious and long-standing interest of political scientists in policy-making, the concept of decision-making has not been defined or developed to any great extent.[4] This is not to say that there are not theories of decision-making[5] or that considerable attention has not been given to the structures within which decision-making takes place. But relatively little has been done to combine these two interests. Also, little has been written about the implications of using this approach, and empirical knowledge of the process of decision-making is not abundant. As one group of authors says, "Oddly enough, the process of decision-making— what a decision is and how it gets made—is still a mystery. . . ."[6] For the most part the available materials bearing on this important area of political behavior have been in the form of case studies[7] and descriptions of concrete agencies.[8]

Whenever writers on international politics get down to discussing the behavior of decision-makers usually one of five kinds of treatment results: (1) the same values and perspectives are assigned to all officials; (2) motivation is assumed to consist of a single drive; (3) the decision-makers' actions are regarded as determined by "conditions" and "resources"; (4) simple descriptions are made on a very low level of generalization; and (5) diplomats are often portrayed as isolated from any governmental organization.

We shall not review existing definitions of decision-making but shall present our own and comment on it.

> A DEFINITION: *Decision-making is a process which results in the selection from a socially defined, limited number of problematical, alternative projects[9] of one project intended to bring about the particular future state of affairs envisaged by the decision-makers.*

Explanation and Assumptions

1. Decision-making leads to a *course of action* based on the project. The term *project* is employed here to include objectives and techniques. The course of action moves along a path (as indicated earlier) toward the outcome envisaged. Adoption of the project signifies that the decision-makers were motivated by an intention to accomplish something. The means included in the project are also socially defined.

2. Organizational decision-making is a *sequence of activities*. The particular sequence is an *event*[10] which for purposes of analysis may be isolated. The event chosen determines in good part what is or is not relevant for the observer's analytical purposes.

To illustrate, if the event in which the observer is interested is American policy-making on the Japanese Peace Treaty, then the focus of attention is the system within the American government which was concerned with this problem and the various factors influencing the decision-makers in that system. NATO, EDC, ERP, the Technical Assistance Program, and so on, were not immediately relevant. If, on the other hand, the over-all cluster of decisions with respect to the policy of containment of Soviet power is the focus, the Japanese Peace Treaty and NATO, EDC, ERP, the Technical Assistance Program, and a number of other factors all become a part of the strategies of implementation.

3. The event can be considered a unified whole, or it can be separated into its constituent elements. A suggested breakdown might be in terms of the sequence of activities: (a) predecisional activities; (b) choice; and (c) implementation. These need not necessarily occur in chronological order, but in all probability they will. Nor are these sealed compartments within the total process.

4. Some choices are made at every stage of the decision-making process. The *point of final decision* is that stage in the sequence at which decision-makers having the authority choose a specific course of action to be implemented and assume or are assigned responsibility for it. At this point the decision becomes official and thus binding on all decision-makers whether they participated or not.

The weeding out of information, condensation of memoranda, and so on, all involve decisions which must be recognized as such by the observer.

5. Choice involves *valuation and evaluation* in terms of a *frame of reference*.[11] *Weights* and *priorities* are then assigned to alternative projects.

6. The *occasion for decision* arises from uncertainty. In other words, some aspect of the situation is no longer taken for granted; it becomes problematical in terms of the decision-makers' frame of reference.

7. The problem requiring decision or the stimulus to action may originate within the decisional system, or it may originate in a change in the internal[12] or external setting.

8. The *range of alternative projects* which the decision-makers consider is
limited. Limitations exist both as to means and ends. Limitations of the
range of alternative projects are due in large part to the following factors: the
individual decision-makers' past experience and values; the amount of available and utilized information; situational elements; the characteristics of the
organizational system and the known,[13] available resources.

Definition of the Decisional Unit and of the Decision-Makers

We have decided to build our analysis around the concept of decisional unit
for a very practical reason. Ordinarily, when we think of foreign policy-making in the United States, for example, we think of the sixty-odd concrete
agencies—such as the State Department, Defense Department, the National
Security Council, and so on—which may be involved in the conduct of foreign affairs. It is tempting, and somewhat logical, to consider these common-sense units as the decisional units we must analyze. But it becomes
obvious at once that there are several difficulties in this "self-evident" approach. First, not all members (or employees) of these common-sense units
are responsible decision-makers under all circumstances. It would be manifestly absurd to include every last file clerk in, say, the State Department. So,
in any case, we have a selection problem on our hands. Second, not all the
sixty-odd agencies are involved the *same way in all* decisions. Each may have
several different kinds of potential roles it can play in various problems or
situations. Third, not all these agencies are equally important. The State Department has, obviously, a larger over-all role than the Department of Agriculture. Fourth, when these agencies do participate, they are not necessarily
related to each other in the same way. Sometimes they are equals, sometimes
not. Fifth, for different problems, different members of the concrete agencies may actually participate. For these reasons we have found it impossible
to attempt to relate concrete units *as such* in the decision-making process.
Rather we insist that it is necessary to abstract from these, so to speak, those
decision-makers who participate in reaching a decision.

The problem here is to establish the boundaries which will encompass
the actors and activities to be observed and explained. We have stated above
that the focus of attention is the analytical concept of an event, that is, decision-making. Moreover, we have said that the type of decision-making
event in which we are interested is one that takes place in an organizational

context. The organizational system within which the decision-making event takes place is the *unit* of observation. The question now is, by what criteria is the decisional unit to be isolated and differentiated from the setting?

The criterion that seems most useful at this time is the objective or mission.

Before we can discuss the nature of the decisional unit, it is necessary to say something further about objectives. We have already spoken of some of the basic characteristics of the concept of the objective. As already noted, the objective is taken as being a particular desired future state of affairs having a specific referent. The aspect upon which we must insist is the specificity, whether this is the production of ten thousand maroon convertibles, a peace treaty with Japan, or any other objective for which it is possible to designate a period of time, a place, and a system of activities.

It is of great importance that the objective be viewed as being specific, because it is only possible to speak of the organization or decisional system with respect to a specified objective. The difficulties which flow from the choice of some broad and inclusive notion of objective such as "the optimization of gain," a "foreign policy," the "saving of souls," seem to be so great that this method was selected as a convenient alternative. It is particularly the specification of a time element that is difficult, given a more general statement of objective.

This posing of the problem has the further appeal of at least bringing into question the assumption frequently made that all organizations having the same general purpose, for example, "foreign policy-making," will be more similar to each other than to other organizations having some other general purpose. In addition to matters of comparability, the virtue of defining the decisional system with respect to the objective is that it allows the observer to distinguish this system of action from other systems of action. It should be clearly understood that the unit is still a concrete one, but we have a relatively simple criterion for inclusion or exclusion, namely, concern with the given objective.

Some general statements about the concept of an objective have been made above, but more needs to be said about it in this connection. Before doing so it may be useful, however, to recapitulate as briefly as possible some of our assumptions. We have said, in effect, that with respect to any foreign policy objective there is an organizational unit so constituted as to be able to select a course of action to achieve that objective. The objective is a concrete envisaged state of affairs.

It is immediately apparent that there is a very large number of different kinds of foreign policy objectives. Seemingly one of the great needs in foreign policy analysis is a typology of these different kinds of objectives. These objectives might be classified on the basis of whether they are political, economic, military, or some other or a combination. The degree of urgency attached to them must be considered. Furthermore, it would be of considerable importance to take into account the time element, that is, whether the objective is considered to be long-term or short-term and what substantive meaning is given to these time spans. This is not to indicate that many treatments of foreign policy-making do not speak of, for example, "short-term military objectives" or "long-term political objectives." What is needed, however, is a systematic classification with clearly stated and easily applicable criteria.

For purposes of an historical study of a foreign policy decision such a typology would be useful but not essential. The student would still be able to isolate the unit which made a particular decision and to analyze the factors influencing the actions of the decision-makers, provided the necessary information is available and accessible. If, however, it is the intent of the observer to predict the kinds of decisions which will emerge from various units, then the typology of objectives becomes essential. That is, the typology will tell the observer something about the kinds of systems that would be involved in these types of decision. And prediction can only be predicated on knowledge of how these types of units act.

The Organizational Unit

Since the *organizational or decisional unit* is at the very heart of the kind of analysis we are suggesting, its constituent elements will be discussed at length below. Here we shall confine ourselves to some fairly general observations. The unit, as we have indicated above, is an observer's analytical device to allow identification and isolation of those actions and activities which are of concern to him. We are assuming that all units will be "organizational" in the sense discussed in a previous section. In our view all decisional units are organizational systems, and by organization we mean the system of activities and the structure of relationships. That is, the activities and relationships will be the outcome of the operation of formal rules governing the allocation of power and responsibility, motivation, communication, performance of functions, problem-solving, and so on. Each unit will have its own organization in this sense. Naturally the particular organizational form which a unit takes will depend on how and why the unit was established, who the members are, and what its specific task is.

It should be apparent that for the observer one and only one organizational unit can act with respect to any one objective. That is, for example, there can be only one set of American decision-makers who were concerned with the Japanese Peace Treaty, since the Japanese Peace Treaty was a unique historical event. This holds true whether the primary institutional affiliation of these decision-makers was the Department of State, the Department of Defense, the Congress, or whatever. Here we must again point to the importance of typification of objectives units. An initial and tentative listing of some of the criteria which units may be typified is the following:[14]

1. SIZE—The number of participants may range from a single member to large bodies such as legislatures. In addition to sheer size the number of participants at any one level would have to be considered.
2. STRUCTURE—Some of the factors that may be relevant here are whether or not the unit is hierarchical, whether the relationships of authority and the communications net are clearly defined or are ambiguous, and the degree of explicitness and conventionalization of the competences.
3. LOCATION IN THE INSTITUTIONAL SETTING—Two factors are pointed to here: first, the primary institutional affiliation of the members; second, the level in the institutional setting at which the unit operates.
4. RELATION TO OTHER ORGANIZATIONAL UNITS—Here the relative dependence or independence, isolation or involvement, would be indicated.
5. DURATION OF THE UNIT—The relative permanence or impermanence of units would be the guiding consideration here.
6. TYPE OF OBJECTIVE—This is probably one of the important criteria, and further exposition of the factors involved will have to await the development of a typology of objectives.

We might indicate at this point that it does not appear likely that all decisional units which can be distinguished are representatives of particular types. Some, and perhaps a substantial number, may be more unique than typical. Perhaps future research will provide us not only with useful typologies of objectives, but will also discover important differences between continuing units and those existing only briefly.

We have tried to indicate here that there are essentially three ways of looking at decisional units. (1) *An actual system existing with respect to a particular concrete objective.* We might call this the historical point of view since it involves the reconstruction by the researcher of a particular past event. (2) *A typical unit existing with respect to a typical objective.* Here the kinds of typologies discussed above come into play, and types of units would be matched with types of objectives. Typification such as that indicated should ultimately permit predictions of the "If . . . then . . ." kind. (3) *Any unit in general.* This is the manner in which we shall discuss the characteristics of decisional units under various headings below. Furthermore, this very general level is also the one of greatest usefulness to the teacher of foreign policy, since, in the absence of complete and specific data, it allows him to characterize the foreign policy decision-making process in various states in general terms. Sufficient information for such general characterizations exists for almost every state.

The Institutional Setting

We have thus far not discussed at all those institutions of government which are the traditional subject matter of the student of foreign policy. We have not done this for two reasons. First, as noted immediately above, the approach to foreign policy analysis we are presenting in tentative form cuts across the departments and agencies of government that constitute the traditional units of study. Second, the regulation of foreign policy has come to involve so many of the activities in the total national governmental structure that it is difficult indeed to locate precisely the foreign policy function within this structure.

How, then, are the various governmental institutions to be treated? It seems most profitable to consider this institutional setting as a great pool of personnel and information for the decisional units. Within this pool, some important kinds of activities and services, notably the collection and analysis of information, are of course carried on continuously. Also, some of the agencies are primarily concerned with the execution of policy and with the carrying out of routine duties.

We do not mean to imply by any means that it is not highly important that systematic studies be made of institutions like the Department of State or the Department of Defense. Indeed, it is vitally important that more and more thorough analyses of these agencies be available, since the behavior of the decision-maker in the decisional unit is largely conditioned by the directives, rules, precedents, and ideologies of these governmental institutions or their subdivisions.

The Origins of Units

We have said that the unit is an analytical tool—a guide to the way the observer reconstitutes the decision-making universe and how its boundaries are to be established. The empirical questions underlying the concept of unit are: *who becomes involved in a decision, how,* and *why?* How does the group of officials (actors or decision-makers) whose deliberations result in decision become assembled? Often the answer to this question is essential to an explanation of why the decision-makers decided the way they did.

This is a major point in the analysis of decision-making, but we shall have to postpone detailed treatment.[15] For the moment we may note two methods of unit construction: *automatic assignment* and *negotiation.* That is, the personnel and activities which we analytically call the unit are specified and established within the total decision-making structure by these two methods. Often the selection of decision-makers from the total number who might become involved is based on a simple classification of problems or decisions. The formal roles of the actors provide the clue as to whether they will be part of the unit. Also there are standing units, that is, committees or groups who are expected to act on given matters. A quite different method of selection is *negotiation* in cases where no routine procedures exist or where new conditions require a special procedure. Some of the great struggles within the total foreign policy-making structure are over *who will decide.* Negotiation may be simply a matter of "springing loose" the right officials for a particular task, or it may represent basic disagreement over the location of authority and power.

The Decision-Makers

One of the most important methodological assumptions we have made is that *only* those who are government officials are to be viewed as decision-makers or actors. In other words, no private citizen—no matter how powerful—can be a member of the analytical unit *unless* he temporarily holds a federal office. It will be argued by some that this is a step backward, a denial of the progress made by a distinguished group of scholars in freeing the study of politics from its narrow, formal institutional focus. There is no doubt that we have clear differences with some of our colleagues on this point. Suffice to say here, we do *not* differ with others on the significance of social factors in the internal setting, particularly opinion leaders and organized group leaders. The issue is whether it is methodologically feasible or advantageous to put nongovernmental personnel in the same action system with governmental personnel. It appears to us more difficult to isolate the decision-making process (or system or unit) and to relate officials and nonofficials when there is no way of assigning recognized roles to *all* actors. Actually there is no state action until *some* officials act, and, no matter how powerful, there is no way of imputing official status to private citizens. Usually the argument is that regardless of the *official locus* of decision-making authority it is where the decision is *really made* which counts. But fundamentally this is a matter of the cruciality of certain determinants not of the location of authority. Furthermore, if interest groups *really make* decisions, the behavior of officials who must translate these into official action must still be accounted for. Except for cases where a private group "owns" a decision-maker, the latter's conduct must also be explained in terms of the other (that is, organizational) factors at work. *Access*[16] bring us right to the decision-maker's door, yet doesn't tell us why he succumbs. Our scheme does not, to repeat, ignore so-called "informal"[17] factors; it does imply a different way of handling them analytically.

Limitations on Decision-Making

The concept of *limitations* constitutes a set of assumptions about *any* decisional system. The assumptions concern the factors or conditions which limit: (a) alternative objectives; (b) alternative techniques; (c) the combination of (a) and (b) into strategies or projects; (d) decision-making resources such as time, energy, skills, information; and (e) degree of control of external setting. In accordance with our general phenomenological approach, we feel that the range and impact of limitations should be considered from the decision-maker's point of view, although many such assessments will be objectively verifiable. The main categories of limitations in terms of their sources are those arising from *outside* the decisional system; those arising from the nature and functioning of the decisional system; and those arising from a combination of both these. It is only necessary here to suggest briefly the possible kinds of limitations under each heading.

external to the system

Although it might seem as though limitations in the setting, that is, internal and external, are "objective" to the decision-makers, it cannot be overemphasized that the estimates of such limitations by the observer and by actors may not be identical. In other words, it cannot—or, rather, should not—be assumed that the observer and the actor will agree.[18] Presumably—by some criteria of rational behavior—it is irrational for a state to select objectives for which it has inadequate means of achievement or to select techniques which are less conducive to the achievement of feasible objectives than others. By implication, these judgments are made from a vantage point *not shared necessarily* by the actor. The actor may have less knowledge than the observer, *or* the actor may also know what the observer knows but be—*in his view*—unable to behave differently.

Once again, what our scheme requires is a classification of *potential* limitations—factors which may restrict the way the decision-makers deliberate and the results of their deliberations. The important point here is that these factors are mediated—or gain their significance—from the perceptions and judgments of the decision-makers. It is also important to remember that for the most part the decision-makers do not confront external limitations directly on a personal, face-to-face basis, so to speak. Rather, their perceptions and judgments result from their participation in a decision-making system.

Judgments of external conditions, objects, events, and other actors as limitations on the action of any particular state may be of two types. First, there are those in which there is relatively little room for doubt or error and in which fewer qualitative appraisals are required. The phenomena being perceived are susceptible to identification and measurement by agreed standards. Such would be quantitative, concrete data. Second—and probably constituting the opposite end of a continuum—are those phenomena which are less measurable by agreed standards and which require qualitative appraisal. In these cases, there is more room for individual judgments which cannot be either proved or disproved merely by an appeal to logical or other criteria. One would expect, accordingly, more possible disagreement between an observer and an actor with respect to the latter category.

internal to the system

Limitations external to the system are by far the best known and most dramatic. We have tried to suggest that decision-making in a complex organizational context is a complicated process requiring the performance of a number of functions and many skills. The limitations traceable to bureaucratic pathology are of course familiar, but they are by no means the only ones. However, aside from these, there are less obvious yet extremely significant limitations having their sources within the system.

1. INFORMATION. The decision-makers may lack information or may act on inaccurate information; in either case the range of alternatives considered may be affected. It would appear to be a permanent liability of the decision-making process that pertinent information is almost never complete and information which is available, that is, present within the system, is rarely completely testable. Furthermore, information within the system may not be "available" to the decision-makers. The necessity to adopt and employ interpretative schemes and compensatory devices such as simplification of phenomena provides a related source of limitation.

2. COMMUNICATIONS FAILURES. Reasonably full information may be present in the decisional unit but not circulate to all the decision-makers who need it to perform their roles satisfactorily. A decisional unit may be resistant to *new* information, or the significance of new information may be lost because of the way messages are labeled and stored.

3. PRECEDENT. Previous actions and policy rules (the givens for any unit) may automatically narrow the deliberations of the decision-makers. Previous action may prohibit serious consideration of a whole range of projects. Reversal of policies is difficult in a vast organization.

4. PERCEPTION. The selective discrimination of the setting may effectively limit action. What the decision-makers "see" is what they act upon. Through perception—and judgment—external limitations gain their significance. Factors objectively identifiable by an observer may be ignored by decision-makers or overweighted.

5. SCARCE RESOURCES. The fact that any unit is limited in the time, energy, and skills (and sometimes money) at its disposal also tends to limit the thoroughness of deliberation and the effectiveness with which certain related functions are performed. Time pressures may seriously restrict the number of possible courses of action which can be explored.

the combination of external and internal limitations
Obviously, the two sets of potential limitations are related and may be combined. While the external limitations have an independent existence, their significance depends on the judgments of the decision-makers, who may be operating under internal limitations as well. One of the crucial questions in the analysis of foreign policy decision-making is whether particular external limitations are assumed or calculated. Another question concerns the degree to which the decision-makers regard certain limitations as subject to their control. Since internal limitations may either reinforce external ones or minimize them, the extent to which internal limitations are known and allowed for in decision-making may be crucial.

How Foreign Policy Decisions Differ from Those Made in Other Complex Organizations—Some Hypotheses

We have insisted that foreign policy-making is most fruitfully analyzed as decision-making in an organizational context. The properties of formal organization outlined would hold for any social organization which met the specifications, whether governmental or nongovernmental, and the properties of decision-making outlined would hold for *any* decisional system. In sum, we would argue that a business organization, a social organization in the narrower sense, a pressure group, and governmental agencies can and should be analyzed by means of essentially the same scheme. To the extent that this conviction is eventually confirmed, comparative analysis of different kinds of decisional systems may be possible, and additional insights into foreign policy-making should result.

Without assuming that foreign policy decisions are unique, it is suggested that the following may be distinguishing characteristics of such decisions:

1. Wider range of *possible objectives and projects* subject to a wider range of *possible interpretations.*
2. Greater *heterogeneity of "clientele"* and thus more potentially hostile or dissatisfied *reactions* and *demands.*
3. A greater *number of perspectives* have to be *integrated* before consensus is achieved.
4. The *"setting"* and *"situation"* of decisions are more complex, less certain, less stable; the consequences of action are therefore *harder to predict and control.*
5. *Sources of information* are broader and less reliable, and the necessity of "classification" constitutes a special problem.
6. Relative lack of *"experimental opportunity"* and infrequency of replicable situations.
7. Difficulty of measuring *organizational effectiveness* and *policy results.*
8. Necessity of discussing alternatives in terms which *do not* meet the simplest test of *verifiability.*
9. *Time-lag* between the arising of problem-situation and the *unfolding of its full implications.*
10. Greater possibility of *fundamental value conflicts* and hence necessity *for more extensive compromise.*

These selected differences are a reminder that the political nature of foreign policy decisions may introduce factors which may make it difficult to generalize to or from nongovernmental decision-making. However, whether differences are a matter of degree or kind, we believe that, analytically, all decision-making in formal organizations can be handled the same way, that is, by the same scheme. While the above list suggests certain special features of the world of the foreign policy decision-maker, these features can be described and explained according to situational requirements and determinants of action as they affect particular decisional units and particular decisions.

6. THE MAJOR DETERMINANTS OF ACTION

The search for explanation of why states behave as they do leads ultimately, according to our argument, to the factors which determine the choices made by the decision-makers. We have said further that decision-makers must be identified in terms of decisional units. The rules, activities, and relationships among the decision-makers constitute the organizational or decision-making system. The point of view from which we take our departure is that of any decisional system.[1]

We now proceed to a more detailed analysis of the determinants of decision-making behavior. The important assumption we are making is that the three major determinants of action in the system are spheres of competence, communications and information, and motivation. It may develop that these are by no means the most significant variables, but until empirical evidence sustains or refutes our assumption, we shall consider that all factors which influence the results of deliberation in foreign policy-making can be accounted for by these variables.

We are not unmindful that this section deals with decision-making from two different perspectives: the properties of the *actor* (decision-maker) and the properties of the *system* (structure and process). Before a theory of decision-making will be possible, of course, logical and empirical relationships among these determinants must he established. At this point only tentative suggestions along this line can be made.

Spheres of Competence

We propose that it is most convenient to treat the organizational unit or decisional system which is the focus of attention as a set of competences and relationships among competences. Frequently, in referring to the structural components of organizational systems, the terms "office" or "role" are used. By using the less well-known term *competence* we are trying to serve two purposes. First, we are trying to avoid the ambiguities characteristic of some of the other terms. Secondly, we are trying to convey a notion of a more comprehensive kind. We are, in effect, trying to convey the idea not only of an *explicitly prescribed* set of activities but also of *conventionalized* activities necessary to the achievement of the organizational objective. To put this into other words, we believe that the structural components of the system of action must include as a minimum some norms and rules of behavior in addition to those set out in the organization's charter or manual.

Definition of Competence

A competence is defined as *the totality of those of the activities of the decision-maker relevant and necessary to the achievement of the organizational objective.* Relating to these activities there is, from the point of view of the actor, what might be called a set of rules. These rules serve, in effect, as guides to action for the actor. A part of these rules is explicitly prescribed, that is, set forth in writing in a job specification or its equivalent. A second part of these rules is accepted by convention and acted upon largely as if the conventionally accepted rules had the same status as the explicitly prescribed ones.

Both the explicitly prescribed and the conventionally accepted rules have two components. One of these is *description of the job itself,* detailing what the actor does or is to do. The other deals with the *relationships of the actor to the other actors in the system.* The dominant relationship indicated by the rules is probably the superior-subordinate relationship. In addition we are assuming that the actor has *expectations* based on his knowledge of the rules about the behavior of other actors.

The rules guiding the activities that constitute the actor's competence are subject to interpretation by the actor. That is to say, the actor's competence is flexible, and its dimensions are empirically problematical. We shall explain this point more fully below, but an example may be helpful here. We shall consider several recent interpretations of the competence of the Secretary of State. The available evidence would appear to indicate that Presidents Eisenhower and Truman left the formulation of foreign policy largely in the hands of their respective Secretaries of State, Messrs. Dulles and Acheson, granting them thereby considerable areas of discretion. On the other hand, it is alleged that the late President Roosevelt took a much more active personal part in the conduct of foreign relations. It would seem then that the competence of the Secretary of State would differ widely on this basis alone in the Roosevelt administrations as compared to those of his successors.

A number of points need to be noted about all the activities constituting the competence. First, if we assume that the decision-maker is not a willful deviant, the pattern of activities is predictable with a high degree of probability to the extent to which it is specified and prescribed in the explicit rules of the organization. From the researcher's point of view, then, a considerable amount of information is generally available on the division of work, structure of authority, flow of information, as well as on the ideology and policies which provide the framework within which the decision-maker operates.

A second consideration in connection with the use of the competence concept rests on the assumption that no organization defined as a system of action, as it has been here, can be planned completely a priori. We assume, that is, that the planner invariably finds himself in a situation of uncertainty and incomplete information. Consequently, the planned or explicitly prescribed structure of the organization is supplemented over a period of time by patterns of action established and sanctioned by precedent, habitual ways of doing things, that constitute the second component of the decision-makers' competence, the one to be called *conventional.*

Together, the patterns of action referred to above as the *prescribed* ones and those referred to as being *conventional* make up what we shall refer to as the *formal characteristics of organization.* It should be emphasized that these are at this stage of development of the conceptual scheme the only ones of interest to us.

Those who are acquainted with studies in the field of organization and administration know that in the last twenty or twenty-five years, attention has increasingly been devoted to the so-called "informal" organizations existing within the larger "formal" structure. Some of the phenomena which have been labeled "informal" bear a considerable resemblance to what we call the conventional component of the competence,[2] but most of them do not. It does not seem appropriate to enter into an extended discussion and criticism of writings on "informal" organization here. Suffice it to say that many of them have been unsystematic and confusing. We do want to make it very clear that when we refer to conventional activities we have in mind activities *strictly necessary* to the achievement of the objective of the system but not specified explicitly in the charter, the job specifications, the relevant legislation, the executive order, or the organizational manual. The precise nature of the conventional activities remains problematical for the observer and will probably tend to differ from system to system. It is to be hoped that ultimately more reliable knowledge will allow the characteristics of the conventional activities to be related to the characteristics of various types of systems.

With regard to the discussion of the conventional component of the competence, it should also be noted that the time element involved also relates to a process of legitimation. Legitimacy does not in this instance need to include the moral dimension Max Weber refers to.[3] It means simply acquiescence in certain patterns of consideration and action as appropriate to a given situation.

There are a number of assumptions underlying this view of organization, and also some consequences stemming from it, which might profitably be considered. First, we have tried to indicate above that the planned and prescribed structure has the status of a kind of assumed prerequisite, a skeleton which is objective in the sense of being known to both actor and observer. To this are added the patterns we have called conventional. *These together may be viewed as a set of rules which constitute guides to the conduct of the actor.* These rules have a greater or lesser mandatoriness depending in part on whether they are explicitly stated or whether they are conventional and also whether they are subject to interpretation by the actors. It is clear that this formulation leads to at least the rudiments of a theory of bureaucratization, since under the conventional category we must consider not only the kinds of activities comprising it, but also the way in which the actor interprets the rules relating to these activities.

The Problem of Bureaucratization

Bureaucracy, or, to be more accurate, bureaucratization, for we are dealing with process and not structure, is an oft-discussed but rarely clarified subject. There is an abundance of descriptive material relating to structure but little precise analysis of the process. Since governmental institutions are generally recognized as being especially vulnerable to bureaucratization, a few words on the subject seem appropriate here. Foreign policy-making would appear to be no less vulnerable than other kinds of policy-making.

Max Weber, in his great treatise, *Wirtschaft und Gesellschaft,* distinguishes three bases of legitimate authority, the rational-legal, the traditional, and the charismatic. He also speaks of transformations of these types of authority, notably of the traditionalization of rational-legal authority.[4] Two aspects of Weber's discussion are relevant and noteworthy for our purposes. In distinguishing among various types of authority and in discussing the transformations of these, Weber calls attention to the different ways in which the actor orients social structures. Secondly, it is not without import that the transformations Weber discusses involve the traditionalization of the other two types of authority.

Weber defines traditionally oriented action as being determined by accepted usage which in the extreme case is "very often a matter of almost automatic reaction to habitual stimuli which guide behavior in a course which has been repeatedly followed."[5] If, then, as we have indicated above, the organizational structure may be treated as a set of rules for the actor, a number of questions arise immediately. Perhaps the most important of these is how does the actor interpret the rules?

The familiar idealization of organization holds that it is the institutionalization par excellence of rationality.[6] It may then be asked whether the actor acts rationally in a social system planned, in theory at least, so as to make the rules of behavior as explicit as possible, to maximize the possibility of obtaining information, and so forth. The findings of numerous writers seem to indicate that he does not. The key point is that it seems necessary to postulate that to a very high degree the orientations of the actor are independent of and vary irrespective of the characteristics of the social system of which he is a member at any given time.

Bureaucratization, we would suggest, is a process whereby more of the rules, precedents, and methods of operation are oriented traditionally, that is, are no longer easily subject to challenge, questioning, or amendment. The reason for the increasing traditionalization of orientations is apparently to be found in large part in the psychological make-up of the actor. It is to be found in the characteristics of the social structure only to the extent to which it reinforces and intensifies the psychological mechanisms involved.

It is by no means our intention to assert that bureaucratization is invariably bad or to depart from a neutral attitude toward this phenomenon. It does need to be pointed out, though, that very little is known about this process and research seems urgently needed. The major problem would be the investigation of the "how" and "why" of the traditionalization of the decision-maker's orientations. The focal point of such research might well be the structure of the "world of the decision-maker." Schuetz[7] suggests a seemingly very useful distinction between "open" and "problematic" possibilities in selecting among alternative courses of action. Open possibilities are those that are not questioned, that is, not considered by the actor, whether he acts in terms of them or simply excludes them from his calculations. Problematic possibilities are those which are called into question and considered. The crucial question for the researcher would then be: what kinds of possibilities are "open" ones for the decision-maker? what kinds are problematic? The time element would, of course, have to be taken into account in doing the research, and the researcher would have to inform himself on the period in the life of the organization with which he is dealing as well as on the history of the organization, at least with regard to crucial decisions taken on matters of organization, objectives, and so on.

It should be apparent that these matters are by no means of exclusive concern or interest to the student of foreign policy decision-making. These questions are relevant to any study of large-scale organization, be it of business, government, voluntary, or whatever. The information is necessary for any study of organizations, no matter what their purpose. While some studies of the consequences of so-called "crucial" decisions are available, material on routine activities and bureaucratization is meager indeed.

A final consideration with regard to bureaucratization is arising in connection with the consequences of this process. We have indicated above that the term is not to have the epithetical connotation usually given it. As Selznick has suggested,[8] the fact that the term bureaucracy is generally so used should alert us to the fact that there is an important phenomenon here worthy of further investigation. Above all it must be remembered that the functionality or dysfunctionality[9] of bureaucratization depends in good measure on the point of view from which it is approached. For example, the unquestioned acceptance of the organization's rules may be very desirable from the point of view of maintenance of the organization's stability or its defense against external attack. On the other hand, bureaucratization may be totally dysfunctional if it impairs the organization's ability to adapt to new or changing circumstances.

The Actor's Interpretation of His Competence

Thus far, we have discussed two major points in connection with the *decision-maker's competence*. First, in defining the competence concept we indicated that it was useful to broaden the usual definition of *formal organizational* characteristics to include the body of conventions, that is, habitual practices, precedents, unelucidated presuppositions, and so forth. Secondly, it was proposed tentatively that a distinction might profitably be made in the analysis of the way in which the actor interprets the body of rules and norms of behavior that, from the point of view of the actor, constitute his competence and the social structure within which he operates.

In addition, one further consideration derived from the competence concept needs to be discussed, and that is the impact of the actor upon his competence. The basic assumption here is that no matter how simplified a model of the actor or decision-maker we wish to use, it must include at least some elements of his values, his prior experience, and his learned behavior, in short, of his biography in this technical sense.[10] At any given instant in time, or over any period of time, then, *we are dealing with the interaction of the actor and his competence.* In addition to the fact that his behavior is affected by the rules, the actor also interprets the rules. He must, in other words, be treated as more than a passive agent in some preordained spectacle. We do not mean, thereby, to get involved in the sterile debate between the advocates of free will and those of determinism. Any effort in the direction of scientific analysis assumes *ex hypothese* that the universe being treated is an ordered one, that there are no random elements in any absolute sense. The assumption of order does not, however, carry with it any implication of omniscience on the part of the observer, nor does it require that the model of the actor omit the possibility of his making choices. Any attempt to treat decision-making without an actor so constructed as to be capable of selecting among alternatives would indeed be wasted effort.

Since the actor's choices may be concerned with the structure of the organization or at least may have consequences for the structure, the capacity to interpret the rules would seem to be required. This capacity would imply that the competence itself must be treated as something flexible, its limits always empirically problematical. The distinction between prescribed and conventional elements would, of course, remain as before. Considerably more extensive discussion will be devoted to the interaction of the actor and the competence under one of our other major categories, motivation.

A few words, though, might be devoted here to some of the implications of the preceding statements. There are apparently no data available on the problem of the reciprocal interaction of actor and social structure. Contemporary organizational theory has rarely analyzed the problem in quite this manner. To permit reasonably adequate prediction along these lines, a taxonomy of personality types would be of great value. We may, however, make some general suggestions without such a taxonomy.

A scale may be postulated ranging from what might be called "strict construction" to very broad interpretation of the rules. The limiting cases seem to be fairly clear. At the extreme of greatest latitude of interpretation, the organizational system would cease to exist or change into another unit because the authority relationships and the patterns of communication would be so altered that another type of unit would come into existence. At the other extreme, obedience of the "letter of the law" would also cause destruction of the system through a kind of "subversion by slow-down." Investigation of the empirical limits is badly needed.

To illustrate this point one might examine the relief of General MacArthur in 1951 from his several positions as American and Allied Supreme Commander in the Far East. If one takes as the organizational system one involving President Truman as Commander-in-Chief and members of the appropriate executive agencies at home and, also, General MacArthur with his aides and subordinates in the Far East, it is apparent that the General's competence involved great and, to a high degree, unspecified areas of latitude. When the General's decisions began to threaten the organization as constituted, the maintenance of that particular system seemed to require, in President Truman's view, the action he took. It should be quite clear that this analysis does not rest on any view of which side was "right" or "wrong" in this instance. From the point of view of organizational analysis, General MacArthur's interpretation of his competence was apparently threatening the organizational system as constituted, and the man at the head of this system felt that it could only be maintained if the General was relieved of his posts. Some of the General's supporters might accept the organizational analysis but insist that a change in the organizational system as constituted would have been better for the country.

The MacArthur episode points to another important factor, namely, the consequences of unknown or incompletely known limits of rules' interpretation for the creation of tensions in the organization. Here again little information on this point is at present available.

In addition to personality type, position in the organizational hierarchy and, also, expertise would seem to be especially closely related to the actor's interpretation of his competence. Since this paper is not intended to be an extended treatise on organization theory, it is hoped that the all too brief allusion to factors needing to be taken into account will suffice. The competence concept is crucial since the competences are the building blocks of the decision-making systems central to our analysis of foreign policy-making. We now turn to a consideration of the ways in which the competences are differentiated from each other.

Differentiation of Competences

The previous section dealt with the definition and to some extent the elaboration of the characteristics of what we have called the actor's or decision-maker's competence. In this section we shall discuss briefly some of the bases for differentiation among these competences. Three bases for such differentiation will be suggested: (1) *authority;* (2) *the degree of generality or specialization;* and (3) *the nature of participation.*

These categories are by no means intended to exhaust all the possible bases for differentiation among the competences. However, they do seem at this point to be a promising point of departure. It cannot be repeated often enough that this is only an initial and tentative formulation of a conceptual scheme and that its adequacy or lack of adequacy remains to be proven by empirical testing.

differentiation on the basis of authority

In discussing differentiation on the basis of authority, it should be clear that authority is used here to denote the relationship between superior and subordinate. Authority may be defined for the purpose at hand as the ability to issue orders, instructions, and commands with the probability that they will be obeyed. Involved, moreover, is the possibility of the availability and the use of sanctions by the bearer of authority.

A number of points need to be made in connection with the discussion of authority. We have already said that authority is a concept referring to a relationship of two or more individuals. It should however be noted that not all organizational relationships need to involve the exercise of authority. Some committees would provide examples of relationships not involving the exercise of authority among members.

Talcott Parsons, who has done more than any other scholar to bring the work of Max Weber to the attention of American social scientists, says that one of Weber's outstanding contributions consisted of the prominent place assigned elements of coercion and compulsion in social relationships. The role given authority in Weber's classic analysis of bureaucracy is central. But those who have used implicitly or explicitly a model of organization similar to Weber's have frequently not taken into consideration the special place the ideal type occupies in Weber's methodology. The ideal type is in effect a device to throw into bold relief certain features of a social structure, features which characterize it and distinguish it from others. It is not a description of an actual concrete structure.

The orthodox view of organization, current among many American social scientists as well as among business executives and government officials, is quite similar in many features to Weber's ideal type. It depicts a steady "downward" flow of orders and instructions and an equally steady "upward" flow of many kinds of information. The picture is obviously much oversimplified, resting as it does on the assumption that the organization is, if we may be allowed to borrow a term from the nefarious vocabulary, monolithic.

In accord with the monolithic view of organization, one frequently sees references to the structure of authority which imply a single set of relationships which is presumed to exist at all times and in all cases. While analysis on the basis of a single structure of authority is probably inadequate and misleading in all cases, it is especially so, given our definition of organization as a system of action discriminated from other systems on the basis of its objective. There is not one structure of authority. On the contrary, there is the probability that in most decisional systems of any complexity there will be several structures of authority.

This point, will, we hope, be considerably clarified in the discussion of differentiation among the competences on the basis of generality and specialization and the nature of participation. It is most important to be sensitive to the possibility of several structures of authority when dealing with such complex decisional systems as interdepartmental committees and, for example, a system involving the President and the Senate.

The relationship of authority involves also, as we have previously mentioned, the probability of obedience and the possible invocation of sanctions. However, we shall here climb out onto a limb by saying that this coercive aspect is not a prominent one in the ordinary day-to-day operation of the organization. Unless the organization is one in which coercion is a prominent feature of operation such as a military organization or a penal institution, we may at least propose that other determinants of action are of greater importance.

There are, nevertheless, instances in which the authority relationship becomes decisive. Most prominently this is true in the following classes of cases: first, where there is a challenge to the source of authority; secondly, where there is a challenge to the bearer of authority; thirdly, where there is equality of authority; and, fourthly, where there are differences in the interpretations of the rules, objective, or similar matters. The challenge or calling into question may be deliberate, or it may be due to ignorance. We shall not at this time draw a fine distinction between these two ways, even though the manner of dealing with them may differ considerably.

By using the term source of authority we do not mean to raise the sordid business of sovereignty. The conceptual scheme used here is one designed for the analysis of operating organizational units. Consequently the question of the "source" of authority does not come up in the ordinary course of organizational operation. It arises only in case of serious challenge to the existing order. To use terminology that we have previously employed, possibilities which had been "open" ones become suddenly "problematic." Generally it would appear that questioning of the "source" of authority would take the form of a challenge to the order as a whole.

The questioning of the bearer of authority would constitute a fairly common occurrence and does not seem to need any further elucidation. The case of equal authority is also a well-known one, but one that raises some very grave questions with regard to the strategies of resolution. One way would be appeal to an outside clientele as in the case of conflict between the President and Congress. Another possible way of seeking resolution brings into prominent focus the problem of institutional leadership. Space will not permit more than a few words on the subject here. There nevertheless do seem to be elements of the role of institutional leader apart from those intangible arts of manipulating individuals of which some writers on administration are so fond, or apart from the attributes of personality of which the psychologists speak. Among these would appear to be, as a minimum, a requirement of neutrality and a concern with general matters rather than specific detail.

The final case of challenge to the interpretation of the organization's objective or rules is well exemplified in one of the few existing studies of large-scale organizations, Philip Selznick's analysis of the TVA.[11] Selznick shows that some serious conflicts as to the TVA's mission had to be settled during the early years of its existence. The phenomenon usually referred to as a "struggle for power" would from the point of view of the organization, though not necessarily from the point of view of the participant's motivation, generally come under this heading.

THE PROBLEM OF RESPONSIBILITY. In concluding the discussion of the authority relationship, a few words might well be said about the problem of responsibility. This term frequently appears in discussions of authority. Levy defines responsibility as "The accountability of an individual(s) to another individual(s) or group(s) for his own acts and/or the acts of others,"[12] a definition we shall use for present purposes. This way of defining responsibility focuses attention on the relational character of the phenomenon, a relationship that is perhaps the obverse of the authority relationship. It is probable that from the standpoint of motivation the two relationships are quite different, for the question of ethical and moral norms of behavior arises in acute form.

Again we are not able to do more here than allude to some of the considerations arising in connection with the analysis of responsibility. One of the more important is that once we sort out from the large majority of cases in which accountability is reasonably clear a class of those actors or decision-makers whom we may call the bearers of greatest authority, the question becomes difficult indeed.

A few examples will serve to illustrate the point. If we consider first the presidency of the United States, it is notable that despite the explicit restrictions provided in the Constitution the latitude of office is enormous. Even greater is the latitude of the dictator, especially if, as in Hitler's case, there are prominent charismatic elements. Surely we cannot assume, at least initially, that fear of the invocation of sanctions is a dominant consideration. The relevant questions would rather seem to be: what kinds of values or ideologies the actor brings to the interpretation of the latitude given him? how are the rules making up the competence oriented in terms of these values or ideologies? what are the means chosen by the actor in his appeal to values or ideologies?

It has been proposed that a balance of authority and of responsibility is necessary over the long run for the stability of social systems. While we may accept this as a possibly fruitful hypothesis, much clarification is needed of the nature and limits of the responsibility that must balance the exercise of authority.

degree of generality or specialization

By degree of generality or specialization we mean what is generally referred to as function. Due, however, to recent efforts to give the term function a more precise meaning in the vocabulary of the social sciences, we prefer to use the more cumbersome terminology.[13]

The general question, then, is how are the competences differentiated from each other on the basis of the specifications for the job. The first point to be made here is that there are elements of the organization which can profitably be treated as "givens." This allows specification of membership in the system of action (unit), and also indicates in a general way the kinds of knowledge and skills required for the achievement of the objective. Thus, the objective provides at least a basis for internal differentiation in terms of the tasks that have to be performed.

In the previous section we have indicated that generality and specialization are closely associated with differentiation on the basis of authority. We shall proceed on the assumption that the more inclusive the generality of the actor's authority, the more general his competence and the greater the latitude of his interpretation of his competence. A distinction must of course be drawn between the generality of the actor's competence with respect to authority and job specification *and* the previous training and learning he brings to the competence. An extremely important empirical question in this connection is the primary values and norms[14] to which the actor is committed.

Thus far we have discussed the division of work requisite for carrying out the objective of the organization. There is also a class of occupations, however, primarily concerned with the *maintenance* of the organization. The housekeeping, policing, and intelligence jobs which would fall into this class are fairly obvious and do not need further elaboration here.

Generally there is available in most ongoing organizations a list of job specifications which make up one element of the actor's competence. But here again the distinction between the prescribed and conventional components is a useful tool. The explicitly stated job description is, for the actor, a way of saying what he is to do, what the special requirements of the job are, and so on, and, for the observer, a kind of initial way of obtaining information. But rarely if ever is the official job specification an exhaustive description of the tasks he carries out. Elements are added by the accrual of new tasks, the way the actor interprets his competence, and so on. The periodic re-evaluation of jobs familiar to all students of administration is the indication of an effort to bring the explicit specification into a more adequate balance with the actuality.

We have already alluded to the distinction that must be borne in mind between the characteristics of the competence and the actor's training. This is especially important where individual's advance from specialized jobs to more general "administrative" positions and may carry with them the commitment to a professional ethic which is quite inadequate to their new competence. These matters will be accorded fuller treatment under the general headings of motivation and communication and information.

Thus far nothing has been said about the traditional distinction which is usually found between staff and line in most of the literature on administration. In some recent writings a considerable amount of dissatisfaction has been expressed with these terms because of vagueness of usage and the difficulty of distinguishing, particularly in organizations composed wholly or in large part of experts, between "staff" and "line" activities. Without going into the matter in any detail, the objections seem to be well taken. It appears at the present time more satisfactory not to prejudge activities in this manner, leaving the characteristics of individual competences problematical. Some of the subject matter generally treated under the staff-line heading will be given consideration in the next section.

nature of participation

The third method of differentiating among the competences is on the basis of the nature of the actor's participation. Provisionally three categories of participation are suggested: (1) *membership;* (2) *representational;* and (3) *advisory.*

Participation on the basis of membership implies obviously and straightforwardly what it says, that is, that the actor or decision-maker as occupant of his competence is a member of the organization or decision-unit. It is participation classifiable under the other two categories which brings up some more complex considerations.

We must emphasize once again that some and perhaps many of the identifiable decisional systems are exceedingly complex. The complexity may take a variety of forms and the deficiencies, already discussed, of using the simple pyramidal model of organization with but a single structure of authority become more apparent. Consequently the second category, participation on the basis of representation, is introduced here to convey the idea that in some systems of action claims are held to participation. In other words, some decision-making systems are so constituted that some individuals or groups or institutions can claim participation as a matter of right, whether this is given explicit statement somewhere or exists on the basis of general consent.

The conception underlying this category of participation is quite similar to but more general than the theories of functional representation which had their greatest vogue during the first two and a half decades of this country. Our category is also devoid of the normative overtones usually associated with these writings.

To illustrate the matter, we may consider the United States Interdepartmental Committee on Trade Agreements previously mentioned, in which all agencies having some right to be heard on matters of foreign trade treaties were given representation. It is to be noted that to the initial participants from the Departments of State, Treasury, Commerce, and Agriculture and the United States Tariff Commission were added participants from the Departments of Defense and Labor and the Economic Cooperation Administration at a later date. Numerous factors are immediately apparent in this connection. First, representation is not primarily based on the fact that these participants are experts on foreign trade but rather on the fact that they are spokesmen for other governmental agencies and, even more broadly, as in the case of the representatives for Commerce and Labor, for major non-governmental interest groups. Secondly, these cases of interdepartmental committees are most frequently in the category of equality of authority in which the role of the institutional leader is heavily emphasized. Thirdly, there seems to be some indication that claims to representation are heavily influenced by changes in the situation or organizational environment. It is, however, also highly likely that once a claim to representation is established, a changed situation will probably not result in abandonment of this claim. This is relevant to our earlier discussion of bureaucracy.

The final basis for participation is the advisory one, or to use the more frequently employed phrase, the role of the expert. The expert or advisory role involves neither a claim to participation nor any involvement in the legitimate relationships of authority and responsibility within any particular decisional unit.[15] It may take the form of the need for expert help by the decision-maker, or it may alternatively take the form of a desire by the decision-maker to inform himself of the views of some individual or group which might possibly be affected by the decision. Hence, formulation of this role as only involving expert recommendations seems too narrow a view for our purposes.

One most interesting aspect of advisory participation should be noted here. The decision-maker who consults the expert may inadvertently be opening a Pandora's Box. The newly established channel of communication may be so heavily used that over a period of time a claim to representational participation may develop. The line between representational and advisory participation is frequently not clear. In actual cases the two often tend to blend most especially as advisory participation becomes representational.

Communication and Information

Thus far we have discussed some of the structural features of decisional systems in terms of the characteristics of the competences, and in terms of the various bases for differentiating among such competences. In turning to our second major determinant we are confronted with a number of choices.

Attention to problems of communication has increased greatly in the past several years. Scholars in a wide variety of fields have brought their specialized techniques and skills to bear on these problems. It seems, indeed, at present that communications theory may develop, together with the theory of choice and organization theory, into one of the most useful and powerful tools available to the social sciences.

It does appear however to be somewhat premature to speak of a communications theory as if it were an integrated and generally agreed upon system of concepts and propositions. We would probably be closer to the fact if we spoke of communications theories, though the amount of agreement among a large number of the proposed formulations is considerable.

Here we shall discuss two of the senses in which the concept of communications is used. The first of these is communications as a basic requisite for any social system. The second is information theory as a tool for analysis.

Communications and Systems of Action

It does not seem necessary to discuss in great detail communication as a requisite for any social relationship. Elaboration of these points is the specific province of a *sociology of knowledge*.[16] From some of the writers in that field we accept the following propositions about the nature of the external world: that the world is constituted *intersubjectively;*[17] that as a consequence *objects, social relationships,* and so on, are perceived in terms of a *system of meanings, values,* and *preferences;* and that, furthermore, these *meanings, values, and preferences* are *learned and communicated.*

It is, of course, possible to discuss in great detail the assumptions undergirding this aspect of communications and to analyze some of the propositions deriving from it, but this is not necessary here. The salient point to bear clearly in mind is that the actor model which we have used throughout is assumed to have, with its contemporaries (that is, other actors), a large number of shared similar experiences so that they can communicate meaningfully about the world they perceive. To put this somewhat differently, they speak the same language, literally and figuratively. The meanings given the objects perceived are similar. It is possible for them to communicate about their everyday experiences.

It is necessary for us to differentiate further the members of various social systems, and this may be done in terms of more and more shared experiences ranging from the general to the particular. In this sense communications is as one recent writer remarks: "Modern organizations are in large part built upon and held together by communications."[18] However, even more than that is involved. The notion of multiple roles[19] is now widely used. Associated with each role are particular demands, perceptions, and expectations.

The point that emerges quite clearly is that the observer is confronted by a tremendous number of choices with regard to his focus of attention. Useful and profitable studies may range from descriptions of the activities of a single actor to highly formalized models of decision-making. In order, however, to be of maximum utility, the observer's methodological choices must be made as explicit as possible. Surely this observation would be banal were it not for the large number of existing studies in which assumptions and categories are implicit or unclear, hindering the kind of pyramiding of knowledge vital to the development of a science.

Communications and Authority

We have thus far noted the role of communications as requisite to any social relationship and any system of social action. In the narrower context of organizational analysis a number of consequences of communicative activity need to be considered. One of these is the relationship of communications and authority.

A social system, as we have tried to indicate, depends for existence on shared, similarly perceived experiences, making for the possibility of the existence of *understanding* among the members. To this we must now add the assumption that the social system is maintained, reinforced, or may possibly be undermined and destroyed by the continuity, discontinuity, and the intrinsic properties of the communicative activity. In the organizational unit one of the consequences of this communicative activity is the maintenance of the existing system of super- and subordination whether the system is the officially prescribed or the conventional one. Alternatively, the existing system may be altered by these communicative activities.

Here again, as in the discussion of the actor's interpretation of the rules, which bears directly on this point, it is necessary to think of ranges of behavior maintaining, supplementing, altering, or destroying the system. The specific character of the actor's communicative activities, that is, the information communicated, the meaning attached to it, the channels chosen or, just as tellingly, not chosen, will depend in great part on his interpretation of the rules of his competence, which in turn is postulated as being a function of the actor's structural position, of his biography, and of his use of the information available to him.

We have already indicated in the previous section that the organizational order is assumed to be a legitimate one, that is, that it involves as a minimum acceptance of the existing superior-subordinate relationships in the organization. It seems to follow that the very concept of legitimacy rests upon similarly perceived aspects of the situation to which a similar meaning is attached, and which has as a consequence a certain conformity of action.

Some of the advantages of communications analysis other than highlighting the conveying of information should be mentioned. This view of social relationships also bears on the preceding discussion of differentiation of competences within the organizational system of action, particularly with regard to the influence of shared experiences on the activities of the actor. We would want to know, for example, with whom the experiences are shared, that is, with what group the actor identifies himself, and its consequences for his orientation. We would also want to know what significance these shared experiences have for the actor, that is, the weight assigned to the shared experiences as against other values he holds. A further important question is the period of time over which these shared experiences developed. For we are assuming that only if the element of duration is included in the conceptual scheme do specific shared experiences make for the emergence of significant shared experiences with particular other actors.

Some further questions grow out of a consideration of what is known as role conflict. For example, what are the consequences for the system of a change of the values and loyalties in terms of which the actor orients his actions? The related question regarding the consequences for the actor of ambiguities arising within his scheme of orientation is one for the psychologist to investigate.

It does not seem useful at this time to explore more fully the character and consequences of this aspect of communications. We hope that we have set forth some concepts which will be useful in the description and analysis of decisional systems. These are some of the variables we believe will have to be taken into account in a proper theory of organizational decision-making, and from which more precise and specific propositions for the guidance of analysis and research may be derived.

Organizational decision-making emerges, then, as a function of organizational structure and goal, subjectively viewed as a set of rules for the actor, information, about which more will be said in the next section, and personality type, which will be discussed under the heading of motivation.

The Concept of Information

The next few pages will be devoted to the concept of information and some of its implications. Communications involve as a minimum a communicator, a message, and a communicatee. Information may be defined rather crudely as that which is being communicated by the communicator. While bearing in mind that the structural and communications factors already discussed are directly relevant to the flow of information, it seems desirable to indicate also the usefulness of information theory as a somewhat separate tool for analysis.

From this point of view, the organization, or decisional system, may be viewed as a *communications net*. Through the channels of this communications net is carried information of varying types and varying significance. Information is stored in the net, and new information enters it. Within the net information is distributed differently. More will be said about all of these matters below.

The System of Action as a Communications Net

The concept of the communications net would seem to have great utility for analysis and research. Armed with this concept and its correlative ones it is possible to undertake what Karl Deutsch has called the *mapping* of the system.[20] This mapping provides the observer with a picture of the actual flow of information within the system. By means of such a map it is possible to locate various kinds of activities in terms of the points of stages in the sequences of all activities at which they take place.

A map or accurate description of the flow of information in the system would highlight the actual *channels of communication*. By channels we are referring to the paths of the messages. In this manner it would become possible to determine whether and where the actual channels of communication coincide with the prescribed ones, and whether and where they deviate.

Moreover, it would be important to know whether the deviations are widely accepted, that is, have the status of conventional practices or whether they are momentary and of little consequence.

It is apparent that the channels of communication are closely linked to the authority relationships discussed earlier. Just as there may be within one decisional system more than one structure of authority, so there can be more than one communications net. The various communications nets, with their linkages and overlapping, would tend to follow the structures of authority. A special case illustrating this point is discussed below.

In addition to describing the communications network, the observer should also know something about the *procedures and rules* governing communications within the system. Generally most organizational systems have very definite prescriptions as to how various types of messages shall be prepared, how these shall be routed, and so on. For example, most readers will be familiar with State Department manuals covering this point. It would be important to know not only the circumstances under which these prescriptions are followed but also the ones under which they are departed from.

The variety of *instruments of communication* must also be taken into account. Oral communications may range from very casual conversation to regular meetings and would include telephonic communication. Written communications may range from brief memoranda to long and detailed reports. With regard to these, questions such as the following would need to be answered: What was the form of communication used for a particular message? Why was that particular instrument used rather than another? Did the form of communications chosen have any significance for the structure of the organizational system? What was that significance? Thus, for example, the telephone may be chosen not only for speed and ease but also because conversation may not commit the initiator of the message as heavily as the written word.

A distinction may be made between various *kinds of information and messages* within the system. In very general terms we may say that there are three major kinds of information in the net: first, information necessary to achieve the goal of the system, that is, the kind of information required to make a decision or a series of decisions; second, information relating to the internal state of the system, that is, information generally concerned with the efficiency and maintenance of the system; and third, information regarding the state of the relationship of the system to its setting. These are not mutually exclusive categories, but the distinctions seem worthwhile from an analytic point of view.

Communications engineers have discussed the concept of *noise* in connection with information. By noise is meant the loss of information from a variety of causes while in transit through the net. The uses of this notion for social engineers to determine inefficiencies and obstacles to the free flow of information are obvious. But the concept also seems to be widely relevant in social analysis. If we make the assumption, now widely accepted in the natural sciences, that every physical system will contain some noise, it would seem possible to correlate the amount of noise from various sources with the adaptability of the system. That is, the amount and location of noise should tell the observer something about the characteristics of the system he is investigating.

Another major distinction between types of information suggested by writers on information theory is that between *primary and secondary messages*. A primary message refers to the information itself. A secondary message is the label attached to the information, that is, the manner in which it is classified. It is possible to draw even finer distinctions by speaking of tertiary messages which would refer to the specific meaning given the information by the actor. For our present purposes, we shall, however, confine ourselves to the distinction between primary and secondary messages. Examples of secondary messages are common enough, since routing slips, the tags conveying the relative urgency and classification of the message, are all of this class. This distinction stresses the importance of the system and instrumentalities for classification and handling of information within the organization.

We have mentioned above that the way in which information is differentially distributed throughout the system is significant. This point relates directly to two matters already discussed, that is, to the way in which the decision-maker interprets the rules constituting his competence, and to the authority relationships. It is possible, for example, to propose to broaden the previously suggested hypothesis relating structural position and interpretation of the rules constituting the competence by suggesting that the more general and extensive the actor's information, the broader his interpretation of the rules. Insofar, then, as the channels of information provide more extensive information to decision-makers in positions of greater authority the system is reinforced. In addition to the need for investigation of the adequacy of this proposition, it would also seem necessary to look into the consequences of its obverse.

One student in this field has suggested that in the case of a closed system of communication, that is, a system into which no new information enters, information will tend, over a period of time, to become equally distributed through all parts of the net.[21] As a consequence one might postulate several alternative resultants of this state of affairs. One might, for example, hypothesize the breakdown of the existing system of super- and subordination in the system, or that existing relationships could be maintained only by increasing traditionalization of orientations; that is, in effect, the existing order would not be subject to questioning.

The Concept of Feedback

Information theory, by means of the concept of "feedback," also seems to provide the student of organizational decision-making with an alternative to the static models of organization based on some approximation of the Weberian ideal type. Feedback refers to the messages about the actions or state of the system which are returned to the system. By means of a continuous flow of such messages it is possible for the decision-makers to have a more or less current picture of the success or failure of their actions and the relative adequacy of the system. This, as everyone knows, is what happens in some actual cases. Nevertheless, the concept of a system of action, including a feedback which may change both objectives and structure of the system, is one that is quite new to organization theory.[22] It seems equally important for the student of organization theory to have some knowledge of the responsiveness of the system to the information about its own activities and state.

It has been the practice of some scholars, particularly in economics and logic, dealing with the theory of choice or decision-making to propose what are essentially rational models of rational action, models in which the actor is not only predicated as acting rationally but also as having complete information. These are not, however, completely adequate for application to situations characterized by risk, uncertainty, and incomplete information. It should be made very clear that it is not our intention to disparage in any way efforts at formalization which must of necessity make numerous simplifying assumptions. These formal models have resulted in discussion and clarification for which any student of organizational decision-making must be grateful.

Nevertheless, in an attempt to devise a conceptual scheme in which sociological and psychological variables play as important a part as in this one, the element of uncertainty and organizational efforts to deal with it must be given some attention. Organization, or, perhaps more accurately, the rationalization and formalization of behavior through the instrumentality of explicit rules, is itself an effort to reduce uncertainty—uncertainty concerning the internal operation of the system. We have already asserted that a part of information feedback relates to the state of the system itself, and this may be viewed as a kind of continuous *monitoring,* providing information about the state of the system.

Similarly, the other information provided by the operation of the feedback mechanism on the relationship of the system to its environment and on its objective-directed activities provides information which reduces uncertainty. Consequently, it seems necessary to take cognizance of three types of activities which take account of the three types of information in the system.

Thus far, we have frequently referred to the adaptability or viability of the system without more explicit discussion of the matter. Adaptability may be looked upon as analogous to the learning capacity of the individual. That is, the learning capacity of the organizational system may be thought of as the extent to which it acts upon the information received through the operation of the feedback mechanism. Thus, we may propose, with a rather crucial *ceteris paribus* assumption to be discussed below, that the viability and objective capacity of the organizational system varies directly with its capacity to learn.

In connection with the discussion of learning, the notions of *information-storage* and *organizational-memory* must be mentioned briefly. Information of all three types is stored in various parts of the net. Some of the questions the researcher would want to answer are: where is the information of each type stored? what is the nature of memory of each kind of information? can this be correlated with other structural features of the system?

Another useful distinction might be made between information in use and information available but not utilized. Some of the causes of nonutilization may then be investigated. The observer may ask whether there are certain factors inhibiting the recognition of information as information, whether there are blockages within the system preventing adequate channeling of messages, whether the secondary messages attached to the information are adequate, and so on.

It should be perfectly clear that, as far as the actors in the system are concerned, information that is not in use or *is* not recognized as information does not exist at all. Files, intelligence reports, research, and all the other paraphernalia of modern administration might just as well not exist at all if they are not used. Moreover, a particular message may have no meaning in an actor's schema of the external world and may consequently be disregarded. Here again it is of great importance for the student to investigate the nature of the world of the decision-maker.

It may be well to return briefly to the *ceteris paribus* assumption made above, relating to the discussion of action in the face of uncertainty and also the responsiveness of the system to information. It seems necessary to mention in this connection at least one class of cases, in addition to those in which information plays no major role because of excessive traditionalization (which brings into question the viability of the system), in which information is not accorded great importance. Here we are referring primarily to instances in which the organizational system has sufficient control over its environment not to have to consider other factors. The limiting case would seem to be almost inconceivable empirically, but there does seem to be a range of control over the organizational situation which is correlated with the treatment given information.

Noncoincidence of the Communications Net and the Formal System

In most of the preceding discussion there has been the at least tacit assumption that the communications net coincided and to some extent was coterminous with the legitimate and responsible formal system of action. Now, in concluding the discussion of information, it may be well to devote a few paragraphs to a special case which is probably empirically the most general one. That is the case in which the communications net and the formal responsible system are not coterminous.

To illustrate, the example of the Interdepartmental Committee on Trade Agreements might once again be used. On this body, at the highest level, participation is, as we have pointed out, predominantly representational in character. Each participant has, in effect, a special information system available to him in his own department or agency. Only a part of all this information is integrated in the specialized subcommittees of the Interdepartmental Committee. Here, then, is an example of information entering the responsible system at various points—information of varying degrees of mandatoriness in defining the actions of the decision-makers.

Reconsideration of the Concept of Access

In general terms, information may enter the system at various points and at varying stages of the decision-making process. The mandatoriness of this information will be dependent on the source, and the manner of entrance into the system, among other factors. The notion of information entering the system also makes possible the isolation of certain points crucial as channels for such information. Secondly, it would be important to know something of the sensitivity of the actors in various positions to the information entering the system. Here it would be useful to make a distinction between fairly specific information, the source of which can be isolated and assessed in terms of a variety of criteria, and general and fairly unstructured expressions of opinion by individuals or the mass media. Analysis might, in the foreign policy field, provide valuable information on whether the Secretary of State, for example, or the National Security Council is responsive to "public opinion," or whether, as some students, including Mr. George Kennan, suggest, decisions are taken and "public opinion" is then expected and allowed to "catch up."

In this connection the concept of the communications network permits a new look at the notion of *access*. The major point that needs to be made here is that our assumption that the decisional system is in all cases a legitimate one is highly relevant, for this assumption provides a clearly defined focus of attention. Involved in the notion of access are precisely the kinds of considerations stated in the preceding paragraph. Some of the questions that arise are the following: what is the source of the information? how is it brought to the attention of the decision-maker? where does it enter the system? how is it considered by the decision-maker?

Elsewhere we have already stated that decision-makers are officials and that they do indeed make decisions. That the decisions may be heavily influenced by the views of pressure groups, or by information obtained from polls and surveys, or by some instinctive reading of the barometer of the "climate of opinion," does not in the least alter what appears to us as a reasonable assumption. Indeed, the legitimate system we assume allows a classification of the relationships between extragovernmental systems and governmental systems in that these relationships can be isolated, their nature can be investigated, and perhaps ultimately generalizations as to the types of these relationships can be made.[23]

Information and the Activation of Decisional Systems

In an earlier section of this presentation we have discussed briefly the source and activation of decision-making systems. Some of the concepts we have presented under the general heading of information are highly relevant to that point. In a very large number of cases decisional systems come into being or are activated in response to information that is received. In some cases activation is the result of the operation of a feedback mechanism.

The information in these cases determines what the characteristics of the system that is activated will be and who the participating decision-makers shall be. Moreover, the nature of the information that is circulated in the activated system also influences the uniformity of the decision-makers' definition of the situation. The character of the communications net is also to a large extent determined by the information, since channels must be provided to those having relevant specialized information and to outside groups having some interest in the particular objective.

Motivation

Anyone who has grappled with the motivational analysis of human behavior knows that it involves very thorny problems indeed. Despite the obvious difficulties we have elected to treat motivation as a major determinant of decision-making in our scheme. There are several reasons for this. First, it is dangerous to suppress assumptions about motivation because they undergird explanations of why states behave as they do. It is impossible to probe the *why* of state behavior without also doing something about the motivation of decision-makers. To *assume* motivation begs many of the most significant questions which arise in the study of international politics. Second, motivational analysis makes it possible to spotlight certain aspects of decision-making which might otherwise be neglected and have in fact been neglected because motivation has remained implicit in various conceptual schemes. Third, if properly conceived and executed, motivational analysis ought to provide a much more satisfactory foundation for linking the *setting* and the *unit,* particularly the internal social setting and the decision-makers—one of the more troublesome areas of research. Fourth, such concepts as personality, perception, values, learning, and attitudes have increasingly become part of the vocabulary which refers to the behavior of decision-makers, and motivation may possibly clarify and synthesize all of them. Fifth, as social scientists improve their handling of motivational theory, the field of international politics ought to be prepared to take advantage of such developments.

Beyond listing highly generalized objectives such as security, power, economic welfare, and so on, little effort is usually made to push the analysis to a more fundamental level. How are objectives defined? Why are certain objectives valued? Why does the pursuit of a general objective take the particular form it does? Why does a nation become interested in some situations, not others? In short, analysis does not usually include an account of how and why situations are *defined* as they are.

As noted earlier, motivation has been ascribed to the *state*—to an abstraction—thus inviting the possibility of reification. This has had one effect, namely, to imply that diplomats and officials are virtual prisoners or servants—by some mystical process—of the spirit of the state whose impulses and drives carry them along.[24] Motivation is also imputed to the decision-makers as a collectivity, which requires more of an analytical operation than is normally characteristic of writing in our field.[25] Most motivational analysis is based on one of three kinds of assumptions: a *single motive* or dominant motive for *all* decision-makers; multiple motives operating *equally* on *all* decision-makers; and the single decision-maker—typical of all—functioning in isolation. Finally, state behavior is often explained in terms of key personalities—Hitler, Mussolini, and so on—*viewed as whole persons.*

Assumptions Underlying the Present Approach

Before discussing motivation per se, we wish to make our own assumptions clear. It is important to recognize that motivation is only *one* component of action. Causation is larger than motivation. The attempt to probe motivation by finding or postulating a single explanation tends to overemphasize motivation. Furthermore, we are not concerned with *all* the motives of *all* participants under *all* circumstances in the decision-making process. Since we view such participants as *actors* (an analytical concept), *not as discrete, "real" persons,* we are interested only in motivational factors which may help us to account for their behavior in a particular system of activities.

We shall assume, further, *multiple motives*—actually, a configuration of motives, a system in the sense that they are related to each other and are expressed in related programs of action. At any one time, there will be an order of relative dominance among these motives. Since there is more than one motive, we shall assume the likelihood of *motive conflict*—especially among the more intense ones. Motives and their expression may change from time to time. Not all motives can be satisfied equally and simultaneously because of scarce resources and limitations on decisional units. Finally, one course of action may satisfy several motives, and one motive may lead to several courses of action. These are rather simple-minded postulates but they serve to point up certain differences between existing analyses and our own and to emphasize the multidimensional quality of motivation.

The Nature of Motivational Analysis

It would be well to have it understood clearly that *motivation* is a concept, not a thing or a datum. Motives are not behaviors but inferences drawn from behaviors. Hence, they are indirectly inferred, *not* directly observed. Motivation is also what Newcomb and others call an intervening variable or construct,[26] that is, motives refer to a process of mediation between organic factors and social factors operating within the individual which results in some form of observed behavior. Motives are postulated as a basis of understanding and are verified by observing behavior. Motivated behavior has an inner-outer nature: there is a condition internal to the behaving organism (the individual human being) and "something" in the external situation which is wanted, and the two are linked.

Definition of Motivation

Since motivation concerns the individual as a human biosocial organism, it has been studied for the most part by psychologists and social psychologists. Naturally there are many types of motivational theories, some of them quite inappropriate for foreign policy analysis. At any rate a review of these theories is not necessary here. We shall simply summarize briefly the consensus among scholars as to the essential nature of motivation as an analytic tool.

Much motivational analysis is cast in terms of the individual organism, but to be consistent with our previous vocabulary we shall refer to the *actor* (the official decision-maker). We are concerned primarily with "why" questions—why does the actor (or why do the actors) *act,* that is, why does a decision get made? why does action take the *particular form* that it does in a *particular situation?* why do *patterns* of action evolve from decision-making?

1. Motivation refers to a psychological state of the actor in which energy is mobilized and selectively directed toward aspects of the setting.[27] This state is characterized by processes essential to the initiation, maintenance, and direction of activity.[28] That which determines the direction of action, that is, the particular objective or configuration of objectives, is called orientation. Hence, the psychological state referred to is characterized by a *disposition* to certain actions or reactions. The motivated actor has a will to act, is prepared to act, and directs his acts toward selected ends, and thus we have *drive, set,* and *orientations.*

2. From the foregoing, two meanings of motivation emerge: *energy* and *tendencies.* The psychological processes leading to the psychological state of willingness and readiness to act in certain ways also consist of behaviors. Motives may also refer, then, to *preparatory* and *promotional* nets which are actually conditional to the acts being observed and are conducive to their performance. These prior acts incline and impel the actor toward immediate overt action. Or to put it another way, the preparatory and promotional acts help mobilize energy.

3. These mediating processes of motivation, in effect, account for the interaction of the *need-dispositions* of the actor and the stimuli which form part of a particular situation. The response will be expressed in the tendency to

acquire certain objectives and to seek their achievement. Another character-istic of the "motivated state" of the actor is the existence of *needs* and *tensions* which impel the actor to seek satisfaction and release. Needs will not be sim-ple and separate, but complex and grouped in a *system.* Tensions are relative and a minimum level always is present. However, it is important to note the tension-reducing concomitants of action—once taken.

4. Any *act* (or action) as we have previously defined it analytically is *actu-ally a sequence or unit of behaviors dominated by a common motive* (or by com-mon motives) and the act includes: *performance, perception, thought,* and *feeling.*[29] The concept of motive ties them all together. Therefore, it is neces-sary to speak of a *motive pattern*—a sequence or unit of behavior characterized by constancy of direction or goal-orientation. (The notion of motive-pattern dovetails nicely with our concept of *event* discussed earlier.) Clues to the exis-tence of motives are to be sought in consistency of direction. The sequence is relatable to a desired end result (objective), and motives are *labeled* either in terms of characteristics of the sequence or its end result (or perhaps a combi-nation of both). Behavior is thus understood by motives attributed on the basis of inferences drawn from observed sequences of conduct.

Further Analytical Properties

In addition to these assumptions we are making concerning motivation, there are certain rather more significant aspects of the concept of motivation as we are employing it.

motives are learned

A distinction is sometimes made between primary and secondary motives on the basis of origin. We do not intend to enter the controversy over innate or instinctual motives. Rather we will say that the motives we are most con-cerned with are *acquired,* and are not inherent in the physiology of the human organism. This still permits us to use the term drive to signify the energy component of motivation. Two kinds of learning will be of direct in-terest to us, given the decision-making actors responsible for any nation's of-ficial actions: first, learning associated with membership in a culture and in a larger social system called society; and second, learning associated with membership in a governmental institution. Our scheme will have to take both kinds of social learning into account. Both involve learning processes of quite different sorts and in quite different contexts.

Two of the attributes of motives which derive from the fact that they are acquired are their *durability* and *persistence.* While whims doubtless play their part in official life (as in other realms), being motivated is more than a momentary state. Motives may be reinforced through the continued performance of acts which satisfy needs.[30] Reward, familiarity, and feedback from success may all strengthen motivational orientations. These factors may arise from the consequences of interpersonal relations among the decision-makers (that is, the system), or they may arise from the relations between the total membership of a decisional unit and the setting. Group influences on motivational reinforcement are notoriously strong. The decision-maker is, par excellence, a group actor.

motives are functionally autonomous

The persistence of motives *does not* depend on the continued presence of the original drive or stimulus. There seems to be general agreement that new motives may grow out of old ones by the simple process of objectives becoming desirable regardless of the original need which gave rise to the selection of the particular objective. One ramification of this is that means employed to satisfy a given drive through the achievement of an objective become an independent source of satisfaction and therefore displace the original objective. Here may be one clue as to why nations pursue objectives which no longer "make sense" in terms of their interests, that is, needs.

motives differ in strength

Because of the energy and directional components of motivation, it is possible to detect variations in intensity. Not only is intensity an important cue to ultimate choice, but the conditions under which intensity increases or decreases may also be important predictors of future action—the occasion for decision, the conditions under which action will take place, and even the way a decision is reached. There are many hypotheses concerning motive strength which cannot be discussed here. But one may be mentioned: the lower the intensity of motivation, the less information will be sought by the decision-makers as a basis for their deliberation.

motives may conflict[31]

Often two drives can be adequately expressed in a single course of action. However, it is a common occurrence that two sets of needs cannot be satisfied simultaneously. In effect, a conflict of motives involves competitive demands for energy focus and alternative directions of action. Foreign policy-making is, of course, an organized activity where the system of need-dispositions is exceedingly complex because of the wide range of influences at work on the participants. Motive conflict will be the rule. The effect of motive conflict on decisions and the resolution of such conflicts are prime objects of inquiry on the part of students of state behavior. Again we would argue that *logical* motive conflict seen by an observer may or may not be so viewed by the decision-makers. As with motive intensity, relevant hypotheses are available. For example, prolonged conflict will inhibit decision-making capacities and may result in decision by fiat.

We have already said that our task is made somewhat simpler by not having to worry about innate drives. We can simplify further by drawing a distinction between *because of* and *in order to* motives. *In order to* motives refer to an end state of affairs envisaged by the actor. Such motives thus refer to the future. What is motivated, as Schuetz points out, is the "voluntative fiat," the decision: "let's go" which transforms inner projection into an act. On the other hand, *because of* motives refer to the actor's *past experience,* to the sum total of factors in his life-history which determine the particular project of action selected to reach a goal. If we had to trace every act back to an ultimate cause, our task would be impossible. Were we required to account for "because of" motivation we should have to explain a particular act in terms of a sequence of past behaviors, something which would necessitate almost a psychoanalytic approach. Whereas in the case of "in order to" motivation, we are concerned with the future consequences of an act—its relationship to an ultimate end from which motive can be inferred. In the first case there is always the problem of whether one has fully reconstructed the antecedents of an act. Explanation would entail dealing with the organism and its psychic structure. One would need a full medical and psychiatric case history of the Secretary of State to explain why he lost his temper at a conference or why he yielded a point to an adversary.

The Vocabulary of Motivation

Fortunately, people talk about their motives and attribute motives to others. This is not only a fact about social behavior; it also provides a basis for clarifying and easing motivational analysis. Following Gerth and Mills,[32] we shall consider motives as terms which persons use in their interpersonal relations. Now this in no way alters what we have already said. We have merely added to the inference of motives from conduct the observation of the social functions served when actors in a system avow certain motives and impute motives to other actors.

It seems particularly fruitful to employ this kind of concept of motivation in understanding and explaining the behavior of foreign policy decision-makers because of the nature of diplomacy and because of the diverse groups which may become involved in decision-making in a complex organization. Regardless of the obvious hypocrisy and sham which has been evident in diplomacy and despite the distorted version of a quotation which has come down to us as "diplomats go abroad to lie for their country," international politics is clearly a realm in which the participants pay a great deal of attention to the reasons they give for their actions and to arguing with others about their actions. We said earlier in this essay that it had gone largely unnoticed, in an analytical sense, that much of the behavior of policy-makers was verbal in form. Acts are verbal acts. Furthermore, much of the discussion among them—and between states—proceeds on a symbolic level. Gerth and Mills note that it is in precisely those social situations (interpersonal) in which purposes are vocalized and carried out with close reference to the speech and actions of others where motive avowals and imputations seem to arise most significantly.[33]

Gerth and Mills go on to characterize those types of social situations as ones in which the actor is most likely to *question himself*—because of the *expectations* of others or because of the importance of their *reception* of the actor's conduct. Also, in these situations, the actor is most likely to *question others*. The existence of alternative purposes and the possibility of unexpected purposes add to the likelihood of questioning. Both elements are present in state action beset as interstate relations often are by crises.

Motives are words which are adequate; adequacy depends on whether such words satisfy other actors who do question or might question an act. Motive statements thus function to coordinate social action by persuading some participants to accept an act or acts. As Gerth and Mills point out, the vocabulary will be limited to those terms acceptable for certain types of social systems.[34] Motives are, then, *acceptable justifications* for present, past, and future programs of action. However, it should be emphasized that it is not *mere justification,* because motive statements serve important social functions. *A crucial point emerges: the decision to perform or not to perform a given act may be taken on the basis of the socially available answers to the question: what will be said?* What will be said by other decision-makers, by the public, and by other nations? In short, can an acceptable motive be attached to the contemplated act? For example, can the United States convince the recipients of foreign aid that no intervention in their internal affairs is intended? Or can they successfully argue that armed intervention in Indo-China is for true liberation of the native population?

We argue above that motives may change from what is originally prompted by a particular stimulus. The same action—or sequence of action—may be accompanied by a new motive or an additional motive. If it is accepted that motive statements by actors may perform the social function of gaining acceptance of given actions, then the acquisition of new motives *may* be an important condition for the continuance of given actions.

Motives Are Chosen

It follows that often motives may be *chosen* in the sense that the decision-makers will be more concerned about how a particular act can be explained motivationally for others (or how others can be motivated by it) than about its other consequences. An act may proceed from any number of diverse motives but ordinarily is based on one. However, in case of motive conflict, where each motive would result in a totally different act, attention may focus on the state of mind which is to accompany the act and on the strategies of inducing the act's acceptance. Generally a consideration of alternative motives is related to some higher motive. For example, decision-makers may decide in a specific case to verbalize their motive(s) in terms of military objectives in order to demonstrate the acceptance of certain political objectives. Thus, sending troops to Western Europe is a token that the United States will not desert this region politically.

As Gerth and Mills point out, the vocabularies of motives change and have trends. Two differences between the motivational statements of nations now and 100 years ago may be noted. First, such statements are now much more numerous and much more explicit. Both suggest important changes in the environment of world politics and in the norms which influence statesmen. Second, it appears much more imperative today than a century ago for nations to make their intentions understood to a large public. Some of the earlier appeals to honor and to investment apparently have been somewhat overshadowed by welfare symbols.

By this time the reader has perhaps begun to think of such words as "rationalization" and has also asked: can vocabularies be taken for *real* motives? do statesmen mean what they say? This last question is a reminder of the common image of diplomacy as a shell-game and propaganda contest. Without blinding ourselves to the difficulties, we may make several points. First, we have already said that much state behavior is verbal, that is, acts or actions as we have defined them may be in the form of declarations. Many declarations by the President or the Secretary of State are in effect motive statements. Now the discrepancies frequently noted between alleged real motives and motive statements *may* be discrepancies between two kinds of action, verbal and nonverbal. Second, it is a well-known principle of behavior that an actor may influence himself, so to speak, by his own declarations.

In short, motive statements—though originally not reflective of real motives—may become guides to conduct. If repeated often enough such statements may reflect, then, a motive change or substitution. Third, motive statements do not just describe or offer reasons (perhaps rationalization) but may result in influencing the behavior of other actors. It is also a principle of behavior that an actor's verbal acts may and usually do alter a situation through the impact on others in the system. Therefore, even if a decision-maker *lied* about his motives (or those of the state he represents), if he repeated the lie often enough, some persons would believe it and act upon it. The notion that a public official can consistently falsify his motives with no consequences for ensuing decisions and the surrounding situation is simply misleading. The more important the official the more likely his motive statements *will* have an effect on the situation.

Fourth, we are interested not only in motive vocabularies expressed in verbal interaction between governments but in the imputations and confession of motives among the decision-makers. As is well known, some of these are made publicly; most are made privately. At any rate, it seems highly unlikely that the decision-makers systematically try to deceive each other.

Our argument amounts to this: there may be circumstances under which real motives cannot be inferred from the factors which governed the choice of vocabulary, but it ought not to be assumed that because motive statements do have social consequences (acceptance), they are necessarily fraudulent.

Motivation, Attitudes, and Frames of Reference

We have said that motivation of foreign policy decision-makers refers to a set of tendencies manifest in their behavior. These are tendencies to respond in uniform ways to certain stimuli in the setting (internal and external), to select certain conditions and factors as relevant, to value certain objectives, to make evaluations of alternative courses of action, to allocate energy to various projects and strategies, and so on. Clearly, such tendencies are related to familiar questions: what is the *attitude* of the decision-makers toward this nation or that condition? *what* do decision-makers *think* about this range of problems? *How* do they think about these problems? Behind direct questions of this type lie complicated behavioral phenomena. To determine how answers might best be sought, it is necessary to specify further derived components of motivational analysis.

Attitude is a familiar yet ambiguous term in contemporary political analysis. Through carelessness and lack of precision it is often equated with *opinion.* For purposes of the analysis being suggested here, it is necessary to regard attitudes as a more basic phenomenon, namely, the *readiness of individual decision-makers to be motivated*—in effect; the readiness to have the tendencies noted *activated.* Thus, the structure of official attitudes constitutes a generalized potential of responses which are "triggered" by some stimuli. The notion of stimuli is, of course, a well-known psychological concept. It should remind the reader of an earlier discussion of changes in the setting of decision-making and the sources of the necessity to decide which may be located within the decisional unit or outside it. At any rate, the structure of attitudes held by the decision-makers is not focused until a particular stimulus invokes it. Let us try to illustrate these points. Assume for the moment that the attitude of the decision-makers of state X toward state A is one of hostility. According to our analysis this simply means that state X is "ready" to respond to a particular action on the part of state A by protest, counteraction, alternation of plans, watchful waiting—any one of which would be an expression of state X's motives, both general motives and those directed toward state A as part of the external setting. One fundamental motive would naturally be self-protection against the designs of state A. Until A actually undertakes an action which triggers X's response, its altitude or altitudes toward A are simply a condition of readiness or, as the psychologist might say, a "set" with respect to a given kind or range of stimuli.

Now the attitudes of decision-makers will presumably be found in clusters and at any given time will have a limited range. That is, there will not be readiness or set with respect to *anything* which might happen in the setting. Furthermore, while we chose a hostile altitude toward state A for our example, it is probable that hostility is also accompanied by other potential reactions toward state X such as suspicion and fear. One of the first things we would wish to know is the *content* of the structure of official attitudes. (We cannot assume a uniform set of attributes shared equally by all decision-makers.) Secondly, we should inquire into the *source* of these attitudes. (An investigation of the sources of attitudes takes us into an analysis of the kinds of data from which motivational inferences are to be drawn. These types of data will be discussed below.) Thirdly, the behavioral consequences of the attitudes held would be of great significance in the attempt to answer the "why" questions of state action.

The concept of attitude being considered here has a direct bearing on one of the problems of foreign policy-making in the United States—the proper role of the military in decision-making. In particular, one aspect of this is the so-called military mind. We are suggesting elsewhere[35] that if the attitudinal structures (along with frames of reference)[36] of military decision-makers can be isolated and described perhaps the way will be open to determine whether *one* structure of attitudes (readiness to invest energy in, and to respond characteristically to, military problems or military aspects of general problems) is distributed with sufficient frequency among military personnel to make it possible to speak of *the* military attitude (mind).

We have said that attitudes are a generalized readiness to respond in certain ways to stimuli. But this does not take us far enough. Why does a hostile attitude take the form of response which it does? Surely there is more than one possible specific response and readiness that must be mobilized with respect to some particular problem or situation. This brings us to the concept of a *frame of reference* which determines the specific responses of decision-makers. In turn, the frame of reference will include as analytical components: *perception, valuation,* and *evaluation.*

Earlier it was stated that perception is an aspect of motivation. Being motivated means that the individual's energy and attention are selectively directed. Motive determines what one selects in perceiving and how one organizes and uses it. To repeat, decision-makers act on the basis of a "definition of the situation." The relevancies which are built into the situation result from events, conditions, objects, and the actions of other states having been "sized up" by the decision-makers. These factors are related to each other, to existing policies and projects, and to other situations. Psychologists are generally agreed that perception in its fundamental sense involves three processes: *omitting, supplementing,* and *structuring.* These processes result from the stimulation of a "prepared organism"—the individual has been prepared by tendencies to react and by readiness to react in certain ways. But preparation also requires knowledge and information—previous experience as well as recognition and appraisal of the stimulus—in this case, a particular foreign policy problem or an action by another state.[37]

The frame of reference also includes values or standards; hence, *valuation* goes hand in hand with perception. In addition to the selection of factors to be related in the situation, there must be a selection of appropriate action. Thus, the motivated action brings to any situation a set of values. Valuation, as an accompaniment of perception, is behavior directed toward the establishment of preferences: it involves discriminating, rejecting, or "caring about" certain elements of the situation. Valuation defines the objective or objectives in the situation and enables the actor to determine the bearing of any act or any factor on any other act or factor.

Valuation basically concerns the nature and range of objectives which will be injected into the situation. But values also concern the preferred paths of strategies which direct specific acts toward the objective or objectives selected. In other words there are process or means values. It seems advisable to confine the term *valuation* to the general direction of the motive pattern as action unfolds, and to call the appraisal of the relationship between specific acts and the state of affairs envisaged as well as the immediate target *evaluation.* Clearly, the combination of perception, valuation, and evaluation can be looked upon as embracing "thinking" or "problem solving."

To conclude, the frame of reference becomes a determiner of behavior *after* an attitude or attitude cluster has been triggered by a stimulus. Operation of the frame of reference results in the construction of a meaningful behavioral environment—an environment congruent with *reality* and with the needs of the state as viewed by the decision-makers. As in the case of attitudes it is necessary to investigate; (a) the *content* of the frame of reference—the processes and patterns of perception, valuation, and evaluation; (b) the *sources* of these processes and patterns; and (c) *the behavioral consequences* of these in particular situations. Again, as in the case of attitudes, it should be possible to locate typical frames of reference among decision-makers and to determine their frequency.

We have separated for analytical purposes *motive, attitude,* and *frame of reference.* Obviously this is an artificial separation. If we were to observe the actual deliberations of a group of foreign policy decision-makers as they grappled with a specific problem, we would be aware of a sequence of behaviors which apparently defied categorization. Nevertheless, if we would "explain" their behavior and the action they decide upon, we must try to find out how—in the psychological sense—the individual decision-makers were prepared for their task. What *purposes* and *attitudinal sets* did they bring to it? What habits of *selection* and *relating* information and previous experience affected the "sense" they made of the situation? What *values* did they think were involved in the situation? How did they *calculate* a proper integration of objectives and techniques?

Such questions do not refer to behavior which unfolds in chronological order. In the actual course of decision-making, the factors alluded to may be completely intermixed. Regardless of how the conversation proceeded among the decision-makers, or even if their exchanges did not take place in person, the considerations, information, argument, reasoning, and deciding would in our view have to be described and explained in part through motivational analysis.

Motivational Data[38]

Unfortunately there is no full-blown theory of motivation appropriate for decision-making in complex organizations which might be modified or adapted for foreign policy-making. About all we can do at this juncture is to suggest some of the basic kinds of data from which motivation must be inferred. These data are, of course, also necessary to probe the attitudes and frames of reference which are expressed in the reactions, actions, and choices of the decision-makers.

1. functions and objectives of the total foreign
policy-making structure and of any substructure

The members of any decisional unit will be motivated by the responsibilities and objectives of the governmental structure, or any part thereof, involved in foreign policy-making and execution. Functions will range from the most general—such as the maintenance of national security through effective and efficient conduct of foreign relations—to the more and more specific such as the rendering of some specialized service such as intelligence reports. Presumably all decision-makers are (or should be) motivated by the general functions of the total decision-making structure, but it seems likely that the lower an actor is in the hierarchy the less significant these will be in his orientations.

So far as general objectives are concerned, it is obvious that at any one time there will be either a coherent strategy (or set of strategies) or a collection of prevailing plans and projects (action contemplated and action under way) which will exert motivational pull on the decision-makers. For example, the creation of "situations of strength" among neutrals, friends, and allies; the "containment of Soviet power"; "support" of the United Nations; and "aid to underdeveloped areas"—all these, once accepted, became a crucial factor in the orientation of decision-makers after 1948. We should also note that, in accordance with our definition of policy, the rules governing future exigencies will motivate decision-makers too.

Furthermore, when we were discussing the concept of successive, overlapping definitions of the situation, we remarked that while each decisional unit defines the situation with respect to its particular task or problem, often one unit knows what other units have done or are doing. In a sense, an aspect of the "givens" for each unit consists of the action taken or contemplated by other units.

We do not mean to suggest that functions, actions, rules, and "givens" have an absolute, precise meaning. One of the most important consequences of perception is the relating of a problem or alternative courses of actions to previous experience. This involves interpretation by the decision-makers. To be sure, there are limits to the discretionary judgment but there is nothing automatic.

2. the objectives of particular units

Decisional units are often not concrete substructures and are often temporary. Thus, decision-makers will be motivated not only by broader objectives binding on the whole structure of foreign policy-making but also by the specific objectives for which a temporary unit was established. An ad hoc interdepartmental committee created to recommend a policy on Universal Military Training will be influenced by the executive directive which sets it up, and it will also be influenced by higher plans and projects. Normally, it will be made explicit what the committee is *not* to do. Yet the decision-makers can hardly escape the motivating force of known over-all defense strategy. Hence, the decision-making unit will be subject to a "system" of purposes and functions.

3. socially defined[39] norms and values internal to the decisional unit

Decision-makers (the particular actors in any unit) have a membership in the total foreign policy decision-making structure and—more significantly—in concrete substructures such as the State Department (or any subdivision thereof), the Defense Department, the C.I.A., and many others. In addition, membership in the decisional unit itself (if it is composed of representatives from concrete units and is thus really an analytical unit) usually carries a formal role assignment. Consequently, decision-makers *may* be motivated by factors which have nothing to do with the *objectives* of the total structure or any unit. Rather, a different range of membership motives may operate: rewards appropriate to position, role expectations (both those of the role occupant and those with whom he interacts), unwillingness to appear ignorant or unorthodox, a desire not to impair continuing contacts or friendships—these and many similar ones.

One of the most important and also one of the most obvious motivational factors is the peculiar traditions of concrete suborganizations and units. When a representative of the State Department serves on a committee, his motives will be in part traceable to the fact that he is acting for the Department and that the Department has a stake. Now presumably, this stake is not unrelated to the purposes and functions of the total organization and the committee itself. However, the Department may have a *vested* interest, that is, an interest related primarily to its position in the total organization rather than to general policies. Therefore, the Department's representative may oppose a course of action in order to retain policy initiative.

Within the State Department, to take another example, a decisional unit might include Foreign Service Officers. These decision-makers will be motivated by the Department's missions and rules as well as by the government's missions and rules, but they *may* also be motivated by their membership in a notably tradition-bound group. The Foreign Service is known to be a homogeneous suborganization, some of whose members are very jealous of their prestige and general position in the Department's hierarchy. Loyalty to the Service might conflict with or at least not be compatible with loyalty to the Department.

4. socially defined norms and values external to the total decision-making structure and internalized in the decision-maker

It is clear from what has been said in the three sections immediately above, that when a person is appointed or elected as an official decision-maker he enters a complex system of objectives, preferences, and rules and becomes also an institutional member. Yet it is true too that the decision-maker enters the government from the larger social system in which he also retains membership. He comes to decision-making as a "culture bearer." Any conceptual scheme for analyzing state behavior must attempt to account for the impact of cultural patterns on decisions. If the decision-maker is viewed as a culture bearer, it would seem possible to lay the foundations for tracing the possible effects of common value orientations[40] shared by most members of a whole society upon the deliberations of members of decisional units.

By internalization is meant that certain patterned responses (which characterize both perception and valuation) are learned by the individuals during the process of socialization and are so much a part of him that they are "his" and are largely taken for granted. It is therefore unnecessary for the decision-maker to be aware or particularly self-conscious of such common values in his own thinking. Nonetheless, it may be a good hypothesis that high-level decision-makers do articulate cultural values as a natural concomitant of their functions. Leaders—political leaders in general and foreign policy leaders in particular—in any mass culture and complex society cannot escape responsibility for articulation of such values. One extremely important role of basic values is to *legitimate*[41] policies; verbalized values are employed to satisfy citizens as to the desirability of pursuing certain courses of action.

Two vital kinds of effects of major common value orientations on decision-making behavior may be noted: (1) effects on the ways in which decision-makers perceive the world and the unproblematic (that is, not open to doubt or choice) ends which they bring to their deliberations; (2) the verbal formulations which decision-makers employ to render official policies acceptable to the society.[42]

In recent years, students of international politics have noted that "cultural bias" may be a crucial factor in national behavior and in the stimulation of conflict. While this phenomenon has not been examined very systematically, we may note here that it seems to mean the following: (1) an attempt *to impose* the values of one culture on another on grounds of their universal validity—a kind of cultural imperialism; the bias is alleged to appear in the implied notion that there is some way of deciding which culture's values are *right* and which are not; (2) the *general judgment* that one nation's practices are abnormal, wrong, or misguided because they do not conform to the standards of another; it often follows that failure to conform to certain norms on the part of other nations relieves the one nation which so judges of any obligation to treat the others fully according to *its own* standards; (3) an attempt to predict the behavior of decision-makers in another state by assuming that they are bound by the same kind of cultural pattern; or (4) an attempt to predict such behavior by making "allowances" for cultural differences—an assumption being that these allowances are in fact sufficient to bridge the gap and are not themselves culture-bound.

Let us illustrate the chief points in section 4 by an example or two. It seems perfectly obvious that the extremely high value placed on human life and the great respect for the individual as a moral being in American society limit the ends and means which United States decision-makers can seriously consider. The course of repatriation negotiations after the Korean armistice demonstrated this clearly. Some nations are regarded by some American decision-makers as "backwards"—particularly if they do not believe that technological improvements necessarily bring social progress. When it came time to deal with the Japanese after World War II, many decision-makers felt that a powerful emperor was incompatible with democratization—a conviction which totally ignored or distorted the social and cultural role of the emperor. Predictions of Germany's reaction to large scale bombing in the latter years of World War II seem to have rested in part on fallacious assumptions concerning German culture. Finally, almost any general policy speech of the Secretary of State can be found to include reference to basic values of American culture—"we are doing so and so because this is the way free people or people who value freedom do act and should act."

So far we have been speaking of common value orientations presumably shared in minimum degree by *all* decision-makers, as members of a given culture.[43] But in addition to general cultural patterns there are subsystems of values which are not necessarily shared by most members of the society yet are also built through social experience. These subsystems will affect *particular* decision-makers. Here regional factors, especially in the case of legislative decision-makers, would be relevant.

5. material needs and values of the society or any
segment thereof not internalized in the decision-making
The line between the data specified in sections 4 and 5 is very thin indeed
and is permissible only for purposes of analysis. In section 4 we were referring to internalized values in the sense that the pursuit of such values
represents the coincidence of the self-interest of the decision-maker and
the interest of the society. Pursuit of these values is almost second-nature
and is taken for granted by the decision-maker. Now very closely related
to these values are other values and needs which are not, strictly speaking,
their "own" values and needs felt by the decision-makers as members of a
society and culture. We would argue that it is worth preserving a distinction between, on the one hand, norms and values external to the decisional
unit which are brought into the unit by the actor as part of his "preparation," and, on the other hand, norms and values which are "accepted" by
the actor *after* his entrance into the unit and which are not his "own" in
the usual sense.

We shall suggest, tentatively, that the needs of the society as a whole or
needs and values of particular segments or groups of the society enter the
motivation of decision-makers in two ways: first, through *estimates* made by
the decision-makers themselves; second, through *expectations* of rewards
and sanctions which the decision-makers feel might be the consequence of
deciding to maintain or not maintain certain general conditions in the society or to accept or reject certain demands by segments or groups within
the society. There seems no way of avoiding the conclusion that the relative
importance or compellingness of the material needs and values of particular, usually organized, groups, which are not necessarily shared by the whole
society, rest ultimately on calculations made independently by the decision-
makers or on calculations accepted by them as accurate—in which case
they become the calculations of the decision-makers. Calculations range
from the welfare of the whole society in a general sense (security) and in a
specific sense (vulnerability to military attack) to the protection of watch
manufacturers from Swiss competition. Thus, the generalized motives of
the whole society are injected into decision-making *only* through the estimates of those who can give those motives official status. While certain
groups will urge these generalized motives on behalf of the whole body of
citizens, normally the calculation of broad social wants and needs will be
carried on because of voluntary recognition of the necessity to do so by the
decision-makers. On the other hand, more particularistic wants and needs
will be vigorously urged on the decision-makers by hundreds of direct appeals by "pressure groups."

In sum, the norms and values being discussed in this section enter the decision-making process more or less through *conscious choice* of the decision-makers. Such become operative on the decision-maker as part of his function and are not taken for granted as in the case of the norms and values mentioned in section 4. Naturally the choice will be related to *expectations*—to an assessment of the consequences which might follow from accepting or rejecting certain norms and values as guides to action. Consequences might range from national disaster to sanctions invoked by groups. Sanctions might range from a "bad press" to a refusal of, say, atomic physicists to cooperate in the making of hydrogen weapons.

6. personality

It would be tempting to leave the personality of decision-makers as a residual category—anything not explainable by other factors is due to "personality." To face up to personality as an aspect of motivational analysis is akin to opening Pandora's Box. On the other hand, it is scarcely possible to avoid it on both common-sense and theoretical grounds. For one thing, we need some method of bridging the analytical gap between those portions of our scheme based on a model of the individual actor and those based on a system or structure. Personality, as we shall suggest, is one way to do this. If the task is defined as trying to ascertain which facets of a decision-maker's total personality structure made him behave a certain way on a given day, we are up against a hopeless search. But in fact we are not in this kind of a box unless we so decree it. Many students have been attracted by the "great man" approach to historical explanation. Take Franklin Roosevelt, Joseph Stalin, Winston Churchill, and Adolf Hitler, analyze the motives of these men, and you have the motives of America, Russia, Britain, and Germany pinned down. Nothing else is really needed. Furthermore, the recent developments in personality theory and psychoanalysis make it tempting also to analyze decision-makers in terms of tension-reduction mechanisms and Oedipus complexes.

Interesting as these kinds of investigation are, we shall have to define our approach to personality data much more narrowly. We took a long step in this direction when we rejected "because of" motivational analysis. This relieves us of the necessity to connect what the Secretary of State had for breakfast with his conduct at a meeting of the National Security Council. For example, the enduring tension between Secretary of State Dean Acheson and Secretary of Defense Louis Johnson can be accounted for in large part by the different attitudes and frames of reference characteristic of the two men in their official roles, not by unique events in the personal lives of either. If the Secretary of State loses his temper in a meeting following a bad night's sleep, motivational analysis would be inappropriate. If this turned out to be crucial, the observer would then talk about the nature of communications or changes in authority relationships as aspects of the conditions under which action took place. We shall now note that, analytically, there is a threefold division of character structure: the physiological organism, the psychic structure, and the person, that is, social being. What is required for our purposes is a sociological conception of personality. Our scheme places the individual decision-maker (actor) in a special kind of social organization. Therefore, we must think of a social person whose "personality" is shaped by his interactions with other actors and by his place in the system. This does not mean that we reject the influence of ego-related needs and tensions but only that the behavior of the decision-making actor be explained *first* in terms of personality factors relevant to his membership and participation in a decision-making system. In this way we can isolate what area of behavior must be accounted for in terms of idiosyncratic factors, that is, self-oriented needs not prompted by the system.

A. INTELLECTUAL SKILLS AND THEIR APPLICATION. Since the essence of decision-making is deliberation, choice, and problem-solving, it would seem important to ask: what kinds of intellectual operations are performed by actors in policy-making roles in a decisional system? Decision-makers, as we have repeatedly stressed, analyze situations, estimate needs, define problems, establish ranges of alternatives, assign relevancies and significance to events and conditions, and interpret information. Students of foreign policy and international politics have come to label all these as "policy analysis" and to collectively label the skills "capacity for policy analysis."

What we are saying here is that the attitudes, perception, valuation, and evaluation of the decision-maker—as parts of his motivational structure—will be expressed in certain intellectual operations. How can these be probed? There are, briefly, three related kinds of data which might be helpful:

1. TRAINING AND PROFESSIONAL OR TECHNICAL EXPERIENCE INSIDE OR OUTSIDE THE DECISION-MAKING ORGANIZATION—Presumably the perspectives and judgments of the decision-maker will be affected by whether he was trained as lawyer or economist, by whether he is a generalist or a specialist, an area or functional expert, a career man or a political appointee, a staff adviser or line operating official, a planner or an executor, and so on. This is one way in which subsystems of values prevalent in the society and internalized in the decision-maker are injected into the process of policy formation.

2. CONTINUED PROFESSIONAL AFFILIATIONS—This is another of the important ways in which value subsystems and group perspectives enter the decision-making process; if, for example, an area expert retains his close intellectual association with other nongovernmental experts, it is worth assuming for purposes of investigation that he will share some of their value orientations and analytical tendencies.

3. WORKING THEORIES OF KNOWLEDGE—These refer to ideas, concepts, formulas, and proverbs concerning human nature and behavior which circulate in any given culture and which may not be inculcated through specialized training and experience, but are absorbed in normal adult socialization.

Despite a fairly extensive if scattered literature on expertise, the social background of decision-makers, and such stereotypes as the "bureaucratic mind" or the "military mind," no systematic attempt has been made to give these various terms operational definitions or to establish empirical referents for them. Nor has the possible impact of continued professional association been studied. The case of the Institute of Pacific Relations and its alleged influence on certain members of the State Department would seem to be a case in point. Yet it is assumed that the diplomat, the economic expert, or the legal adviser all have special skills requisite to sound policy-making. But we know relatively little about these skills, why their possessors have different perspectives, and what difference it makes in their actions.

"Working theories of knowledge" suggests a very fundamental point. Foreign policy decision-makers must either make their own predictions and interpretations of human behavior or use the predictions and interpretations of intelligence or other experts inside or outside of government. Basically, these intellectual operations can be reduced to the collection and interpretation of data—the data concerning the behavior of foreign decision-makers and populations as well as the relevant behavior of domestic groups and individuals. On the basis of these data, generalizations and calculations must be made with regard to potential reactions to contemplated actions. Therefore, it becomes important to the observer of state action to know what notions the decision-makers (or the preparers of background papers or action papers) have about *how much verified or verifiable knowledge about human behavior is possible, what the most fruitful ways of analyzing it are, and to what extent it can be predicted.* Such "working theories," that is, the ideas and concepts which partially guide the decision-makers' manipulation of the information at their disposal and which also influence the very collection of the information, can become part of the personality through specialized training and professional experience. But such theories also abound in any given culture and in the organizational system. Concepts of human nature which may be passed on to the individual through socialization either before or after his accession to a decision-making role may play a significant part in his judgments.

Several examples will suggest the kind of data which may be pertinent here. National *stereotypes* circulate in all cultures which are exposed to outside contacts. Decision-makers are not necessarily immune to stereotypes which circulate with popular acceptance, though it seems unlikely that they will all share the same ones or even the more naïve varieties. However, a combination of stereotypes based partly on cultural myths and partly on diplomatic experience or organizational experience may develop. When stereotypes are found to be part of the intellectual equipment of decision-makers, it means their predictions and interpretations are based on prior classification of behaviors according to type rather than on close examination of such behaviors. It is quite conceivable, for example, that when United States decision-makers characterize the behavior of British policymakers, they are, in subtle fashion, classifying, and not explaining. Yet this may be accepted as an explanation and thus become the basis for a self-fulfilling prophecy.[44]

Many decision-makers appear to believe only in *intuition* as the basis of knowledge. A Foreign Service officer may feel he can learn more about the mood of public opinion in Austria by visiting a few bars and restaurants than by employing survey techniques. In effect, most officials who believe largely in intuition reject the possibility of systematic analysis and low-level accurate predictions. What kinds of intellectual operations are concealed by the word "intuitive"? What are the consequences of the decision-maker's regarding himself as an "educated guesser"? Often decision-makers say, give us the facts and only the facts! But what is meant by *fact* in this context? Particularly in the social realm, the meaning of fact is crucial. An insistence upon only facts—as noted earlier in this essay—implies a concealed assumption that no previous choice of criteria is necessary.

Usually decision-makers have to "put together" many factual elements and interpretations with respect to any problem or, if they do not do so, the intelligence experts will. How are many disparate, seemingly unrelated data integrated into an action hypothesis? How are conflicting data reconciled, if at all? If an expert in anthropology and an expert in economics come to different conclusions as to the potentialities of economic growth in an underdeveloped area, which is to prevail? A great deal of attention has been paid to the estimate, say, of Soviet capabilities by American decision-makers, yet relatively little attention has been paid to the impact of unquestioned concepts of knowledge on the estimate. What we are saying is that answers to these questions must be sought in part in the views held by decision-makers as to *what constitutes verified or verifiable knowledge of human behavior and how predictions are to be formed.* This is one aspect of personality which is organizationally relevant and can be isolated from other characteristics.

It is extremely important to note in passing that these intellectual qualities—certain personality traits relevant for decision-making—will be affected by the group process of decision-making. There will presumably be both a pooling and modification of intellectual skills. An individual decision-maker—a specialist for example—if he is making a decision alone might be inclined consciously or unconsciously to push his professional perspective to the limit. On the other hand, in a group, the interplay of specializations will result in some modifications. The area expert may disagree with the demographer, and the primarily intuitive thinker may be called upon to make his assumptions explicit. This *pooling* of intellectual skills will itself be data for the observer. Closely related to the integration of the perspectives (ways decision-makers think about foreign policy problems) will be the creation of *composite estimates or predictions.* In the total decision-making organization there will be a number of agencies and individuals interpreting data on the setting—particularly of course, the external setting. Another kind of intellectual operation may enter in, one which may not be appropriate to the data per se. For example, in the United States decision-making system the *national estimates*[45] prepared under the leadership of the Central Intelligence Agency may often represent "shadings" of true convictions held by various intelligence agencies. To put it another way, the estimate is primarily an organizational compromise rather than a genuine merging of the soundest intellectual operations. One question which arises here is: what intellectual criteria, if any, are applied to choices between irreconcilable conflicts of judgment?

Group decision-making appears to have another possible effect on intellectual skills, namely, that a wider range of alternatives may be considered initially and that a more thorough exploration of consequences may result. This is problematical, but social research indicates it is at least a good working hypothesis. Thus, a committee chairman or an agency director or the presiding officer of top policy-making groups may broaden or narrow the actual impact of the intellectual skills of participants in the decision-making process. Leadership thus may be a skill of crucial importance to decision-making.

Organizational norms and group interactions have some other consequences for the nature and effectiveness of intellectual skills—which confirms our view that a fruitful conception of personality for foreign policy analysis must be more sociological than psychological. First, one of the types of data to be observed under the heading of intellectual skills is the *techniques* of *legitimation*.[46] By legitimation is meant the ways in which action or proposed action is made "acceptable,"[47] that is, consonant with experience and proper motives. It is highly doubtful if any decision-making group ever agreed to a policy which called forth a sense of incongruity and which was clearly in conflict with the range of officially acceptable motives. Among the decision-makers themselves the chief techniques seem to be: appeal to past experience, to ultimate values, to personal reputations, and to alleged consequences. More is involved here than policy selling, rationalization in the usual sense, and rational argument. The selection of motives is not the same thing as logical analysis and arguing about whether aircraft or ground troops or both should be sent into Indo-China. Nor is a two plus two equals four calculation the same as the acceptance of a proposed action because the decision-makers have faith in its leading proponent. Particular decisional units may have characteristic techniques. An ad hoc unit may not have a large reservoir of specifically relevant experience to guide them. Another unit may rely exclusively on the reputation of experts.

Second, the intellectual aspects of motivation remind us to look for the devices whereby the decision-makers minimize the psychological tensions which accompany decision-making under *circumstances of uncertainty and lack of complete information.* The business man has accounting rules and the baseball manager has "the percentage." What devices, if any, are available to the foreign policy-maker? How does he learn to live with unavoidable error? If devices to compensate for uncertainty are used, what effect do these have on deliberations? Third, what notions do decision-makers entertain concerning the *limitations* of their position? Is there an acceptance of minimal limitations operative at all times? What kinds of factors in the setting are deemed subject to control and what kinds are not?

B. INTERPRETATION OF COMPETENCES. So far we have dealt briefly with the decision-making personality in terms of intellectual skills and their application. Equally important is the interaction between the actor and the sphere of competence as defined in an earlier section. Any competence in any decisional unit will have what we have called prescribed and conventional aspects. Within these there will be a minimum set of rules and requirements which would be binding on any occupant. In other words, it is possible to isolate dimensions of the role (in our vocabulary, sphere of competence) of Secretary of State which would persist regardless of the particular person who is actually filling it. However, beyond this conventional boundary it is largely a matter of individual interpretation and discretion on the part of the occupant as to what is done and how. This area of the competence consists of activities which depend on the actor's discretion. But undertaking such activities—in effect adding to the basic minimum of the competence—may not be accomplished merely by simple choice of the incumbent actor. Since he interacts with other decision-makers in a system, he may have to "feel his way" in order to have his "extra" behavior accepted beyond a certain point. Practically speaking, the acceptance of other actors limits the area of new activity which can be undertaken. If these limits are ignored by the actor, the conditions under which the decisional system can be maintained may ultimately disappear. Thus, any competence will have associated with it a set of potential role-strategies which the particular actor may employ in interpreting the basic minimum and in adding new dimensions. One strategy, for example, would be to adhere closely to the minimum requirements and rules of the competence.

Now this line of argument postulates a choice in "role interpretation." Clearly, here is an opportunity for so-called personality factors to operate. Nevertheless we should note that there are two basic sources of pressure for changes in role interpretation, that is, for different answers to the questions: will this decision-maker act? and how will he act? One source lies *in requirements of the group situation* (an organizational decision or forcing conditions), and the other lies in *ego-oriented needs and tensions.* Before it is too quickly assumed that Secretary Dulles acts differently from Secretary Hull *only because* the two men are different human beings, many other questions ought to be asked. And before the student of foreign policy burdens himself with an embarrassingly large residual category of "personality" (meaning unique factors), he ought to exhaust other analytical alternatives first.

What we have done is to attempt to isolate the idiosyncratic element in the motivation of decision-making. Tentatively, we feel that it is better to try to account for the impact of personality on state behavior by eliminating all the organizationally or situationally relevant aspects of personality first. If we remember that idiosyncratic behavior is not necessarily random—that is, unpredictable and unpatterned—the whole notion of personality does not at least open up the possibility of either unexplainable or a hopelessly wide range of behavior patterns.

C. PERSONALITY TYPES AND DECISION-MAKING. Earlier in this essay we suggested that the orderly analysis of foreign policy would require carefully worked out typologies—kinds of states, decision-making systems and units, situations, objectives, and decisions. Further control over the personality variable may be possible through the construction of a typology of person-alities in terms of decision-making in complex organizations. Such a typology would be constructed on the basis of certain crucial characteristics typically present among decision-makers. Obviously what we are thinking about is a role player—an actor whose discretionary choices in relating him-self to his position and whose contributions to the decision-making process result in part from the expression of certain organizationally relevant, dom-inant personality traits.

To illustrate our point we shall suggest a very crude and incomplete set of decision-making types:

1. THE COMMUNICATOR—a leader type who has definite skills in trans-lating specialists to each other, in identifying common properties of otherwise conflicting approaches to problems, and in providing bases on which the different perspectives of decision-makers may be inte-grated; a coordinator on the intellectual level, he is a consciously self-styled go-between and mediator.

2. THE INNOVATOR—may be, variously, a rebel against the existing nor-mative order, a risk taker, or an original thinker; in any case he is likely to be a catalyst so far as the intellectual processes of decision-making are concerned and is likely to press toward the outer limits of the negotiable area of his sphere of competence; he is also likely to be a primary source of internally generated demands to redefine situa-tions or to focus the energies of the decisional system.

3. THE TRADITIONALIST—the conservative counterpart of the above type, a repository of precedent and the embodiment of organizational memory; a value-saver with respect to long-standing habits of proce-dure and thought; his actions contribute to a slowing up of organiza-tional change and to rigidities of approach to policy problems.

4. THE LITERALIST—the decision-maker who insists on a strict (narrow) interpretation of the rules of the system; a subtype is the self-styled "realist" who perceives (or thinks he perceives) only the major essen-tials of situations or problems; usually a passion for unadorned facts and a willingness to deal only with specifics rather than generalities accompanies the realistic and strict-construction posture toward deci-sion-making activities.

5. THE POWER-SEEKER—the upward mobile official whose position in the total decision-making organization and in the internal political setting tends to dominate his behavior; he may violate procedural

norms and take public stands on policy issues if it serves his purposes; he is likely to take a broad view of his sphere of competence and to inflate its functional aspects; it might be expected that he would personalize his official relationships even if this meant departing from normal channels of communication.

6. THE CAREER SERVANT—the decision-maker who maintains a carefully correct attitude with respect to his role limitations, who is likely to identify himself with a concrete membership group, and who is self-consciously an *expert* having a specific contribution to make to decision-making; ordinarily the career servant will have a strong sense of organizational mission.

Now such a list of types suggests only that it may be possible and desirable to isolate certain dominant, characteristic responses to decision-making roles and situations. It is, of course, nonsense to imply that any real person fits neatly into just one of these categories and that his total personality can be interpreted in these terms. What the types do imply is the possibility that typical responses may be sufficiently frequent to speak of an organizational personality. Hence idiosyncratic behavior—behavior not predictable or describable in terms of formal or situational factors—may be accounted for nonetheless by organizationally relevant factors. In other words, ego-oriented sources of difference in role interpretation may be expressed in patterns of behavior which are not unique to the individual decision-maker and to particular situations.

Summary

We have attempted to specify six important types of data which might be brought to bear on motivational analysis. The sources, content, and consequences of the attitudes and frames of reference which influence the behavior of decision-makers can be analyzed through the collection and interpretation of such data. Naturally the discussion of the six categories of data is suggestive, not exhaustive. It will be noted that the data lead to certain major areas of contemporary social research and intellectual interest: cultural analysis, bureaucracy and administration, group problem-solving, the psychology and sociology of personality, the political process, recruitment and training of government officials, the application of social science knowledge to policy-making, and so on. However, the significance of the data and techniques implied under these headings must be assessed on the basis of their help in explaining the conduct of foreign policy-makers.

We think it worth stressing that these data are related and that no one category is or ever can be sufficient to explain decision-making behavior. Cultural values are, for example, mediated (through the individual decision-maker's participation in a system) by the operation of forces implicit in categories 1, 2, and 3—or what might be called influences deriving from organizational membership. In turn, these are mediated by personality factors. Aside from the interrelationships among the six classes of data, the impact on action of the structure of competence, and the network of communication and information must be remembered. Finally, the situation confronting the decision-makers may have varying kinds and degrees of compellingness which is, in effect, "imposed" on the decision-makers.

Motivational analysis is, of course, on the level of the individual decision-maker rather than on the level of the decisional system considered as relationships among individual decision-makers. We have been building throughout the discussion of motivation a model of the typical decision-maker—an actor in the analytical sense. This actor (decision-maker) participates in a particular kind of social system of which we have described the essential features. We have built into this actor certain properties which we assume—until we discover differently—will partly account for his behavior.

The six kinds of data which we have specified as relevant for an explanation of the possible motives of foreign policy decision-makers imply a general concept of multiple membership for the individual actor:

1. Membership in a culture and society
2. Membership in noninstitutional social groupings such as professional, class, or friendship
3. Membership in a total institutional (political) structure
4. Membership in a decisional unit

Presumably these place the individual decision-maker under a set of simultaneous—and not always compatible—role obligations (in the broad sense) and expectations, both his own and those of others, with whom he interacts. While his participation in a decision-making system tends to structure or condition the behavior much more rigidly than is normally supposed, there are choices among acceptable responses all along the line. Out of the collective choices of the decision-making group emerges policy and action. These choices will be influenced by the organizationally relevant personality factors and by what we have called idiosyncratic factors (those stemming from ego-oriented needs and conditions). Our model of the actor really is intended to circumscribe analytically the area of behavior which might only be explainable in terms of the "whole person," that is, in terms of ego-oriented needs and conditions.

We restate our conviction that if the student of state action is interested in describing and explaining the nature of foreign policy objectives, the multiplicity and relative priorities of objectives, conflicting objectives, scarcity and appropriateness of techniques and strategies, and the expression of acceptable gratification of national wants and needs, some kind of motivational analysis is necessary. We have only been able to suggest the groundwork for such analysis.

7. RECAPITULATION

We began the brief exposition of our frame of reference by stating our conviction that the analysis of international politics should be centered, in part, on the behavior of those whose action is the action of the state, namely, the decision-makers. We insisted, further, that state action grew out of and was embodied in the "definition of the situation" by the decision-makers. Finally, we have attempted to demonstrate that the definition of the situation resulted from a decision-making process which took place within a decisional unit. In our scheme, decision-making is accounted for in terms of the activities and relationships of the members of the unit. The unit is viewed as functioning in an internal and external setting.

We then attempted to define the concept of decision-making and to specify what we meant by treating decision-making as "organizational behavior." To explain the actions of decision-makers we employed three basic determinants: spheres of competence; communication and information; and motivation.

We shall suggest certain obvious connections among the three sets of variables, leaving for a later time a more systematic joining of the concepts:

First, the knowledge and information which comprise some of the ingredients of perceptions are *communicated* throughout a decisional system or are usually available for communication other than by individual memories. Second, motives—that is, attitudes and frames of reference—must be *communicated* throughout a decisional system in order that an agreed range of objectives, integration of perspectives, and hence a common definition of the situation on the part of decision-makers is possible and likely. Third, *motives* are linked to *spheres of competence* because the latter provide cues as to the decision-maker's values (location in the total hierarchy and organizational membership), his actual range of choice (responsibilities and power relationships), and his skills and training (specific functions). Fourth, the communication network helps to carry rules and commands and also confirms or supports the *structure of competence*.

About the decision-makers in any decisional system concerned with any particular problem we want to know: what are the characteristics and relationships of the spheres of competence? what are the motivational influences at work? what is the nature of the communication network? what is the nature, amount and distribution of information? and, finally, what is the reciprocal impact of these on each other? Answers to these questions should provide a basis for adequately describing and explaining state action. It should be remembered that any one of the three fundamental concepts to which these questions point can serve as a separate tool of analysis independent of the other two.

We shall have to postpone consideration of two concepts which can be derived from our analysis, namely, *intellectual process* and *policy attention*. Both can be used to probe certain behavioral patterns and conditions without elaborate organizational analysis in the structural sense. The first points to the patterns of thought or problem-solving which may be typical of certain decisional systems or issues. The second points to the distribution of the total organization's resources with respect to policy problems.

The Essence of Decision-Making Analysis: The Nature of Choice

We shall terminate our essay with an attempt to characterize our central focus. We have thus far discussed a variety of factors relevant to the formulation of a scheme for the analysis of foreign-policy decision-making. We have sought to stress the interaction of the decision-maker with the various elements of his situation and to point to some of the consequences of this interaction. But we have not said much about what precisely it is that the decision-maker does when he decides. In the following paragraphs we shall try to deal briefly with this matter.

In another context we have alluded to some contemporary work in economics, philosophy, and psychology dealing with the Theory of Choice. A number of these suggested models show extensive agreement in certain of the assumptions made by their proponents.[1] First the actor or decision-maker is generally represented by a *scale of preferences,* that is, the values of the decision-maker are assumed to be ordered from the most to the least highly regarded. Some of the writers presenting somewhat more complex models assume further that, let us say, decision-maker A will take into account the reaction of decision-maker B to his (A's) suggestion. Secondly, it is usually assumed that a *set of rules* governs the actions of the decision-makers. These rules determine the manner in which the alternative choices shall be presented, the procedure of voting, and so forth. It should be remembered that most of the models are logical and mathematical in character and that the scales of preference and rules are logical devices. They are not intended to be relevant to every empirical choice situation.

These models, to which we have probably not done justice in our all too brief characterization, do provide a convenient point of departure for a discussion of choice. No matter how much certain situational elements are stressed, and we have of course stressed these considerably and (we believe) justifiably so, choices are in the final analysis made by the decision-makers. Decision-makers have preferences; they value one alternative more highly than another. Though the scales of preference may not be as highly ordered as the logical ones referred to above, decision-makers may be assumed to act in terms of clear-cut preferences.

The key questions, then, are: what is the nature of these preferences? what are the factors influencing them? The first statement that may be made in very general terms is that these preferences do not appear to be entirely individual. In other words, we would propose the hypothesis that one element of the scales of preference derives from the rules of the organizational system within which the decision-makers operate. Here we might mention both prescribed rules and conventions and precedents.

A second element might be a shared organizational experience over a period of time. A third has been treated under the general heading of biography, the decision-maker's past experiences. Here the expectation would be that similarities and divergences of class background, education, and so forth would make for similarities and divergences in preferences.

An additional factor that must be considered together with the various elements of the decision-maker's preferences is the information the decision-maker has. We have spoken earlier of a process of deliberation in connection with the making of choices. This would presumably involve taking into account, in selecting one of several alternatives, the information available. The information, as we have tried to indicate, is assessed selectively in terms of the decision-maker's frame of reference.

It has probably been apparent to the reader that there is considerable difference between what we have called rules and the kinds of rules discussed in connection with the models of choice. We would assert at least initially that the rules governing the decision-maker's behavior are expressed directly through a component of the scale of preferences. The rules which relate to such factors as the presentation of alternatives, the order of voting, and so on are considerably more difficult to deal with, since in the empirical situation there is a great variety of forms that these rules take. For example, in some choice situations, a vote is avoided at all costs, and in others a vote may be used as a punitive measure against some member of the system. In the face of very little evidence, it seems difficult indeed to generalize about the effects of the various procedures that may actually be found. Suffice it to suggest here then that on the basis of various elements of the scales of preference we would expect considerable similarity in these preferences to the extent that the elements are similar.

In conclusion, we might summarize our comments on the nature of choice as follows: information is selectively perceived and evaluated in terms of the decision-maker's frame of reference. Choices are made in the basis of preferences which are in part situationally and in part biographically determined.

NOTES

Introduction

1. Although the present essay centers on decision-making, our whole framework of analysis will give due attention to state interaction.
2. We shall later explain the meaning of this phrase in detail.

1. Scope and Method

1. Richard C. Snyder, "Decision-Making as an Approach to the Study of Politics," paper prepared for a conference at Northwestern University, June 15–19, 1954.
2. The reader may wish to consult the following selected bibliographical items which deal with basic aspects of concept formation: Ernest Nagel, "Some Problems of Concept and Theory Formation in the Social Sciences," in *Symposium of Science, Language and Human Rights* (American Philosophical Association, Eastern Division, 1952). Vol. I, pp. 43–64; Carl G. Hempel, *Fundamentals of Concept Formation in Empirical Science* (Foundations of the Unity of Science, 1952), Vol. II. No. 7; Herbert Feigl and May Brodbeck (eds.), *Readings in Philosophy of Science* (New York: Appleton-Century-Crofts, 1953), Secs. IV, VII; Philip Wiener (ed.), *Readings in the Philosophy of Science* (New York: Scribner, 1953), pp. 443–570.
3. Karl Deutsch, *Political Community at the International Level,* Foreign Policy Analysis Series No. 2, 1953.
4. Talcott Parsons and Edward Shils (eds.), *Toward a General Theory of Action* (Cambridge: Harvard University Press, 1951); David Easton, *The Political System* (New York: Knopf, 1953).

5. See Robert Merton, *Social Theory and Social Structure* (New York: The Free Press of Glencoe, 1949), pp. 5–10 for a discussion of the nature of such theories.

6. Deutsch, *op. cit.* is an example of middle range theorizing which illumines the analysis of state interaction.

7. Cf. Easton, op. *cit.*, pp. 52–63; 64–89. Needless to say, the phrase is employed here in quite a different meaning from that normally employed by social psychologists. Later on we shall employ the concept in the social psychological sense.

8. Gardner Murphy, *In the Minds of Men* (New York: Basic Books, 1953).

9. Hadley Cantril (ed.), *Tensions that Cause Wars* (Urbana: University of Illinois Press, 1956).

10. See Alfred Schuetz, "On Multiple Realities," *Philosophy and Phenomenological Research,* 5 (June, 1945), 533 ff.

11. See Karl Deutsch, "Mechanism, Teleology and Mind," *Philosophy and Phenomenological Research,* 12 (December, 1951), 185–222; "Communication Models in the Social Sciences," *Public Opinion Quarterly,* 16 (Fall, 1952), 356–80.

12. In the technical sense. See Parsons and Shils, *op. cit.,* Chap. I.

13. Glenn Shortcliffe, "Class Conflict and International Politics," *International Journal,* 4 (Spring 1949), 95–108. A useful article which clearly illustrates the point being made here.

14. Percy Corbett has reminded us that only a general theory can ultimately do full justice to these purposes.

15. This problem of the kinds of knowledge possible for humans about themselves and others has been generally neglected by political scientists. The phrase "we all *know* that . . ." covers a multitude of different things. The differences ought certainly to be at least recognized by scholars.

16. The term low-level prediction has two meanings. First, it means a prediction having a wide margin of error. Thus we might say: in six cases out of ten the President will be forced to defend his Secretary of State from attacks by his own party under specified conditions. This is not very exciting perhaps but is better than pure hunch and, above all, it is a good test of the reliability of our knowledge. Second, and perhaps more commonly, it means a prediction covering only a limited range of phenomena and therefore having "limited generality."

2. Some General Characteristics of the Present Study of International Politics

1. Frederick L. Schuman, *International Politics* (New York and London: McGraw-Hill Book Co., Inc., 1933).

2. Nickolas J. Spykman, *America's Strategy in World Politics* (New York: Harcourt, Brace & World, Inc., 1942).

3. The pages of *World Politics,* which began publication in 1948, perhaps best exemplify the search for new approaches and insights. Its excellent articles represent pioneering efforts to re-examine the field.

4. It is a reasonable assumption—subject to disproof—that the range and types of interactions among states have increased and hence the number of factors which must be taken into account has also increased. However, it must be emphasized that the analytical problem is no different. We do not wish to imply that international politics "began" twenty years ago.

5. In particular, Samuel A. Stouffer *et al., The American Soldier* (Princeton: Princeton University Press, 1949); also, the Office of Naval Research studies, e.g., Harold Guetzkow (ed.), *Groups, Leadership and Men* (Pittsburgh: Carnegie Press, 1951).

6. Cf. William Y. Elliot, *et at., United States Foreign Policy* (New York: Columbia University Press, 1952), pp. 229 ff. for examples.

7. Both as policy prescriptives and as descriptions of the role of Values in policy formation.

8. Easton, *op. cit.,* pp. 267–90.

9. Having been critical of reification we should remind the reader that purely for convenience we have employed the phrases "state as actor" and "state behavior." See below for a detailed explanation of our conception of the state—one of the central concepts in our scheme.

10. See Marion J. Levy, *The Structure of Society* (Princeton: Princeton University Press, 1952), pp. 88–89.

11. For example, the rational man of eighteenth-century political thought.

12. We shall state our objections in an indiscriminate use of the formal-informal distinction at a later time. Most of the discoveries of informal factors were made in the field of industrial relations and by students of industrial organization. These were found to be applicable to public administration.

13. We shall also withhold for the moment our reservations on this concept.

14. David Truman, *The Governmental Process* (New York: Knopf, 1951).

15. All relationships of political significance whether strictly political or not.

3. Contemporary Approaches to the Study of International Politics

1. See for example: Harold Guetzkow, "Long-Range Research in International Relations," *American Perspective,* 4 (Fall, 1950), 421–40. A. E. Heath, "International Politics and the Concept of World Sections," *International Journal of Ethics,* 29 (January, 1919), 125–44. Charles Rothwell, "International Relations in a World of Revolutionary Change," *World Politics,* 1 (January, 1949), 272–76. Waldemar Gurian, "On the Study of International Relations," *Review of Politics,* 8 (July, 1946), 275–82. Georg Schwarzenberger, "The Study of International Relations," *Yearbook of World Affairs,* 1949, pp.

1–24. Kenneth Thompson, "The Study of International Politics: A Survey of Trends and Developments," *Review of Politics,* 4 (October, 1952), 433–67. R. Snyder, "The Nature of Foreign Policy," *Social Science* (April, 1952), pp. 61 ff. William T. R. Fox, "Interwar International Relations Research," *World Politics,* 2 (October, 1949), 67–79. Frederick S. Dunn, "The Present Course of International Relations Research," *World Politics,* 2 (October, 1949), 80–85. Grayson Kirk, *The Study of International Relations in American Colleges and Universities* (New York: Council on Foreign Relations, 1947).

2. Hans Morgenthau, *In Defense of the National Interest* (New York: Knopf, 1951); and George Kennan, *American Diplomacy 1900–1951* (Chicago: University of Chicago Press, 1951).

3. Though once reality is described, deductions from it seem to follow as a matter of faith.

4. Inadvertently or otherwise, writers sometimes argue that "reality" *should* govern conduct.

5. We shall return to the basic problem of rationality in another publication.

4. Toward a New Frame of Reference for the Study of International Politics

1. Obviously these difficulties are not unique to this branch of political science but they are either more serious or are largely unrecognized.

2. Marion Levy, Jr., "Some Basic Methodological Difficulties in Social Science," *Philosophy of Science,* 17 (October, 1950), 287–301.

3. Cf. James K. Feibleman, *Ontology* (Baltimore: Johns Hopkins Press, 1951), pp. 301 ff. To avoid confusion later on, we should make it clear that we are assuming a social order within which decision-makers operate and therefore there is no chance element in *their* actions. Here we are discussing the possible *results of their actions* in the realm of interstate relations generally.

4. Frank Knight, *Freedom and Reform* (New York and London: Harper and Bros., 1947), pp. 335–69.

5. The distinction between social action and behavior is an important one analytically, though we shall continue to use state action and state behavior synonymously.

6. We shall have occasion later on to suggest the necessity for other typologies.

7. Some social scientists argue that a collectivity cannot properly be regarded as an actor as the term is used in the analysis of social action. However, see Parsons and Shils, *op. cit.,* pp. 192–95.

8. The vocabulary of action analysis has become fairly common, yet there are several kinds of action theories (for example, note the differences between Levy, *op. cit.,* and Parsons and Shils, op. *cit.*).

9. In particular, "Choosing Among Projects of Action," *Philosophy and Phenomenological Research,* 12 (December, 1951), 161–84; and "Common-Sense and

Scientific Interpretation of Human Action," *Philosophy and Phenomenological Research*, 14 (September, 1953), 1–37.

10. Compare this concept with Arthur Macmahon, *Administration in Foreign Affairs* (University, Ala.: University of Alabama Press, 1953), Chap. I, entitled "The Concert of Judgment."

11. We are indebted to Professor Harold Sprout for calling our attention to this point. See our more detailed discussion of limitations below.

12. Introduction to Deutsch, op. *cit.*, FPA Series No. 2.

13. See Karl Deutsch, *Nationalism and Social Communication* (Cambridge, Mass.: Technology Press; New York: Wiley, 1953); and *Political Community at the International Level* (New York: Random House, 1954).

14. See below, Secs. 6 and 7.

15. This raises a number of issues which will have to be treated in the monograph referred to earlier.

16. Situational analysis is discussed in: Easton, *op. cit.*, Chap. 6; Lowell J. Carr, *Situational Analysis* (New York: Harper, 1948), pp. 1–38, 45–61, 90–100; Lawrence E. Cole, *Human Behavior* (Yonkers-on-Hudson, N.Y.: World Book Co., 1953), pp. 357–88; Dorwin Cartwright (ed.), Lewin's *Field Theory in Social Science* (New York: Harper, 1951), pp. 30–60, 238–304.

17. The terms "objective," "end," "goal," and "mission" are generally used interchangeably. There seem to be good reasons to employ the last named, but we will not press the distinction here. Only limited aspects of the concept of objective are covered here. Further analysis will be found under the headings: *Definition of the Decisional Unit and the Decision-Makers; Motivation.*

18. Cf. Arnold Wolfers, "National Security as an Ambiguous Symbol," *Political Science Quarterly,* 67 (December, 1952), 481–502.

19. Sec Wolfers, op. *cit.*

5. The Decision-Making Approach

1. Earlier in this essay we employed the term "system" in a somewhat looser sense. Here it is a key concept and we employ it in its specific analytic sense. See Parsons and Shils, op. *cit.*, p. 197, and Levy, *op. cit.*, pp. 19–22.

2. Consult the essay by Dwight Waldo, "Administrative Theory in the United States," *Political Studies,* Vol. II, No. 1 (February, 1954); Cf. W. E. Moore and R. C. Snyder, "The Conference on Theory of Organization," SSRC, *Items* (December, 1952).

3. W. E. Moore, Memorandum No. 5, Organizational Behavior Section, Princeton University, 1952. See also, *Organizational Behavior: Report on a Research Program,* Organizational Behavior Section, Princeton University, 1953, pp. 7–10.

4. See, however, Herbert A. Simon, *Administrative Behavior* (New York: Macmillan, 1947).

5. Most of the current work on the theory of choice is being done in economics, philosophy, and psychology. See references noted in connection with Section 7 below.

6. Edmund P. Learned, David N. Ulrich, and Donald R. Booz, *Executive Action* (Boston: Division of Research, Graduate School of Business Administration, Harvard University, 1951), p. 55.

7. See, for example, Harold Stein (ed.), *Public Administration and Policy Development* (New York: Harcourt, Brace & World, 1952).

8. James McCamy, *The Administration of American Foreign Affairs* (New York: Knopf, 1950); The Brookings Institution, *The Administration of Foreign Affairs and Overseas Operations* (Washington, 1951); Arthur W. Macmahon, *Administration in Foreign Affairs* (University, Ala.: University of Alabama Press, 1953).

9. We employ the term "projects" here because of the nature of our definition of decision-making and because more than a synonym for "objective" is needed.

10. "Event" is not used differently in this context than in connection with Diagram 4 except that here event refers to a unit-act in effect performed by many actors and corresponds to the definition of the situation.

11. The term is used in its social-psychological sense, not in the sense employed in the introductory section of this essay. The concept is defined below under motivational analysis.

12. In an earlier section we did not define the term *internal setting* beyond saying it referred in general to the *society or to the total social structure* in which the decision-makers function. Now we must note that internal setting really has two components: the total social structure *and the total governmental institutional structure* which is discussed immediately below.

13. This is consistent with our earlier formulation of the concept of setting which alerts the observer to factors which may become conditions of action for the decision-makers without their directly perceiving such factors in the usual sense.

14. A number of terms introduced in this classification will be defined and discussed below.

15. At numerous places we have said that further discussion must be deferred to our larger work. We have done so in order to get the main outlines of our scheme laid out as economically as possible without omitting anything crucial.

16. Our notion of "access" is discussed below under *communication and information* and *motivation*.

17. We have referred to this concept in connection with organizational theory, but here we refer to the fact that many students also call nonspecified relationships between any organization and its social setting informal.

18. This touches on the concept of rationality, discussion of which must also be deferred.

6. The Major Determinants of Action

1. See above the discussion of *Organizational Unit.*
2. Thus Philip Selznick's definition of informal as "deviations from the formal system (which) tend to become institutionalized" is quite closely related to our conventional category. See "Foundations of the Theory of Organization," *American Sociological Review,* 13 (February, l948), 27.
3. See *Wirtschaft und Gesellschaft* (1947), Pt. I, Chap. 1 and Pt. III, Chap. 5.
4. See *ibid.,* Pt. I, Chap. 3, Pt. III, Chaps. 7. 8, and 10.
5. *The Theory of Social and Economic Organization,* tr. A. M. Henderson and Talcott Parsons (New York: The Free Press of Glencoe, 1947), p. 116. This is a translation of Part I of *Wirtschaft und Gesellschaft.*
6. Rationality may here be defined as the selection of the most appropriate means to a given end after careful weighing of all available information.
7. See Alfred Schuetz, "Choosing among Projects of Action," *Philosophy and Phenomenological Research,* 12 (December, 1951), 161–84.
8. Philip Selznick, "An Approach to a Theory of Bureaucracy," *American Sociological Review,* 8 (February, 1943), 47–54.
9. For detailed discussion of these terms see Robert Merton, *op. cit.,* Chap. 1.
10. This point is expanded in the section on motivation.
11. *TVA and the Grass Roots* (Berkeley: University of California Press, 1949).
12. M. J. Levy, Jr., *op. cit.,* p. 332.
13. Merton, *op. cit.,* Chap. 1 and Levy, *op. cit.,* Chap. 2.
14. The range and nature of possible clusters of values and norms (i.e., ideology) which may govern the actor's interpretation of his competence are discussed below under motivation.
15. The observer has an option of including or excluding such roles so far as the unit and the communications net is concerned.
16. Sec Alfred Schuetz, *Der Sinnhafte Aufbau Der Sozialen Welt* (1932). "Sociology of knowledge" is here used in the sense of a *Verstehende Sociologie.*
17. For the meaning of intersubjective see above, section on the objective-subjective dichotomy.
18. Charles E. Redfield, *Communications in Management* (Chicago: University of Chicago Press, 1958), p. 7.
19. See below, section on motivation.
20. See "Communication Theory and Social Science," *American Journal of Orthopsychiatry,* 22 (July, 1952), 469–83, and "On Communications Models in the Social Sciences," paper presented at the Conference of Model Construction in the Social Sciences, sponsored by the Organizational Behavior Section, Princeton University at Princeton, N.J., March, 1952.
21. Harold Garfinkel, O.B.S., Memorandum No. 3, *Notes Toward A Sociological Theory of Information* (1952).

22. See, for example, the *path of action concept* discussed earlier.
23. As noted earlier, our approach on this point is not a widely accepted one in political science at the moment. The assumption is equally useful for the analysis of totalitarian regimes. Indeed, the discovery of similarities and differences between totalitarian and nontotalitarian regimes ought to be enhanced.
24. This is not to deny that policy-makers often talk as though the state or the decisional organization had an existence of its own.
25. Parsons and Shils, *op. cit.,* pp. 192–95.
26. Theodore Newcomb, *Social Psychology* (New York: Holt, Rinehart & Winston, 1950), p. 74.
27. Newcomb, *op. cit.,* pp. 74–75.
28. Seward, "Dialectic in the Psychology of Motivation," *Psychological Review,* 59 (1952), 406.
29. Newcomb, op. *cit.,* p. 96.
30. Motives may be acquired through canalization, i.e., needs become specific in consequence of being satisfied in specific ways.
31. Incompatibility of different means to the same end should not be regarded as motive conflict.
32. Hans Gerth and C. Wright Mills, *Character and Social Structure* (New York: Harcourt, Brace & World. 1953), Chap. 5.
33. *Op. cit.,* p. 113.
34. *Op. cit.,* p. 118.
35. Burton Sapin, Richard C. Snyder, and H. W. Bruck, *An Appropriate Role for the Military in American Foreign Policy-Making—A Research Note* (Foreign Policy Analysis Series No. 4, Organizational Behavior Section, Princeton University, July, 1954).
36. See below.
37. This ties in with a Hypothesis-Information Theory of Cognition being developed by Leo Postman and Jerome Bruner which we will discuss at a later time. See Leo Postman, "Toward a General Theory of Cognition," in John Rohrer and Muzafer Sherif (eds.), *Social Psychology At the Crossroads* (New York: Harper, 1951), pp. 242 ff.
38. This raises the whole question of the *evidence* which is to be accepted concerning motivation. Professor Harold Sprout has reminded us that legal interpretations of intent are relevant here. However, the problem will have to be treated at another time.
39. That is, as defined by the actors, not by the observer.
40. We are using Robin Williams' phrase here. See his *American Society* (New York: Knopf, 1951), pp. 372–442 for an informative treatment of values in general.
41. This important concept will be mentioned again later, but fuller discussion must be postponed.

42. This does *not* include, of course, *all* rationalizations, arguments, explanations, and so on, but only those which represent explicit wordings of basic shared values.

43. This is one of the places where motivational and communications analysis interconnect. See above the discussion of *Communications and Systems of Action* and *Communications and Authority*.

44. Merton, *op. cit.*, Chap. VII.

45. The technical term applied to composite analyses prepared by the Central Intelligence Agency. Such estimates refer to the strengths and weaknesses as well as the objectives of other nations.

46. We shall treat this concept in greater detail at another place. It applies not only to intellectual operations internal to the decisional unit but to external discussion in the setting as well. This is a more inclusive concept than that employed by Weber and which was cited above.

47. Acceptability may be defined in other ways, of course. Here we have in mind a broadly psychological phenomenon which includes feeling as well as reason.

7. Recapitulation

1. See Duncan Black and R. E. Newing, *Committee Decisions with Complementary Valuation* (London: Wittodge, 1951); Duncan Black, "On the Rationale of Group Decision-Making," *Journal of Political Economy*, 56 (February, 1948); 23–24; Kenneth J. Arrow, *Social Choice and Individual Values* (New York: Wiley, 1951); Felix E. Oppenheim, "Rational Choice," *The Journal of Philosophy*, 50 (June, 1953), 341–50.

The Scholarship of Decision-Making: Do We Know How We Decide?

Derek H. Chollet and James M. Goldgeier

In American political science, macro-level theories of world politics remain the predominant focus of international relations scholarship, whether these works involve realist arguments about the enduring nature of balance-of-power politics, liberal contentions about a democratic peace, or constructivist efforts to demonstrate the roles played by normative understandings. These political scientists seek to build theories of general patterns of behavior not from an analysis of individual behavior but, rather, from an understanding of factors such as relative military capabilities or domestic regime types or the strength of international institutions. Not satisfied with the ability of the grand theories to explain particular foreign policy choices made by particular decision-makers leading particular states faced with particular circumstances, other scholars have continued to probe the nature of foreign policy decision making at the micro level.

Forty years ago, Richard Snyder, H. W. Bruck, and Burton Sapin (henceforth SBS) argued that a bottom-up approach was needed for the study of international politics. But efforts to synthesize levels of analysis never developed in any sustained way. Kenneth Waltz's (1979) contention that international politics was a separate domain from foreign policy ruled the IR roost, and so those interested in decision-making focused on understanding processes of choice within national governments while leaving grand explanations for global affairs to the realists, neo-liberals, and later constructivists.

In the foreign policy literature, as Herbert McClosky (1956) correctly predicted, the pursuit of a single theory has proven to be a chimera. Instead, scholars have rightly pursued different factors that Snyder, Bruck, and Sapin were among the first to discuss—namely, bureaucratic politics, organizational routines, and individual psychology—to develop mid-range theories of how individuals, small groups, and institutions make choices.

Looking at current approaches in these areas, one realizes how far we have come. In psychology, for example, prospect theory is now widely accepted across a wide array of disciplines; scholars recognize that individuals react much differently to prospective gains than they do to prospective losses. Bureaucratic politics approaches have used detailed case studies to explore, test, and refine the hypothesis that where you stand depends on where you sit, and organization theory has deepened our knowledge of how standard operating procedures and organizational culture shape outcomes.

But these approaches also show how far we have to go. Despite many important insights, we still do not fully understand the essence of decision. We are still a long way from adequately capturing the interplay between domestic politics and bureaucratic politics. Moreover, the gap between what factors policy-makers consider important to determining outcomes and what outside analysts believe is important is still too wide—in fact, it has probably only gotten wider in the four decades since SBS first appeared. For example, outside analysts do a poor job of understanding in any systematic fashion the importance of individual relationships formed within governments as well as between them. And despite the centrality of prospect theory and of notions of "satisficing" and other ideas drawn from psychology to understand individual choices (especially in the field of behavioral economics), psychology is still too marginal to the field of international relations (Goldgeier, 1997; Goldgeier and Tetlock, 2001).

We do not argue that one can create a theory of international politics by starting from a decision-making perspective. In this sense, Waltz is right: understanding foreign policy is not the same as theorizing about international politics. Nor are we ignoring the fact that much of the foreign policy literature since SBS has tried to explain particular foreign policy decisions, contributing to knowledge about specific outcomes but not necessarily to grand theory. Nevertheless, over the past four decades, a large body of literature from political science, economics, and psychology has developed generalizable propositions to explain broad patterns of choice. And many of these generalizations are widely accepted and understood—among scholars as well as policy-makers.

Thus, we start where SBS left off and look at how themes they raised have led to the formulation of generalizable propositions regarding bureaucratic politics, organizational routines, or individual responses to the external environment. As McCloskey argued, the goal is to go from questions to hypotheses to testing and refinement in order to develop limited theories of behavior. And, over time, research has developed some core generalizable propositions about both behavior and process—even if there is not and probably will never be a general theory of decision-making (or, for that matter, international politics).

In addition to discussing the successful development of these generalizable propositions, we also want to discuss issues that SBS raised (and that anyone who has been involved in the decision-making process knows are important) but that scholars have not been able to develop in any systematic fashion. One is the problem of integrating individual and organizational levels of analysis: we need to know not only why people act the way they do but also what the outcome is of a number of individuals interacting in a process. In other words, it is one thing to understand how people act alone, but quite another to understand how they act together. A second is the influence of relationships and trust both within a government and between governments. Ask any policy-maker and they'll tell you that personal relationships and "trust" matter greatly to their perceptions, but for the most part scholars have ignored this factor. Two more issues are process based: the use of public communication not so much for sending signals but rather for settling intragovernment debates, and the role of policy entrepreneurship in shaping outcomes. A fifth is the need to understand the challenges of responding to new opportunities in the international system and how those differ from challenges posed by the rise of new threats to security. A sixth is the problem of isolation: all too often, scholars who study a decision process forget that the process was only one problem among many that a decision-maker was facing at the time; "failures" of decision-making are sometimes explained by inattention because of overwhelming demands within the system.

Finally, SBS remind us that analysis that focuses on crisis decision-making may well bias our understanding of the process and the explanations we develop. The literature on decision-making developed during the Cold War. And a chief foreign policy problem of the Cold War was the danger of crisis escalation. No crisis epitomized this problem as much as the one over Cuba in 1962, and scholars flocked to it. But as SBS point out, crises are likely atypical of the larger class of foreign policy problems, where time is not urgent and the stakes at each moment do not seem high. And in fact, it may be the routine decisions that are more important for long-term outcomes.

GENERALIZABLE PROPOSITIONS ABOUT BEHAVIOR

Much of the work on decision-making has focused on the issue of deviations from rationality and the resulting "suboptimal" outcomes. We tend to look at bureaucratic politics, standard operating procedures, the use of historical analogies, and so on, for how they skew a process away from the rational utility maximizing pursuit of the "national interest." This was the legacy of the generation that followed SBS: Graham Allison, Morton Halperin, and others explained the influence of bureaucracies and organizations, Robert Jervis helped bring psychology into IR, and so on. And following this scholarship, the policy relevant work has focused on how to minimize biases and improve one's ability to make decisions "rationally" (e.g., make sure you have a devil's advocate to minimize groupthink).

From a decision-making perspective, there are at least two problems with such approaches. First, while the behavior in question may result in "irrational" or "suboptimal" outcomes, it may be quite rational from an individual or organizational perspective. Government officials rationally pursue the self-interest of their agency; organizations cannot function effectively or efficiently without standard operating procedures; without the use of analogies or heuristics, leaders would be overwhelmed by information.

Therefore, rather than ask whether behavior is rational or irrational, it seems more fruitful to ask what kind of behavior is most likely under what conditions. Policy relevant work may still seek to minimize bias, but theoretical work should focus on understanding typical patterns of behavior.

For example, when we study the decision process in the U.S. Executive Branch, we often want to know whether or not the president trumped his bureaucracy. If he did, then we tend to argue that the national interest was served. John F. Kennedy's actions in the Cuban Missile Crisis are often held aloft as examples of how a strong and smart president can overpower the bureaucratic pulling and hauling beneath him. But if the bureaucracy stymies the president, or if the president is weak and indecisive and therefore lets the pulling and hauling whipsaw him, then we argue that turf battles hindered a rational pursuit of interest. Here, U.S. policy during the Vietnam War is usually the case in point. But what if the president has a really bad idea? For example, recently released tapes of Richard Nixon's private White House conversations show that the president mused casually with Henry Kissinger about using nuclear weapons in Vietnam—if he had actually done so, surely every analyst would justifiably call this an "irrational" outcome.[1] But even if it is usually considered more optimal for the country if the president wins rather than the bureaucracy, the theoretical question is under what conditions do presidents succeed in having their policies adopted—and then implemented?

Individual Behavior

The first step in addressing such questions is to understand how individuals make the choices they do. An early breakthrough for understanding choice was Herbert Simon's (1957, 1982) recognition that individuals do not have unlimited time, resources, and information to maximize their utilities. They may be rational, but that rationality is bounded. Rather than having the ability to weigh fully the pros and cons of all available options to make the optimal choice, *individuals satisfice*. We can be pretty confident that individuals will settle on the first acceptable option rather than continuing the search for something more optimal.

Decision-makers are trying to solve problems. And as Lindblom (1959) argued, the resulting tendency toward incrementalism is not only to be expected given cognitive limitations, it is smart policy. When faced with difficult situations—such as preventing or ending a war—an incremental step is often better than no step at all. Moreover, with incremental decisions, those making decisions can both test new policies better if they are just slightly different than preceding ones and not presented as "either-or" choices, and they can get a better sense of any unanticipated results.

Any student of negotiations like the 1978 Camp David Accords or the 1995 Dayton Peace Accords for Bosnia understands the pressures placed on policy-makers to satisfice in order to get results (Quandt, 1986; Holbrooke, 1998). Put simply, in many situations the optimal choice is not an option. This is particularly true in situations—such as Camp David and Dayton—in which policy-makers are working with complex, multiparty issues under intense pressure and tight deadlines, and when the stakes for failure are high (e.g., a return to bloodshed). Of course, with the benefits of hindsight, even the negotiators themselves can point to things that they could have done differently or lament missed opportunities, but as analysts trying to understand why they made the decisions they did, it is essential we try to understand the environment that bounded their framework of choice.

What we learned after Simon, developed in the International Relations field by scholars such as Jervis (1976), Deborah Larson (1985), and Yuen Foong Khong (1992), is that individuals, short on time and operating in uncertain environments marked by ambiguous information, rely on history and their own personal experiences to draw analogies for understanding how to operate in the current situation. If we want to understand why decision-makers picked a particular option, we need to know how they framed the situation. When approaching a problem, every policy-maker asks: Have we faced these circumstances before? What should we look out for? What worked or did not work before? Decision-makers draw lessons from history, and those lessons shape how they define what options are acceptable and these lessons can be from domestic politics (c.f. Goldgeier, 1994; Hemmer, 2000).

So, we know that individuals satisfice, and we know that they use analogies to interpret information. The psychologists Gigerenzer and Goldstein (1996) argue that Simon's notion of bounded rationality—in which this behavior is viewed as "adaptive within the constraints imposed *both* by the external situation and by the capacities of the decision maker" (Simon, 1985)—means that using heuristics, or "rules-of thumb" and shortcuts, is *not* nonrational behavior. Their experiments in fact show that making inferences in a "fast and frugal" way works pretty well in terms of outcomes, which is the opposite of what many IR scholars usually argue. "Models of inference," they argue (666), "do not have to forsake accuracy for simplicity. The mind can have it both ways."

What we want to understand in international relations is when does the use of analogies lead to better decisions and when does it lead decision-makers astray? (c.f. Neustadt and May, 1986) Sometimes analogies work; sometimes they don't. For example, in the days after Iraq's invasion of Kuwait in August 1990, many U.S. policy-makers (as well as many of their counterparts abroad) warned of repeating "Munich." They believed that Saddam Hussein, like Hitler in 1938, was determined to change the status quo and would not be satisfied by appeasement. Therefore, the prescription drawn from the Munich analogy was that the U.S.- led coalition had to "draw a line in the sand" and stand up against Saddam to roll back his ambitions. Although the use of the Munich analogy in this case was a powerful justification for action to push Saddam out of Kuwait, its usefulness was limited. President George H. W. Bush frequently compared Saddam to Hitler, but he did not follow through on the same conclusion: overthrowing Saddam and occupying and rebuilding Iraq. Once Kuwait was liberated and Saddam's Republican Guard troops were on the run, other historical analogies—ones that taught the costs of occupation and insurgency warfare, such as the Soviet experience in Afghanistan in the 1980s—became more powerful, and policy-makers decided not to push action.

Historical analogies also influenced the way U.S. leaders approached problems of ethnic conflict during the 1990s—and, more often than not, these efforts at analogical reasoning led leaders astray. Richard Holbrooke

(1998), Samantha Power (2002) and others have described the power of Vietnam and of the 1993 disaster in Somalia, in which soldiers were ambushed and killed, on shaping U.S. actions (or inaction) in places such as Bosnia and Rwanda. The lesson many Washington policy-makers took from these events—which Holbrooke describes as the "Vietmalia syndrome," and many called "quagmire"—was that some situations were simply too tough, too intractable, and too dangerous for America to get involved, and that therefore U.S. interests did not warrant military intervention. As Holbrooke describes it (216), "[T]wo less pleasant memories still hung like dark clouds over the Pentagon. Phrases like 'slippery slope' and 'mission creep' were code for specific events that had traumatized the military and the nation; Mogadishu, which hung over our deliberations like a dark cloud; and Vietnam, which lay further back, in the inner recesses of our minds."

In addition to better understanding the mental tools policy-makers use to make decisions, we've also gained great insight into common ways policy-makers perceive (or misperceive) situations or behavior. A large body of work has shown that decision-makers are predisposed to attribute cooperative behavior by adversaries as situationally induced, and to see conflictual behavior by adversaries as dispositionally induced, what is known as the "fundamental attribution error" (c.f. Mercer, 1996). Part of the problem is that, as the choice literature has demonstrated, individuals are not natural Bayesians, in which the accuracy or strength of a perception is repeatedly tested and adjusted by new evidence; they are slow to adjust to new information (Edwards, 1962; Tetlock, 1998, 1999). The tendency toward making fundamental attribution errors combined with the problem of slowness in updating leads to the generalizable proposition that decision-makers more often miscategorize status quo powers as expansionist (Type I errors) than they miscategorize expansionist powers as status quo (Type II errors) (Jervis, 1976; Goldgeier and Tetlock, 2001).

Consider the "pause of 1989" in U.S. policy toward Gorbachev's Soviet Union and *perestroika* and *glasnost*. Many leading figures in the Reagan Administration—in particular, Secretary of State George P. Shultz—were astonished that the new administration of George H. W. Bush did not recognize in January 1989 that the Cold War was over and Gorbachev was "for real." But Bush's National Security Adviser Brent Scowcroft was concerned that Gorbachev was simply lulling the West to sleep. Given his own experiences with failed détente in the 1970s, Scowcroft had the attitude of "once burned, twice shy": he perceived Gorbachev's actions as situationally induced, and did not believe that he was a new type of Soviet leader. And, as policy-makers such as Scowcroft now admit, they were slow to change this view. It took an entire year to get the new administration comfortable with the notion that the Soviet Union was a different beast than the one they had known previously (Chollet and Goldgeier, 2003).

Perhaps most powerfully from an experimental standpoint, we know that in general, individuals are more risk-acceptant when they find themselves in the domain of losses and more risk-averse when dealing with gains (Kahneman and Tversky, 1979, 1984). Individuals are also prone to the endowment effect: something increases in value to you after you possess it. Experimental results in the psychological literature suggests that prospective gains need to be twice as large as prospective losses to be of commensurate value from the standpoint of risk-taking. Framing issues and choices as involving potential losses or gains thus becomes crucial to the conduct of foreign policy as well as to notions of fairness: there is a bias toward the status quo (Kahneman et al., 1991; Goldgeier and Tetlock, 2001; Levy, 1992, 1996; Farnham, 1997; McDermott, 1998).

The fate of Kosovo during the 1990s serves as an especially tragic example of such thinking. In retrospect, it is quite clear that the Serbian dictator Slobodan Milosevic was willing to accept considerable punishment in order not to "lose" Kosovo and to rid it of Albanian Muslims. In fact, the West's policy toward Milosevic would have been better informed if it had taken into account the lessons from prospect theory; many U.S. policy-makers assumed he would not be willing to endure significant costs to continue his policy toward Kosovo. But Milosevic clearly was willing to accept considerable risk—and endure considerable punishment—to keep from "losing" Kosovo. Drawing lessons from Bosnia, where Milosevic was forced to withdraw support for his local allies because of political, economic, and eventually military pressure from the United States and Europe, was unhelpful precisely because, for Milosevic, Bosnia was in the domain of potential gains, whereas Kosovo was squarely in the domain of potential losses. Those who thought he would back down in Kosovo because he did in Bosnia missed the significant difference in how the two cases were framed and thus Milosevic's resulting risk-taking propensities.

The Foreign Policy Process

Much in SBS is a precursor to later analyses of bureaucratic politics or small group dynamics. They cite as possible individual motives "rewards appropriate to position . . . role expectations . . . unwillingness to appear ignorant or unorthodox . . . a desire not to impair continuing contacts or friendships."

There has been a significant debate over time regarding the role of organizational position versus prior beliefs for shaping individual attitudes and behavior in the decision process. For the rank and file, the notion that *where you stand depends on where you sit* is fairly generalizable. Individual preferences are shaped by organizational role. For the most part, office directors in the Treasury Department recommend different policies than office directors in the State Department (Allison, 1971; Allison and Halperin, 1972; Halperin, 1974; Allison and Zelikow, 1999).

Understanding how individuals at these levels are likely to behave is useful not just for studying the process; it is useful for those who participate in the process. Bureaucrats themselves understand well how predicting other bureau and agency behavior is valuable for working the process on the inside. One knows precisely where State or the Department of Defense (DOD) or Treasury is likely to be, and this arms one with the knowledge of how to push forward a particular project.

For example, when then-Deputy Secretary of Defense William J. Perry and Assistant Secretary of Defense Ashton Carter sought to pursue the safe and secure dismantlement of Russian nuclear weapons in 1993, they immediate recognized a structural problem. The funds authorized and appropriated for such use—the so-called Nunn-Lugar money—was at that point drawn from existing Pentagon budgets rather than having its own appropriation. They understood that no existing unit in the Pentagon would support taking money from its programs for this endeavor, and they pushed to get separate appropriations as the only way to build support within their own building. And so they did (Carter and Perry, 1999).

What is important to recognize is that while the literature on decision-making focuses on the suboptimal outcomes that are supposedly produced by individuals acting not in the name of national interest but, rather, to protect their bureaucratic turf and therefore emphasizes departures from a "rational actor" norm, the behavior of these individuals is quite rational indeed (Allison and Halperin, 1972). These individuals are part of a competitive process: they want to maintain the flow of resources for their programs, they want to look good to their superiors (who come from within their agency), and they are the products of particular institutional cultures (e.g., military, foreign service, developmental economists).

We thus have a good sense of the kind of bureaucratic pressures at lower levels that produce predictable behavior. In many ways, these behaviors are as predictable and probabilistic as the notion that international power structures induce balancing among states. This does not mean that it makes no difference who staffs a given position. But that is just as true when we are talking about the pressures imposed by international structures. And again, not only can outside observers expect to see the pursuit of bureaucratic behavior at lower levels, but those inside the system base their own behavior on expectations about what "State" or "Treasury" or "DOD" is likely to pursue.

Organizations rely on Standard Operating Procedures to make decisions as routine as possible (Allison, 1971; Perrow, 1984; Sagan, 1995). They have to. It allows them to function but reduces flexibility in ways that can be downright frightening (Sagan, 1995). But, as Bendor and Hammond (1992) have noted, how one understands organizational routines depends on the benchmark. They argue that if one assumes that individuals are boundedly rational, then organizations are required for dealing with technically challenging problems. Thomas Carothers (1999) has described well how those in the U.S. foreign policy bureaucracy in the 1990s had to have a template for democracy promotion around the world; developing country-specific strategies would have been impossible for those responsible in the functional bureaus responsible for these issues. But, as he also points out, pushing the same general policy in different countries with different political cultures led to less than optimal outcomes in many cases.

It would seem that we have a fairly good handle on how bureaucrats and organizations typically behave. What has proven problematic is explaining individual choices at the highest levels of government. Most of the critiques about individual choices in foreign policy argue: first, that at these higher levels, shared beliefs of the president and his adviser matter a great deal; and, second, there is a clear hierarchy in the process: presidents trump bureaucracies (Art, 1973; Ball, 1974; Krasner, 1972; Steel, 1972; Snyder and Diesing, 1977; Welch, 1992; Bendor and Hammond, 1992; Hammond and Thomas, 1989; Goldgeier, 1999).

One reason for this critique was that, in the 1970s, many opponents of U.S. involvement in Vietnam worried that arguments about bureaucratic pulling and hauling producing policy let the president off the hook for the policy disaster. But, from a theoretical standpoint, the more important question is: When does the president matter and when does he not?

On this score, Art's (1973) argument is pretty clear cut: on the really important decisions, it is the president and his politics that matter most, not the bureaucracy. And what scholars care about are the really big decisions. Art's argument about LBJ and his decision to pursue a missile defense system is as true today with George W. Bush as it was then: LBJ wanted to pursue a system; he did not care about the details. Bush entered office politically and ideologically determined to pursue missile defense and jettison the Anti-Ballistic Missile Treaty. The particular technology that emerges (subject to bureaucratic politics and industry lobbying) will be less important to him. And, after all, the big decision was the one to go forward.

The power of the president can be seen in those cases in which most individuals in the bureaucracy opposed a policy that was adopted anyway because the president favored it. For example, when the United States began in 1994 developing a policy to enlarge NATO into Central and Eastern Europe, there were very few supporters inside the Executive Branch. Had the president opposed enlargement, that policy never could have gotten off the ground (even with some in Congress pushing it). That case is even more interesting than many because within the bureaucracy, leading policy proponents were entrepreneurial in arguing to opponents that the president supported enlargement, even if his views were neither well known nor well defined for some time. But again, if the president had opposed the policy, it would not have been adopted, either by the United States or by NATO (Goldgeier, 1999).

That case and others also raise the question of how we understand the role of presidential politics in shaping decisions. A standard two-level game approach (Putnam, 1988) collapses bureaucratic and domestic politics into one level. But these are very different issues (Mayer, 1998). And understanding how to integrate what Kingdon (1995) calls the "policy and political streams" is not an easy task. Those working in government understand that presidential politics are much more relevant for the daily business of officials on the National Security Council staff (who serve the president) as opposed to those officials working in the Cabinet agencies. Even those who are political appointees in an agency like the State Department usually come to believe their job is to make *their* boss (i.e., the Secretary of State) look good.

Combining Individual and Structural levels

One of the major problems for understanding foreign policy behavior is that understanding individual choices is only part of the problem. There remains the question of how outcomes emerge, particularly if they do so as a bargaining process. There are several ways to look at the problem. One is to consider the pros and cons of different types of presidential management styles, which George (1980) labels formalistic, competitive and collegial. No one approach is cost-free, and each leads to different tendencies for the decision process. The formalistic approach, for example, utilizes a hierarchic structure to conserve the president's time and to provide for a more orderly process, but that same hierarchy can distort the information that reaches him more than the other two approaches.

Another is to focus on the problem of small group dynamics. Groups tend to stifle dissent in order to reach decisions, but reaching decisions can be crucial for busy presidents and supporting him can be important for his confidence. Janis (1982: 9) defined groupthink as occurring "when the members' strivings for unanimity override their motivation to realistically appraise alternative courses of action." He cited eight symptoms of group-think, including an "illusion of vulnerability" that increases risk-taking; efforts to rationalize in order to discount information that might lead to reopening of the question; and self-censorship.

But group-think does not always occur, and what we want to know is when certain structures or political cultures cause more self-critical information processing, thus attenuating typical biases (and of course, which types of structures or institutional cultures exacerbate bias). Here, a key issue is accountability pressure, which is why the policy proposals coming out of the decision literature focus on issues like multiple advocacy or mechanisms to minimize groupthink (George, 1980; Janis, 1982; Tetlock et al., 1992). A second is the pressure of competitive market settings. The more open the game is in which players are interacting, with high degrees of transparency and repeated play, the more that the punishment for bias should be clear to those who might tend to stray (Kagel and Roth, 1995; Camerer and Hogarth, 1999). The extreme version of this is Thomas Friedman's (1999) argument about economic globalization, in which swift moving electronic herds impose a "golden straitjacket" on decision-makers. If you miscalculate, you'll find out pretty quickly, because billions of dollars will move out of your country that day (Goldgeier and Tetlock, 2001).

Finally, we need to consider ways in which "errors" in international politics may be smart from the standpoint of states wishing to survive in the international system. Let's revisit the problem of attribution error and Scowcroft's slowness in not understanding the Gorbachev phenomenon as early as others. That the bias occurred is quite predictable from a choice perspective. But that bias also may be an "adaptive error" in international politics, since the penalties for being wrong can be so severe. Is it not better to miscast a status quo power as expansionist and lose an opportunity than be fooled into believing an expansionist power is merely interested in the status quo, and suffer great loss? Unless one ends up in a spiral of escalation, then the answer is yes from a decision-maker's perspective (Tetlock and Goldgeier, 2000; Goldgeier and Tetlock, 2001; Chollet and Goldgeier, 2003).

A NEW AGENDA: FIVE AREAS TO EXPLORE

With the benefit of four decades of hindsight, it is clear that SBS set the foundation for much of the subsequent research of foreign policy decision-making. Looking back, scholars can be satisfied that as a field of research, decision-making analysis has proved extraordinarily fruitful. The academy has established not just a vast body of knowledge about what shaped critical decisions in American foreign policy, but developed a set of generalizable propositions about how decisions are made.

Yet, as we hope the above discussion has made clear, the more we think we've learned about decision-making, the more we need to know. In fact, once one really stops to consider how difficult it is to fully understand the process of human decision-making—and the complex roles that psychology, history, sociology, economics, and personality all play—it is easy to see why so many political scientists are happy not to look inside the "black boxes" and instead choose to spend their careers thinking abstractly about billiard balls and balances of power. But given this complexity, and the fact that there will always be new decisions to explain and understand, there is every reason to hope that the future of decision-making studies can be as fruitful as its past. For those scholars willing to forge ahead in the tradition that SBS helped pioneer, there are many areas to explore, including: (1) the interplay between cognition and emotion; (2) personal relations and trust; (3) the role of speeches and policy entrepreneurs in the policy process; (4) perceiving opportunities; and (5) the role of time constraints on decision-making.

Cognition and Emotion

Drawing from psychology, we now understand a great deal about the role of cognition and emotion in decisions. But we need to do better at understanding the interplay between the two. This is not unique to political scientists: even cognitive psychologists tend to try to factor out emotional variables in their research. As Lebow (1982) and others (e.g., Crawford, 2000) have taught us, decision-makers may develop biases not simply because they are rationally bounded from a cognitive standpoint, but also because they are motivated to certain kinds of behavior for emotional reasons. Many prominent scholars have explored the relationship between "motivated" biases (when people's preferences or opinions motivate them to interpret information to be consistent with their views) and "unmotivated" biases (when people's theory-driven beliefs about how the world works influence their interpretations), but much more work needs to be done to understand under what conditions these biases operate—and how they operate together (Jervis, Lebow, and Stein, 1985).

To get a sense of the challenge of sorting out what is cognitive and what is emotion, let's return to the case of Saddam Hussein's Iraq, and the first Bush Administration's controversial failure to deter Saddam from invading Kuwait prior to August 1990. The prevailing explanation for this failure is the first Bush Administration's belief that its policy of "engagement"—trying to influence the Iraqi dictator's behavior by providing him carrots like economic ties and trade—was the best policy (Jentleson, 1994). The central strategic assumption of U.S. policy toward Iraq was that Iraqi actions could be influenced by engagement with incentives; Saddam Hussein, while brutal, could be encouraged to play a moderate, constructive role in the region (such as supporting the Arab-Israeli peace process). Once the engagement policy was adopted, policy-makers stuck with it, even as evidence mounted that the approach might not be working. The desire to avoid difficult trade-offs, or justify the policy to support other priorities, proved powerful. Once U.S. policy-makers adopted a specific image of Iraq, they were motivated to interpret behavior as being consistent with that image, and therefore failed to understand Saddam's true intentions or act to deter him.

Usually the story ends there. But what is both interesting and normally ignored is that, prior to August 1990, Saddam's behavior (including statements about "burning" Israel with chemical weapons and threatening Kuwait) was so egregious that most Washington policy-makers overcame their emotional bias toward engagement. In fact, what influenced their decisions in the days leading up to the August 2 invasion of Kuwait were not the "motivated biases" discussed above, but policy-makers' core assumptions about behavior and rationality—the cognitive "unmotivated bias." When policy-makers held a firm conception of a policy approach, their motivation to adhere to this led them to a sort of policy inertia; when this inertia was largely broken and policy-makers were left without their road map, unmotivated assumptions dominated their thinking. American policy-makers believed that the United States and Iraq were caught in a security dilemma, assuming that Iraq was defensively minded but would interpret any U.S. action as offensive, sparking a conflict spiral.

The perception of a security dilemma illustrates the difficulties policy-makers face when choosing whether to pursue a strategy of deterrence or reassurance. It is extraordinarily difficult to determine whether one's opponent is a like-minded state trapped in a security dilemma or an aggressor state with expansionist intentions. As explained earlier, we should expect the problem is more often that leaders mischaracterize a status quo state as expansionist rather than the reverse. But August 1990 was one of those cases in which policy-makers in Washington and, important, throughout the Arab world, actually believed that an expansionist power was status quo. That is one reason why the United States never really tried to deter Saddam and instead pursued a strategy of restraint and reassurance. If the United States acted tough, it was afraid it would spark the exact response it sought to avoid.

This is only one example of how cognition and emotion interact to shape policy-makers' perceptions. It is not surprising to find such factors present: almost any decision could be analyzed in the same way. Scholars should therefore continue to probe the questions of under what circumstances emotion trumps cognition (or vice versa), and explore what kinds of generalizations can be made about the roles cognition and emotion play when policy-makers confront particular challenges.

Personal Relations and Trust

A second area to be explored is the importance of personal relationships and trust both within government and between governments. These are areas of decision-making analyses that most policy-makers regard as indispensable but most scholars ignore. Decision-makers intuitively understand the importance of personal relationships and trust. They refer to these issues all the time publicly, privately, and with one another. Scholars intuitively understand this, too—just ask faculty members how decisions get made in their own department—but not when explaining the making of foreign policy. Indeed, one of the first challenges any leader faces in foreign policy is his or her ability to interact constructively with diplomatic counterparts. As former U.S. Defense Secretary James R. Schlesinger observed, "a belief that slowly overcomes all presidents after they are in office [is] that personal relationships are more important than they seemed before they are in office. They become less interested in what their subordinates call the fundamentals of a relationship, and more interested in what other leaders tell them."[2] Sour personal relations, Harold Nicolson (1939) noted long ago, diminish the chances for cooperation even when mutual interests are at stake.

In recent years, some scholars have explored the role of "trust" and "distrust" in shaping policy-makers' perceptions. For the most part, such research has focused on how trust enhances the chances for cooperation, or how distrust might explain why opportunities were missed (Larson, 1997). But such research, while important, has not done enough to explore the ways trust actually develops—or in some cases fails to develop—between policy-makers. Such a contribution would be valued for both its contributions to our theories about trust as well as for its policy-relevance.

Work that has been done on trust in organizations has demonstrated that these relations typically evolve in several phases. Trust first begins as a set of simple cost-benefit calculations. Decision-makers gauge the shadow of the future and try to minimize the costs of being wrong. What gets interesting is how they then go from this initial "feeling out" period to internalization, which develops through personal experience and direct communication, and create "knowledge-based" trust (Kramer and Tyler, 1996).

Developing trust through personal relations can have a profound effect on policy outcomes. Again consider the "pause of 1989" in the first Bush Administration's policy toward Gorbachev. A close examination of the history of that period shows that lack of personal relations was one of the reasons for the "pause," and that developing strong personal relations was a critical factor for trust developing between Americans policy-makers and their Soviet counterparts. The inability of truly understanding the Soviets personally caused American policy-makers to interpret concessions as cynical efforts to cooperating to compete.

But as they met their counterparts and established a personal basis for interaction, U.S. officials felt they could better understand Soviet leaders' motives. They started to empathize with them, and saw first hand that Soviet promises were credible—that their deeds could match their words. Personal relations gave U.S. policy-makers more "knowledge" to base their perceptions. Significantly, different U.S. policy-makers came to trust Gorbachev's intentions at different times. And this strongly correlates with the development of personal relations. Secretary of State James Baker, for instance, came to trust the Soviets sooner than his colleagues, primarily because of the personal relationship he developed with his counterpart, Eduard Shevardnadze. On the other hand, President George H. W. Bush and Brent Scowcroft did not have the opportunity to develop personal relations with Gorbachev until several months later, and were therefore slower to believe that Gorbachev was "for real" (Chollet and Goldgeier, 2003).

This process serves as an example of a positive outcome: personal relationships helped build trust, which in turn enhanced cooperation. But at the same time, one could argue that under different circumstances, personal relationships and trust can lead to negative outcomes. For example, many believe that the interpersonal trust established between Bush and Gorbachev later impeded the U.S. Administration from understanding the depth of Soviet change, the unpopularity of Gorbachev, and the importance of Russian president Boris Yeltsin. According to this argument, the Bush Administration became so enamored of Gorbachev that it missed the true dimensions of Soviet change both prior to and after the failed August 1991 coup. In this sense, while the *absence* of strong interpersonal relations and trust caused U.S. leaders to miss opportunities for cooperation in 1989, the *presence* of interpersonal relations and trust blinded U.S. leaders from a different set of opportunities in 1991–1992. And this is not just a problem with the first Bush Administration: analysts have made the same arguments to criticize President Bill Clinton's or George W. Bush's embrace of leaders such as Boris Yeltsin and Vladimir Putin, claiming that the "overpersonalization" of relations colored Washington's understanding of Russian intentions, causing the United States to make bad decisions.

Finally, one could argue that even though two leaders might know each other well, this does not mean that it necessarily enhances trust or cooperation. Put simply, some leaders, like some people, just might not like each other—and the more they get to know each other, the more the dislike grows. In some cases, there is such a thing as knowing someone too well. It is very unlikely that such relationships would lead to conflict, but often the case that they might make cooperation more difficult. But regardless of the outcomes personal relationships and trust lead to, at least one fact is clear: they matter, and the decision-making literature would be stronger if it took such issues into account.

Speech-making as Policy-making

In addition to understanding better what shapes beliefs in the heads of decision-makers, there are still important aspects of the policy-making process that have to be explored further. One area is the role of public communication, particularly speech-making. Typically, scholars have studied foreign policy speeches from a communications perspective—exploring how they are used to convey signals or even as data points (by studying words or phrases used) to derive policy-maker beliefs. But speech-making should be recognized as a critical part of the foreign policy process. Any close study of high-level decision-making shows that senior officials—Presidents, Cabinet officials, National Security aides—spend an enormous amount of time and energy planning, creating, editing, debating, and delivering public speeches. But few scholars actually study this. In many instances, the process of speech-making is the one in which decisions get made—even whether all the players know it at the time or not. Therefore, scholars must consider speeches important not just for sending signals to others, but for agenda-setting and settling intra-government debates at home.

Like trust and personal relations, the role of speeches in foreign policy is an area in which most policy-makers understand the importance. Two recent Secretaries of State, Henry Kissinger and Warren Christopher, have written about speechwriting as a process. Both agree that while the ostensible importance of speeches is the ways they influence external audiences, they are frequently even more important for the ways they send signals to the bureaucracy and serve as vehicles for bureaucratic fighting and settling internal debates. In Warren Christopher's four-part typology for the uses of foreign policy speeches, the "bureaucratic" purpose of a speech is important because the "drafting of a speech almost always reveals the differences among the bureaus of the [State] Department, and the clearance process outside the Department frequently involves sharp and illuminating clashes with other elements of the government" (Christopher, 1998: 9; see also Kissinger, 1977). Christopher—himself a former speechwriter for California Governor Edmund G. Brown—has made the case for speechwriting's role in policy-making so strongly that he is worth quoting at length:

> Policy debates [are] the lifeblood of government. . . . [but] in any given week as Secretary, I received dozens of memoranda advocating various particular policy directions. However persuasive their contents, they did not constitute U.S. policy unless they were incorporated into a speech, public statement or formal government document. The challenge of articulating a position publicly compels leaders to make policy choices. Often decisions on what to do and what to say publicly are made simultaneously. The process of speech preparation is one of the most overlooked aspects of foreign policy decision-making (Christopher, 1998: 9–10).

Policy-makers may tend to stand where they sit, but just as often, deciding what to say determines where they stand.

In the policy world, speeches are often seen as action-forcing events that serve as endpoints for internal debates. To a certain extent, this is intuitive: when forced to articulate a policy publicly, senior policy-makers are forced to clarify their objectives and justify their actions. Deciding what to say (or not to say) therefore becomes a policy decision. For example, the question of whether or not U.S. policy-makers highlight human rights issues in statements about China is a policy decision about how important such issues will be to the relationship. Or the decision to use a speech to make public demands against another actor is, obviously, a policy decision to influence behavior. As Christopher explains it, speeches were "valuable tools of day-to-day diplomacy . . . statements made on the public record were often more effective and credible than private ones" (Christopher, 1998: 9).

More often than not, leaders see major speeches as opportunities to announce specific policy initiatives—and in preparing the speech, the bureaucracy is sent scrambling to come up with meaty "deliverables" to be announced. The most famous of these, of course, is a president's annual State of the Union message before the Congress. But statements made on the public record are also used by skillful bureaucratic players to push their policy agendas ahead. For example, in the Clinton Administration's effort to enlarge NATO during the early 1990s, senior officials such as National Security Adviser Anthony Lake understood that if they could convince the president to say that NATO would expand, then they could command the bureaucratic struggle over the issue. The question over enlargement would be, as Clinton famously put it in early 1994, a question of "not whether but when," and this would shape the internal debate (Goldgeier, 1999).

But getting Clinton to utter words like these was only the beginning. Over the next few years, U.S. officials used speeches to push the NATO enlargement process forward. As Christopher reflected (1998: 10), "The calendar for [NATO] meetings forced the Administration to make decisions. Once we had done so, I used the speeches to chart a course for our Alliance partners, such as by setting timelines for future decisions." Frequently, speeches were used to create a reality that the bureaucracy had to respond to. As discussed above, NATO enlargement's proponents used the president's statements as weapons against their bureaucratic opponents, brandishing these words as evidence that a policy decision had been made, when in fact one had never been determined through any formal inter-agency process.

The highly motivated individuals who use speeches as a tool for surmounting bureaucratic lethargy or opposition in order to win bureaucratic battles are what John Kingdon (1995) has called "policy entrepreneurs." These entrepreneurs can come from outside the formal government structures as well as inside but, in either case, they use good access to key decision-makers as well as a strong commitment to an issue to outmaneuver others (Goldgeier, 1999; Daalder, 2000).

Therefore, major foreign policy speeches deserve more scholarly attention both as policy processes to be understood and as tools individuals use to win bureaucratic fights. There have been numerous nonscholarly accounts of the role of speeches in policy-making—such as the excellent recent books by Peggy Noonan (1999), Michael Waldman (2000), and Benjamin Barber (2001)—but these tend to be mostly memoirs and anecdotal. Scholars should give the speech-making process systematic attention. Such research will benefit decision-making scholarship for at least two reasons: first, because it is a part of the decision-making process that has been heretofore ignored; and, second, because it will bring scholarly research that much closer to understanding the decision-making process in government.

Perceiving Opportunities

More attention must also be paid to how policy-makers respond to new opportunities as opposed to new threats. When scholars study "mistakes" in international relations, they often focus on the failure to identify threats, since the inability to balance rising powers adequately often has such harsh consequences. The buck-passing of the 1930s, for example, is widely credited with allowing Hitler to unleash military aggression that the West might have checked at far lower cost several years before the attack on Poland. But, fortunately, even the most Hobbesian analysts would agree that the world is not made up solely of threats; it is also full of opportunities. And, just as policy-makers can suffer the costs of misperceiving threats, their perceptions also can get in the way of taking advantage of opportunities.

For example, the end of the Cold War and the West's tentative reaction to the Soviet Union's transformation is one such case. This raises the theoretical issue of the failure to take advantage of opportunities that arise when countries that have formerly posed threats now seem open to accommodation. These missed opportunities pit different theoretical issues against one another: the psychological constraints on processing new information correctly versus the structural constraints on responding to conciliatory behavior. Studying missed opportunities is also more difficult because unlike those cases of misperception of threat, in which the penalties for failure are obvious, it is less clear what tangible benefits would occur if only decision-makers had understood their new and improved environment sooner (Chollet and Goldgeier, 2003).

Understanding Time Constraints

Finally, scholars of decision-making still need to do better at understanding that senior government leaders are pressed for time and forced to deal with many urgent decisions every day. This is a call to understand the context of decision. Snyder, Bruck, and Sapin referred to this as the problem of "simultaneity." As they explained it, " . . . Simultaneity grows out of the fact that no state engages in separate, isolated actions, with one following the other in chronological sequence. Within governments a number of actions are being decided upon and implemented at the same moment in time. Between states a number of interactions coexist." All too often, they argued, scholars tend to discuss "examples and cases as though these were all that was happening." This brings real costs to understanding why decisions were made. As Snyder, Bruck, and Sapin put it, "the burden of simultaneous responses to external demands may be a crucial determinant in the timing of actions and the nature or amount of policymaking resources which are devoted to specific actions."

Anyone with senior government experience understands the stressful realities of simultaneity. If there are any doubts, just consider the daily schedule of high level policy-makers. From dawn until dusk, they confront a wide array of issues and decisions to be made. In his memoir of his years as President Jimmy Carter's National Security Adviser, Zbiginew Brzezinski (1983) reprints one day of his schedule. One can see that nearly every minute is occupied by meetings and discussions on an extraordinarily diverse set of issues. Even in times of crisis, decisions must be made on seemingly "less important" issues and, in retrospect, these decisions might become more important than they seemed at the time. For example, in the spring of 1994, the Clinton Administration was seized with the Bosnia crisis, and therefore did not pay as much attention to the genocide in Rwanda as it otherwise might have (Power, 2002).

The simultaneity challenge is obviously not only restricted to foreign policy questions—Presidents also must face domestic decisions as well. An example of this is the account of President Lyndon Johnson's decisions on Vietnam during the summer of 1965. In an excellent study of these crucial deliberations, Larry Berman (1983) reconstructs the decision-making process among LBJ and his top advisers that led to the increase of U.S. troops deployed to Vietnam. In Berman's account, it is very easy to see the decision-making process as a linear narrative. But in re-reading his account alongside the transcripts of LBJ's telephone calls during the same period (Beschloss, 2001), one gets the sense of an even more complex story: a president who is grappling with many issues at the same time, from domestic politics to personnel questions to civil rights to Berlin to Vietnam. What's said in these telephone calls does not refute any of Berman's key insights, but it does give analysts a better sense of the pressures placed on these policy-makers during this important period. Making choices seems hard enough when we treat them as the only choices to be made—but when we consider how policy-makers deal with many worries and decisions simultaneously, we better appreciate the full context of decision.

Also, scholars and policy-makers alike will be wise to remember what Jervis (1976) and others have argued: that other leaders are often focused on their own troubles or different issues, rather than foreign policy. This is a kind of an attribution-error problem—we assume that others' actions are governed by foreign policy reasons or in response to our actions, but in fact they are guided by other unrelated factors like domestic politics.

The challenge of simultaneity was true when Snyder, Bruck, and Sapin pointed it out 40 years ago. But it is even more of a challenge as information and resources become even more available. Visit any senior policy-maker's office, and one will be impressed by the overwhelming information resources at their disposal, giving them real time information on just about every problem in the world. On their computers alone, modern policy-makers have access to thousands of classified cables from hundreds of embassies around the world, as well as intelligence reports and classified e-mail. And this is in addition to traditional stacks of paper memos, intelligence, and aides buzzing in and out for oral briefings. Add to this multiple telephones, a humming fax machine, a split-screen television continuously tuned in to every 24-hour news network, the Internet, unclassified e-mails, a coffee table lined with every major news-magazine and newspaper, and instant messaging through hand computers, and it's a wonder that policy-makers can concentrate on any one thing at all.

Scholars have just begun to understand how this influences decision-making. Foreign policy analysts (and former policy-makers) such as Joseph Nye (2002) have discussed this "paradox of plenty," in which a "plenitude of information lead to a poverty of attention." It is very hard for policy-makers to focus when in an environment with so much information. In modern policy-making, as Nye explains it (67), "attention rather than information becomes the scarce resource, and those who can distinguish valuable signals from white noise gain power."

All this reminds scholars that they must do more to understand the context of decision: more care must be taken to get the fullest sense of the policy-making environment—what sort of other choices they are facing, what other pressures they are under, and what kind of information they are getting. A policy-maker's attention and intellectual resources are finite. How they grapple with time pressures and simultaneity will therefore continue to be a necessary (and fruitful) area of research.

ANOTHER 40 YEARS OF SNYDER, BRUCK, AND SAPIN . . . AND BEYOND

Snyder, Bruck, and Sapin began their landmark work by explaining that they "would be more than satisfied if our effort stimulates others in a modest fashion and if it provides a point from which more accurate bearings could be taken." By every measure, they succeeded. The study of decision-making has proved to be more than a fad: although often forced into the academy's back seat by structural theorizing or formal modeling, studies of decision-making have been indispensable to our understanding of foreign policy outcomes. But, at the same time, more must be done to assure that decision-making scholarship is better integrated into our understanding of international politics. Recall the full title of SBS: "Decision-Making as an Approach to the Study of International Politics." What we want in fact is to integrate propositions about decision-making in specific situations with larger structural factors in international politics to generalize about behavior. Scholars should therefore continue to refine propositions about individual behavior under certain conditions and within certain structures.

But we must remember that perhaps more than any other area of IR, we aren't just trying to explain decision-making processes and choices, we are also trying to be policy relevant in order to help decision-makers do better with processes and choices. And, as the above discussion has shown, policymakers have learned from scholarship on decision-making—whether it concerns "standing and sitting," "groupthink," or the "uses" (and "misuses") of historical analogies. All too often, scholars tend to ignore this fact. There is much to be said for maintaining distance from what one is trying to explain, but when studying politics, it makes little sense not to try to address reality and be policy relevant—especially when one is trying to understand why and how people make the choices they do.

Finally, we need always to remember one key fact about decision-making that academics also often overlook: it's hard. Sometime we critique decisions in a way that makes the "right" choices seem so easy and fingers inept policy-makers for making the obviously "wrong" decisions. Gary Klein (1998) has studied a wide array of people making choices—from firefighters to air traffic controllers to policy-makers—and reminds us that to define problems and then to generate a new course of action requires that one make many judgments: about goals, about possible anomalies, about urgency, about the merit of the opportunity, about proper analogues, about "solvability." One has to be able to use intuition and make mental simulations to figure out a problem and to gauge where things are headed. And one must do all this under immense time constraints. This is as true in our everyday lives as it is for policy-makers making choices. So we shouldn't be surprised that the emphasis in the field has been on how often decision-makers get it wrong—because often it's only in retrospect that the correct choices seem so obviously clear.

All that said, one hopes that the next 40 years of scholarship in the tradition of Snyder, Bruck, and Sapin will be as creative, innovative, and insightful as the last. Based on the work reviewed above, and the new directions to be explored, there is every reason to be confident. And that's worth acknowledging. For, as long as there are decisions to be made, there will be perceptions and processes to be understood.

NOTES

1. "Nixon Proposed Using A-Bomb in Vietnam," *New York Times* (March 1, 2002), pA10.
2. David Sanger, "Leaving for Europe, Bush Draws On Hard Lessons of Diplomacy," *New York Times* (May 22, 2002) pA1.

REFERENCES

Allison, Graham T. *Essence of Decision: Explaining the Cuban Missile Crisis* (New York: HarperCollins, 1971)

Allison, Graham T. and Halperin, Morton H. "Bureaucratic Politics: A Paradigm and Some Policy Implications," *World Politics* 24 (Spring, 1972), pp. 40–79.

Allison, Graham T. and Zelikow, Philip D. *Essence of Decision: Explaining the Cuban Missile Crisis.* 2nd ed. (Addison-Wesley, 1999).

Art, Robert J. "Bureaucratic Politics and American Foreign Policy: A Critique," *Policy Sciences* 4 (1973): 467–90.

Ball, Desmond J. "The Blind Men and the Elephant: A Critique of Bureaucratic Politics Theory," *Australian Outlook* 28 (April 1974): 71–92.

Barber, Benjamin R. *The Truth of Power: Intellectual Affairs in the Clinton White House* (New York: W. W. Norton, 2001).

Bendor, Jonathan and Hammond, Thomas H. "Rethinking Allison's Models," *American Political Science Review* 86 (June 1992): 301–22.

Berman, Larry. *Planning a Tragedy: The Americanization of the War in Vietnam* (New York: W.W. Norton, 1983).

Beschloss, Michael, ed. *Reaching for Glory: Lyndon Johnson's White House Tapes, 1964–1965* (New York: Simon & Schuster, 2001).

Boettcher, William A., III. "Context, Methods, Numbers and Words: Prospect Theory in International Relations." *Journal of Conflict Resolution* 39 (September 1995): 561–83.

Brzezinski, Zbigniew. *Power and Principle: Memoirs of the National Security Adviser, 1977–1981.* (New York: Farrar Straus & Giroux, 1983).

Camerer, Colin F. and Hogarth, Robin M. "The Effects of Financial Incentives in Experiments: A Review and Capital-Labor-Projection Framework," *Journal of Risk Uncertainty* 19 (1999): 1–3, 7–42.

Carothers, Thomas. *Aiding Democracy Abroad: The Learning Curve* (Washington, D.C.: Carnegie Endowment for International Peace, 1999).

Carter, Ashton B. and Perry, William J. *Preventive Defense : A New Security Strategy for America* (Washington, D.C.: The Brookings Institution, 1999).

Chollet, Derek H. and Goldgeier, James M. "Once Burned, Twice Shy? The Pause of 1989," in *Cold War Endgame,* edited by William Wohlforth (University Park: Penn State University Press, 2003);

Christopher, Warren. *In the Stream of History: Shaping Diplomacy for a New Era* (Palo Alto, CA: Stanford University Press, 1998).

Crawford, Neta C. "The Passion of World Politics: Propositions on Emotion and Emotional Relationships," *International Security* 24 (Spring 2000), pp. 116–56.

Daalder, Ivo H. *Getting To Dayton: The Making of America's Bosnia Policy* (Washington, D.C.: Brookings Institution Press, 2000).

Dawes, Robyn M. "Behavior, Decision Making and Judgment," in *The Handbook of Social Psychology,* edited by Gilbert, Daniel T, Fiske, Susan T. and Lindzey, Gardner, 4th ed. (New York: McGraw Hill, 1998), pp. 497–548.

Edwards, Ward. "Dynamic Decision Theory and Probabilistic Information Processing," *Human Factors* 4 (1962), pp. 59–73.

Farnham, Barbara R. ed. *Avoiding Losses/Taking Risks: Prospect Theory and International Conflict* (Ann Arbor: University of Michigan Press, 1994).

Farnham, Barbara R. *Roosevelt and the Munich Crisis: A Study of Political Decision Making* (Princeton, NJ: Princeton University Press, 1997).

Friedman, Thomas L. *The Lexus and the Olive Tree: Understanding Globalization* (New York: Farrar Straus & Giroux, 1999).

George, Alexander L. *Presidential Decisionmaking in Foreign Policy: The Effective Use of Information and Advice* (Boulder, CO: Westview, 1980).

Gigerenzer, Gerd and Goldstein, Daniel G. "Reasoning the Fast and Frugal Way: Models of Bounded Rationality," *Psychology Review* 103 (1996): 650–69.

Goldgeier, James M. *Leadership Style and Soviet Foreign Policy: Stalin, Khrushchev, Brezhnev, Gorbachev* (Baltimore: Johns Hopkins University Press, 1994).

Goldgeier, James M. "Psychology and Security," *Security Studies* 6 (1997):137–66.

Goldgeier, James M. *Not Whether but When: The U.S. Decision to Enlarge NATO* (Washington, DC: The Brookings Institution Press: 1999).

Goldgeier, James M. and Tetlock, Philip E. "Psychology and International Relations Theory," *Annual Review of Political Science* 4 (2001), pp. 67–92.

Halperin, Morton H. *Bureaucratic Politics and Foreign Policy* (Washington, DC: The Brookings Institution Press 1974).

Hammond, Thomas H. and Thomas, Paul A. "The Impossibility of a Neutral Hierarchy," *Journal of Law, Economics, and Organization* 5 (Spring 1989): 155–84.

Hemmer, Christopher. *Which Lessons Matter?: American Foreign Policy Decision Making in the Middle East, 1979–1987* (Albany: SUNY, 2000).

Holbrooke, Richard C. *To End A War* (New York: Random House, 1998).

Janis, Irving L. *Groupthink: Psychological Studies of Policy Decisions and Fiascoes* (New York: Houghton Mifflin, 2nd ed. 1982).

Jentleson, Bruce. *With Friends Like These: Reagan, Bush and Saddam, 1982–1990* (New York: W.W. Norton, 1994).

Jervis, Robert L. *Perception and Misperception in International Politics* (Princeton: Princeton University Press, 1976).

Jervis, Robert L., Richard Ned Lebow and Janice Gross Stein. *Psychology and Deterrence* (Baltimore: Johns Hopkins University Press, 1985).

Kagel, John H. and Roth, Alvin E. *The Handbook of Experimental Economics.* (Princeton, NJ: Princeton University Press, 1995).

Kahneman, Daniel, Knetsch, Jack L. and Thaler, Richard H. "Anomalies: The Endowment Effect, Loss Aversion, and Status Quo Bias." *Journal of Economic Perspectives* 5 (Winter 1991): 193–206.

Kahneman, Daniel and Tversky, Amos. "Prospect Theory: An Analysis of Decision Under Risk," *Econometrica* 47 (March 1979): 263–91.

Kahenman, Daniel and Tversky, Amos. "Choices, Values and Frames," *American Psychologist* 39 (April 1984): 341–50.

Khong, Yuen Foong. *Analogies at War: Korea, Munich, Dien Bien Phu, and the Vietnam Decisions of 1965* (Princeton, NJ: Princeton University Press, 1992).

Kingdon, John W. *Agendas, Alternatives, and Public Policies.* 2nd ed. (New York: HarperCollins, 1995).

Kissinger, Henry A. *American Foreign Policy.* 3rd ed. (New York: W.W. Norton & Co., 1977).

Klein, Gary. *Sources of Power* (Cambridge, MA: MIT Press, 1998).

Kramer, Roderick M. and Tyler, Tom R, eds. *Trust in Organizations: Frontiers of Theory and Research* (Thousand Oaks, CA: Sage, 1996).

Krasner, Stephen D. "Are Bureaucracies Important? (Or Allison Wonderland)," *Foreign Policy* 7 (Summer 1972), pp. 159–79.

Larson, Deborah Welch. *Origins of Containment* (Princeton: Princeton University Press, 1985).

Larson, Deborah Welch. *Anatomy of Mistrust: U.S.-Soviet Relations During the Cold War* (Ithaca, NY: Cornell University Press, 1997).

Lebow, Richard Ned. *Between Peace and War: The Nature of International Crisis* (Baltimore: Johns Hopkins University Press, 1982).

Levy, Jack S. "Prospect Theory and International Relations: Theoretical Applications and Analytical Problems," *Political Psychology* 13 (1992): 283–310.

Levy, Jack S. "Loss Aversion, Framing, and Bargaining: The Implications of Prospect Theory for International Conflict," *International Political Science Review* 17 (1996): 179–95.

Lindblom, Charles E. "The Science of 'Muddling Through.'" *Public Administration Review* 19 (Spring 1959): 79–88.

McClosky, Herbert. "Concerning Strategies for a Science on International Politics." *World Politics* 8 (January 1956): 281–95.

McDermott, Rose. *Risk-Taking in International Politics: Prospect Theory in American Foreign Policy* (Ann Arbor: University of Michigan Press, 1998).

Mayer, Frederick W. *Interpreting NAFTA: The Science and Art of Political Analysis* (New York: Columbia University Press, 1998).

Mercer, Jonathan. *Reputation and International Politics* (Ithaca, NY: Cornell University Press, 1996).

Neustadt, Richard E. and May, Ernest R. *Thinking in Time: The Uses of History for Decision Makers* (New York: Free Press, 1986).

Nicolson, Harold. *Diplomacy* (New York: Harcourt, Brace and Company, 1939).

Noonan, Peggy. *On Speaking Well: How to Give a Speech With Style, Substance, and Clarity* (New York: Regan, 1999).

Nye, Joseph S. Jr. *The Paradox of American Power: Why the World's Only Superpower Can't Go It Alone* (Oxford: Oxford University Press, 2002).

Perrow, Charles. *Normal Accidents: Living With High-Risk Technologies* (New York: Basic Books, 1984).

Power, Samantha. *A Problem from Hell: America and the Age of Genocide* (New York: Basic Books, 2002).

Putnam, Robert D. "Diplomacy and Domestic Politics: The Logic of Two-Level Games," *International Organization* 42 (Summer 1988): 427–60.

Quandt, William B. *Camp David : Peacemaking and Politics* (Washington, DC: The Brookings Institution Press, 1986).

Rosati, Jerel A. "The Power of Human Cognition in the Study of World Politics." *International Studies Review* 213 (Fall 2000), pp. 45–75.

Sagan, Scott D. *The Limits of Safety* (Princeton, NJ: Princeton University Press, 1995).

Simon, Herbert A. *Models of Man* (New York: Wiley, 1957).

Simon, Herbert A. *Models of Bounded Rationality* (Cambridge, MA: MIT Press, 1982).

Simon, Herbert A. "Human Nature in Politics: The Dialogue of Psychology with Political Science," *American Political Science Review* 79 (1985): 293–304.

Simon, Herbert A. "Information 101: It's Not What you Know, It's How you Know It," *The Journal for Quality and Participation* (July-August 1998), pp. 30–33.

Snyder, Glenn H. and Diesing, Paul. *Conflict among Nations: Bargaining, Decision Making, and System Structure in International Crises* (Princeton, NJ: Princeton University Press, 1977).

Steel, Ronald. "Cooling It." *New York Review of Books,* October 19, 1972, pp. 43–46.

Tetlock, Philip E. "Close-call Counterfactuals and Belief System Defenses: I Was Not Almost Wrong But I Was Almost Right." *Journal of Personality and Social Psychology* 75 (1998): 639–52.

Tetlock, Philip E. "Theory-Driven Reasoning about Possible Pasts and Probable Futures: Are we Prisoners of our Preconceptions?" *American Journal of Political Science* 43 (1999): 335–66.

Tetlock, Philip E. and Goldgeier, James M. "Human Nature and World Politics: Cognition, Identity and Influence," *International Journal of Psychology* 35 (2000): 87–96.

Tetlock, Philip E., C. McGuire, R. Peterson, P. Feld and S. Chang, "Asssessing Political Group Dynamics: A Test of the Groupthink Model," *Journal of Personality and Social Psychology* 63 (1992): 402–23.

Waldman, Michael. *POTUS Speaks: Finding the Words that Defined the Clinton Presidency* (New York: Simon & Schuster 2000).

Waltz, Kenneth N. *Theory of International Politics* (Englewood Cliffs: Addison-Wesley 1979).

Welch, David A. "The Organizational Process and Bureaucratic Politics Paradigms: Retrospect and Prospect," *International Security* 17 (Fall 1992): 112–146.

Index